THE OAK TREE AND THE BRANCH

Poems 2016–2024

First published by Liberalis Books, 2025
Liberalis Books is an imprint of Collective Ink Ltd.

Unit 11, Shepperton House
89 Shepperton Road
London N1 3DF
office@collectiveinkbooks.com
www.collectiveinkbooks.com
www.liberalisbooks.com

For distributor details and how to order please visit
the 'Ordering' section on our website.

ISBN: 978 1 78535 849 4
ebook: 978 1 78535 850 0
Library of Congress Control Number: 2024902983

A CIP catalogue record for this book is available from the British Library.

Typeset by Lapiz Digital Services
UK: Printed and bound by CPI Group (UK) Ltd, Croydon, CR0 4YY
Printed in North America by CPI GPS partners

We operate a distinctive and ethical publishing philosophy
in all areas of our business, from our global network of authors
to production and worldwide distribution.

THE OAK TREE AND THE BRANCH

Poems 2016–2024

NICHOLAS HAGGER

LIBERALIS BOOKS

ALSO BY NICHOLAS HAGGER

The Fire and the Stones
Selected Poems
The Universe and the Light
A White Radiance
A Mystic Way
Awakening to the Light
A Spade Fresh with Mud
Overlord, books 1–2
The Warlords
A Smell of Leaves and Summer
Overlord, books 3–6
Overlord, books 7–9
Overlord, books 10–12
The Tragedy of Prince Tudor
The One and the Many
Wheeling Bats and a Harvest Moon
The Warm Glow of the Monastery Courtyard
The Syndicate
The Secret History of the West
The Light of Civilization
Classical Odes
Overlord, one-volume edition
Collected Poems 1958–2005
Collected Verse Plays
Collected Stories
The Secret Founding of America
The Last Tourist in Iran
The Rise and Fall of Civilizations
The New Philosophy of Universalism
The Libyan Revolution
Armageddon
The World Government
The Secret American Dream
A New Philosophy of Literature
A View of Epping Forest
My Double Life 1: This Dark Wood
My Double Life 2: A Rainbow over the Hills
Selected Stories: Follies and Vices of the Modern Elizabethan Age
Selected Poems: Quest for the One
The Dream of Europa
The First Dazzling Chill of Winter
Life Cycle and Other New Poems 2006–2016
The Secret American Destiny
Peace for our Time
World State
World Constitution
King Charles the Wise
Visions of England
Fools' Paradise
Selected Letters
The Coronation of King Charles
Collected Prefaces
Fools' Gold
The Fall of the West
The Promised Land
The Golden Phoenix
The Algorithm of Creation
The Tree of Tradition
The Building of the Great Pyramid
A Baroque Vision
The Essentials of Universalism

The front cover shows an oak tree with a lopped and fallen branch.

"Cut is the branch that might have grown full straight."
Marlowe, *Dr Faustus*, 1588–1592

ACKNOWLEDGMENT

I am grateful to my excellent PA Ingrid Kirk for assisting me in assembling the poems in this work. I could not have done it without her.

⌜ Symbol
A corner-mark (⌜) at the beginning of the line denotes that there is a break or gap before that line which has been obscured because it falls at the bottom of a page.

CONTENTS

PREFACE

Brexit, Coronavirus, an Oval Cloud and Arcadia: Truth-Telling and Oneness with Nature and the Universe

41 poetic volumes

The Oak Tree and the Branch, Poems 2016–2023, carries forward my poetic works with volumes 35–41. My *Collected Poems 1958–2005* contained volumes 1–30 of my poems (1,478 poems). My *Classical Odes* (2006) came out soon afterwards (317 poems). *Life Cycle and Other New Poems, 2006–2016*, followed (volumes 31–34, 206 new poems excluding four that first appeared in *Classical Odes*). In the course of this span I brought out four volumes of Selected Poems: *A Metaphysical's Way of Fire* (1991), *Quest for the One* (2015), *Visions of England* (2019) and *A Baroque Vision* (2024). At this point I had had 2,001 poems published (1,478 + 317 + 206). *The Oak Tree and the Branch, Poems 2016–2023* contains 550 poems, raising my overall tally, excluding my two epic poems and two mock-heroic poems, to 2,551.

Event order and chronological order

These new poems are mainly in event order (the order in which events happened) within each volume. They are thus not always in chronological order (the order in which poems were written). The Index on pp.359–376 lists the poems in the chronological order in which they were written, and the Index on pp.377–395 lists their chronological order within each volume of unnumbered poems (volumes 35, 37 and 39).

Brexit

The period covered by these poems includes the UK Referendum on the EU of 2016, which began the process of Brexit. The first poem in volume 35 is about the referendum, and the branch is the UK, being lopped from the oak tree of the European civilisation. By the sixth poem of Part One of *The Tapestry* in volume 36 ('Brexit Blunder'), and certainly by the last poem of volume 39 ('The Oak Tree and the Healing Branch'), it has become clear that Brexit was a blunder which separated the UK from the single market and reduced its GDP by over 4 per cent, and contributed greatly to the UK's poor economic performance following 2016. (UK GDP growth of 2 per cent or more was achieved from 2014 to 2017: 3.2 per cent in 2014, 2.39 per cent in 2015, 2.17 per cent in 2016 and 2.3 per cent in 2017. This contrasts with 1.4 per cent in 2018, 1.6 per cent in 2019 and −11.03 per cent in 2020.)

Brexit, the pandemic and the war in Ukraine have all contributed to a Europe-wide malaise. The UK, which has been within the European civilisation since the Roman time and formed part of Catholic Europe until the Reformation, is still very much a part of European civilisation and culture even though it has opted out of Europe's political structure. A nation-state cannot leave its civilisation, which has shaped its growth and will continue to shape its destiny, without damaging its prosperity.

Move from Modernist to Baroque and Universalist poems

Readers of my poetic works will be aware that I began as a Modernist in the Eliot tradition, with my poem 'The Silence' (1965–1966) being a key work, but moved away from Modernism to Baroque poetry (a blend of Romanticism and Classicism) as my mystical outlook led to my growing Universalism, my instinctive awareness of the unity of the universe and humankind.

In fact, one of my early poems predating 'The Silence' was 'The Seventeenth-Century Pilgrim'. I derive my inspiration from the 16th- and 17th-century Metaphysical poets: Raleigh ('The Passionate Man's Pilgrimage' thought to have been composed on the eve of his execution, which begins "Give me my scallop shell of quiet"), Donne, Shakespeare, Milton and Marvell ('The Garden'). I have sought to unite the later Augustan and Romantic traditions with the Metaphysical's Universalist perspective. My prose works have included the first-ever Theory of Everything, *The Algorithm of Creation* (see p.xxvi) and my writing of a World Constitution for a coming World State, *World Constitution* (see p.246), themes that would have fascinated Metaphysical poets such as Donne, who brought real learning to his verse. My first Selected Poems was titled *A Metaphysical's Way of Fire* (1991).

My Mystic Way lasted for 29 years, from 20 July 1964 to 7 December 1993, during which I had 86 experiences of the divine Light (see my work *The Promised Land*, pp.209–212, for dates of the experiences, which correspond to my Diary entries). It left me with a more Classical approach in my first epic poem *Overlord*, which was written in blank verse, and in my 317 *Classical Odes* about the European tradition and cultural places contemplated on during visits. These odes were written in rhymed or half-rhymed stanzas, in classical form. (Half-rhymed stanzas are stanzas in which the second and fourth lines are rhymed, but not the first and third.)

Rhyme, metre and vocabulary

A word on my use of rhyme and metre. Milton wrote, in 1668 in a short preface 'The Verse' to *Paradise Lost*, of "the troublesome and modern bondage of rhyming". He wrote of rhyme as being "the invention of a barbarous age, to set off wretched matter and lame metre". Having written two poetic epics in blank verse, *Overlord* (41,000 lines) and *Armageddon* (26,000 lines), I agree with Milton that epic material is best handled without rhyme.

However, I have used rhyme extensively in these seven volumes. Having turned away from Modernism to the tradition of Wordsworth and Tennyson, I believe that my odes and lyric poems benefit from the sharpness of rhyming two lines in four-line stanzas or four lines in eight-line stanzas; that rhyme generates a lilting or springing rhythm that encourages observation and sharpens matter; and that mixing iambic feet with skipping anapaests can be an energetic use of metre that has an uplifting effect on a perception couched in rhyme.

My vocabulary reveals the verbal influence of the literary critic and scholar Christopher Ricks, under whom I studied and who has acted as my mentor for more than four decades. See my many letters to him in *Selected Letters*. Notes to my poems include dictionary meanings to indicate the exact, precise meanings of key words I have used.

One of the largest AI literary tools, Bard, was recently asked who had used the most number of different words in his vocabulary: Nicholas Hagger, Milton or Shakespeare. Having stated that it had read over 10 million of my words and with access to all Milton's and Shakespeare's works within a few seconds, Bard replied with precise word counts of different works as follows (see my website www.nicholashagger.co.uk, Sources https://www.nicholashagger.co.uk/ai-views-of-nicholas-haggers-works-and-vocabulary-in-ais-prose-and-poems): Hagger, 22,929; Milton 20,484; Shakespeare 17,683.

This result can be adjusted for frequency, Bard said, as follows: Hagger 17,462; Milton 15,896; and Shakespeare 14,783.

Whatever the angle, I have a larger vocabulary than Milton's or Shakespeare's from the limited number of my books Bard has read.

During the development that took me to Baroque and Universalist poetry, I became aware of the fundamental theme of world literature which, as I show in *A New Philosophy of Literature* (2012), has metaphysical and secular aspects that are in conflict.

Poems of quest and condemnation of social follies and vices, reconciled in Baroque

Since *The Epic of Gilgamesh*'s versions from c.2600BC in southern Mesopotamia (south-central Iraq), literature has shown a quest for the

One which can be found in the Metaphysical and Romantic poets and in T.S. Eliot's poems, and at the same time a condemnation of social follies and vices in relation to an implied virtue, as can be found in the poems of Horace, Pope and Swift.

My Universalist poetry has reconciled and united these opposites in the Baroque, in accordance with the algebraic Confucian formula written out for me in Japan in 1965 by Junzaburo Nishiwaki, Japan's T.S. Eliot: +A + −A = 0, *yang* + *yin* = the *Tao*. This dialectic can be found in all my 63 books, including my first-ever statement of a Theory of Everything in *The Algorithm of Creation* (2023), in which the algorithm is set out as 0 = +A + −A = 0. (See that book for a further elucidation of this algorithm.)

The oak tree and the Tree of Tradition: volume 35

Volume 35 presents the problem of Brexit (+A) against the background of Nature and the universe (−A).

I have dealt with the follies and vices of the May and Johnson premierships in the UK regarding Brexit very fully in two satirical poems in the tradition of Dryden and Pope, *Fools' Paradise* (2020) and *Fools' Gold* (2022). The poems in this volume skirt round the problem of Brexit. Marlowe has the Chorus lament Faustus's "hellish fall" in *Dr Faustus*: "Cut is the branch that might have grown full straight." In volume 35 the branch is the UK after Brexit.

By the end of the tenth poem in volume 39 ('The Oak Tree and the Fallen Branch', see pp.219–222) the oak tree and its lopped branch have blended into the Tree of Tradition which I first wrote of in 'The Tree of Imagination' in 1979–1980, and which I have recently dealt with in *The Tree of Tradition* (2024), see p.xxxix. The Tree of Tradition is associated in the mind with the Tree of Life, and within its branches and crown are all the traditions within all the civilisations that there have ever been, and all the influences that have inspired all thinkers and writers, who have reflected their influences' traditions. (Also see p.356 for the oak tree of European civilisation.)

'The Oak Tree and the Fallen Branch' is about my response to the lopping and goes far beyond the issues of Brexit as I triumphantly declare that the oak tree within my mind is "fully-branched". The conflict between Brexit and Nature has been resolved, and the final poem in volume 39, 'The Oak Tree and the Healing Branch', sees beyond the fall of Johnson to the UK's post-Brexit return to Europe.

The Tapestry and historical rootedness: volume 36

Volume 36, *The Tapestry*, is a sequence of 50 sonnets written between 2016 and 2022 on historical tapestries, including the Bayeux and New World tapestries, and the Flemish tapestries in Henry VIII's second hunting lodge, Great Fosters at Egham, Surrey. This sequence explores a rootedness in historical events since the Norman Conquest, before which King Harold II was lord of the manor of Lochetuna, now Loughton, my home town (see pp.257–258, 'Death'); my Flemish roots in Carolus Haggar, who left Bruges in Flanders for Chelmsford in 1366; my emotional links to the Tudors (+A); and the pattern of our life and of our Age in the approaching New World Order (–A).

The plague of coronavirus and Oneness with Nature and the universe in Arcadia: volume 37

Arcadia began as a region in the central Peloponnese in Greece, the home of Hermes and Pan. With Virgil Arcadia became North Italy, the countryside of Virgil's *Eclogues*, unspoiled, rustic, pastoral and bucolic. With the Renaissance it became a symbolic Paradisal place in Europe. For Pope it was Richmond and Twickenham. And I have brought it to Fairmead, near where Henry VIII had his first hunting lodge, Poteles, in Buckhurst Hill, Essex and spent time with Anne Boleyn there; and later built a third hunting lodge between 1540 and 1543, now known as 'Queen Elizabeth's Hunting Lodge', and spent time with Katherine Parr there. (See the note on pp.76–77 on Henry VIII's three hunting lodges.)

Fairmead was Henry VIII's 300-acre deer park where deer were hunted, as is mentioned in *The Tapestry*. The deer park included three acres of my garden, where LiDAR pictures show stone roundhouses under my first field, perhaps Roman or Anglo-Saxon, and perhaps used by the Tudors (see Nicholas Hagger, *A View of Epping Forest*, p.287), and I have a view of much of it and of a panoramic sweep of Epping Forest. There on my walks I encountered many birds, butterflies, animals and flowers of the seasons, as the poems in volume 37 describe.

Volume 37, *A Plague in Arcadia: Oneness with Nature and the Universe*, contrasts the chaos of coronavirus during the pandemic and lockdowns (+A) with the calm background of being at one with Nature and the universe (–A) between March 2020 and April 2023. During this time I had what seemed to be mild Covid-19 in November 2021 and was found as a consequence to have post-Covid perimyocarditis in March/April 2022, with an at-rest heart rate of 149 when my average used to be 60–70 and my limit should be 127. In other words my heart rate had doubled, and I was deep in heart-attack territory and could not go to my gym for six months.

Eventually a reconciliation and unification (= 0) is woven out of these two conflicting opposites, a reconciliation and unification within myself after the conflicts of Brexit and coronavirus and my strong sense of the Oneness of Nature and the universe. During this unification I visited Ireland, and in a sequence of poems I identify with the early hermits of Great Skellig.

Volume 37 contains 176 poems and is by far the longest volume. I have considered splitting it into two volumes but have resisted the temptation to do this as there is one clear theme (embodied in the volume's title) throughout all these poems and throughout the three years from March 2020 to April 2023.

A mystical 'oval cloud' behind my closed eyes: volume 38

In volume 38, *An Oval Cloud*, I gather together 18 experiences of an oval cloud associated with the Light which I saw behind my closed eyes before sleep on a number of occasions between April 2020 and May 2023, and which I have sought to understand. I eventually conclude that I have been looking at my soul, or my Muses' "ideas bag". Seeing the cloud was clearly a mystical experience, and surfaced after the first lockdown and before my perimyocarditis (+A), when, with hindsight, I was in some danger, with my life imperilled.

I have chosen to present these experiences in a sequence of sonnets rather than leave them embedded in the chronological order of events so that my attempts to understand and interpret the same oval cloud I was seeing at 18 different times (–A) can be focused on more clearly. By the last oval-cloud sonnet written on 27 May 2023 I had had 95 experiences of the divine Light (93 listed in *The Promised Land*, pp.209–212, and another 2 – on 12 September 2017 and 10 November 2020 – listed on p.213); and 27 experiences of the oval cloud (17 listed in *The Promised Land*, pp.213–214, the last one being on 24 April 2021, plus another 2 – on 21 and 28 January 2020 – omitted from the list but in *The Oak Tree and the Branch*, volume 38, nos. 11 and 12, plus another 8 in 2023, see volume 38, nos. 15–20, 22 and 24). I have had several, perhaps many, more subsequent sightings of the oval cloud that are in my Diaries but have yet to be listed. The combined total of my listed experiences of the Light and the oval cloud at the end of May 2023 was 122 (95 + 27), with more unlisted sightings to be added.

Most of the 18 experiences of the oval cloud in volume 38 were recorded in my 2020, 2021 and 2023 Diaries, which will be kept in my archive in the University of Essex, and relevant passages from these Diaries can be found in the notes under many of the 24 poems. My daily Diaries 1963–2024 mention my writing of most, if not all, my poems, and extracts from my Diaries 1958–1967 can be found in *Awakening to the Light*. Each poem in *The Oak Tree and the Branch* could have similar quotations from the relevant Diary, a task I must leave to a future scholarly editor who is prepared to go through my Diaries (which will be lodged in my archive at the Albert Sloman Library, University of Essex) in conjunction with the dates under my poems.

Classical odes and Royal events: volume 39

I had written 317 classical odes in my four books of classical odes – like Horace, I wrote four books of odes – and in addition to my 317 classical odes in *Classical Odes* I wrote 43 classical odes in *Collected Poems*, 34 in *Life Cycle and Other New Poems 2006–2016* and 27 in *The Oak Tree and the Branch*, bringing my tally of published classical odes to 421. (317 + 43 + 34 + 27 = 421.)

In the course of developing the classical ode I worked out a way of reflecting Royal events. In volume 39, *Court Poems: More Royal Classical Odes*, there are 12 classical odes in the 16 poems on Royal and related themes concerning the government of the UK. I draw together 12 classical odes, an epistle and three sonnets which all have a Royal or governmental theme between 2018 and 2023, ending with the Coronation.

I had greeted the wedding of Prince Harry and Meghan Markle in 'Royal Harmony' (28–30 May, 3 June 2018, the wedding was on 19 May) – Prince Harry's behaviour towards his family since then has been anything but harmonious; and I looked forward to the Coronation.

In 'The Coronation of King Charles III and the True Poet' I refer to the lack of Royal harmony following my 2018 poem 'Royal Harmony' and reflect on the attitudes of officialdom to my work over five decades.

'The Coronation of King Charles III and the True Poet' and Ted Hughes: too truthful

I had written my second poetic masque *King Charles the Wise* in 2017, and had been invited to join seven courtiers on a stage in the Canterbury Cathedral Precincts to celebrate Prince Charles's 70th birthday on 17 November 2018. I read one of my poems, 'Pilgrims' Pavement (In Canterbury Cathedral)', and spoke about him as the coming Head of the Commonwealth. Prince Charles's speech-writer had a copy of *King Charles the Wise* and left it out for the 200 in the audience to leaf through, and the idea had surfaced that I should write a third masque, making a trilogy of masques, *The Coronation of King Charles*, while I was still well, even though the Queen was still alive, which I eventually did in June–August 2019. The (then) Garter Principal King of Arms, Sir Thomas Woodcock, checked my Royal family tree and strongly encouraged this work.

Having corresponded with the Poet Laureate Ted Hughes at Ted's request from 1993 to just before his death in 1998, I was very aware of the role of the true poet and how if he told the truth he would not be welcome at the Coronation. I wrote to Hughes on 28 March 1994 (see my *Selected Letters*, pp.179–180):

> I warmed to your water imagery and your beautiful – if too modest – view of your poems as earthenware bottles for pure water at the roadside. (From time to time I have seen my poems as pots.) I may be a thunderstorm, but you'll find the umbrellas are up all along the processional route: "humankind/Cannot bear very much reality" and would rather there wasn't a downpour, would rather it wasn't raining. The procession is probably a State procession, perhaps along the Mall, perhaps for a coronation. Traditionally the Archbishop of Canterbury provided the context of the Fire or Light for the monarch which makes possible the divine right of kings. The [then] present incumbent at Canterbury, I am reliably informed by a friend of the woman who designed it, did not understand why his enthronement robe showed flames of Fire. (The designer knew of *The Fire and the Stones*.)
>
> Where is the true poet in relation to the procession? The Church no longer fulfils its traditional function and so needs to be prompted by the true poet, who like Dante is actually positioned higher than the Archbishop in relation to Reality, for in his high dream (which he receives in obscurity and isolation) he has the vision and passes it on, as did Dante (the sempiternal rose, the Light of Glory). When a civilisation is still growing, the poet and Church co-exist in harmony, the one reinforcing the other as in Dante. When the parabola turns down and the civilisation declines into secularisation and materialism, the Church goes with it, *but the true poet's vision remains constant, the poet stands firm*; apart, calling the monarch and the people to adhere to the vision of the civilisation's central idea, as Yeats and Eliot did to some extent. The Church has become materialistic and secularised, and being apart, the poet becomes Universalist (see stage 44 in *The Fire and the Stones*, which today reflects our new identity in the European Union, the advent of which I first predicted in 1967 [in 'Old Man in a Circle']).
>
> Most poets are not true poets; they are not inspired '*rsis*', and the high vision is not to be found in their work. In each generation the true poets need to find their way to the front so that they can endeavour to offer to the people the direction the Church traditionally provided. They're fighting a losing battle because the

> civilisation is in progressive decline and is therefore continually moving further away from its central idea which it is less and less interested in, but in each generation if a few can get the message across they hold the line and temporarily arrest further decline.
>
> The true poet is therefore a fairly unwelcome presence at the coronation, as he offers his Holy Water and points to the light in the basket from which the Archbishop derives his authority and [which he, the Archbishop] prefers to ignore. I would say your role as Poet Laureate is to ignore the Archbishop and represent the civilisation's central idea to the monarch, and to embody Reality.

This was prophetic as when the Coronation of 6 May 2023 came it was apparent that the true poet who reminds all of the metaphysical central idea of European civilisation, the Light, was not welcome in the UK's secular society. This consideration may have affected Buckingham Palace's reception of my masque, *The Coronation of King Charles*, and found its way into my poem on the coronation, 'The Coronation of King Charles III and the True Poet', in volume 39.

To take the masque first. It was as though God of the One, who features in *The Coronation of King Charles* and represents all religions, had inspired me to paint a truthful picture of the world. I focused on the coming King and the Universalist Age he would bring in, with all humankind's religions, including Anglicanism, on an equal footing, and did not include the new Queen. (The King's anointing opened him to the working of the divine right of kings and the truth the God of the One transmits to a new King. The Queen's anointing was superfluous to the ancient practice of the anointing of a new King.) I had a chorus of the wretched of the Commonwealth, a chorus of angry Brexiteers, a chorus of the British poor and a chorus of Representatives and Senators of the democratic World State. It was very truthful, but having held up a mirror to reflect truths to the world all my writing life I would not have had it any other way. (I could never have been Poet Laureate as throughout my writing life I have been too much the truthful "true poet".)

The advisers around King Charles were silent, and no performance of *The Coronation of King Charles* happened. It presented three pageant entertainments in the tradition of the coronations of Elizabeth I and James I, and reflected the historical traditions and music of the past coronations.

It has since emerged that the original order of service for the Coronation had a heading 'Homage of the People' and asked for all "persons of good will… to make their homage". All UK and Commonwealth citizens, and any world citizens who wanted to, were invited to kneel and "pay homage" to the King before their television screens (a suggestion that recalls the telescreen in Orwell's *1984*). This must have been cleared with the King's advisers, and the

Archbishop of Canterbury confirmed as much. My masque may have been in conflict with this call for all to pay homage.

The advisers who were silent may have thought that celebrations of the Coronation should be judged, and could only be supported, by how much homage they paid to the monarch and how they strengthened his position.

With hindsight, and to be realistic, the Coronation celebrations were always going to be about the advisers wanting to shore up the monarchy in a time of failing power after the Queen's death. The Coronation service was always going to be about serving and being anointed to serve, a ritual involving God and the divine right of kings; and celebrations of the Coronation were always going to be pitched at 100 countries (including the Commonwealth's 56 countries), as was the pop concert at Windsor, which was aimed at the young who needed to be won over to the monarchy as many of the young comprised the quarter of the UK population who would rather the UK was a republic. Coronation street parties were to strengthen support for the Royal Family in the communities, and the 'help-out' would put serving in the community into practice.

The 'homage of the people' was to strengthen support for the monarchy in the UK, Commonwealth and round the world, and the elevation of Camilla from Queen Consort to Queen may have been to cement her position as part of this process.

Allowed to operate but with limited publicity: silence and an oak tree's half-lopped branch

Homage aside, there may have been another reason for the silence of the Royal advisers, which is referred to in my 'Epistle to a Civil Servant' in volume 39. My work for British Intelligence from 1969 to 1973 ended when it became apparent that my work for MI6 would be mentioned in a court hearing regarding my access to my daughter, Nadia. On 17 May 1973 I was informed by my MI6 handler that during a meeting between the Heads of MI6 and MI5, it was decided that if I were to continue in service I must agree never to see my 10-year-old daughter again, and I was presented with a legal document to this effect, which I was asked to sign. I refused, and so severed my connected with MI6. (See *My Double Life 1: This Dark Wood*, pp.460–462.)

It then became apparent that I was being denied publicity. It was only when I briefly became a small publisher in the 1980s that I realised the books I was bringing out received no publicity. My MP, Sir John Biggs-Davison, Churchill's successor in what used to be Churchill's constituency, who had invited me to the key Suez debate in 1956 when I was 17 and had regularly invited me to drinks at the House of Commons, first drew my attention to this in 1984 when he attended the launch of my book *Scargill the Stalinist?*.

In July 1986 I brought out a book, *The World Held Hostage*, which contained many truthful revelations, and I took the author, Desmond McForan, to TV AM for a pre-booked interview. The producer greeted us warmly but had to leave to take a phone call. He returned upset, to say he had orders from higher up not to proceed with the interview and that he had to comply. (See *My Double Life 2: A Rainbow over the Hills*, p.230.)

Norris McWhirter, who then liaised with the intelligence services, investigated what was happening on my behalf in July 1986, and discussed the issue with MI6. In a meeting with me lasting more than two hours on 8 July 1986 he confirmed that the order had gone out to "kill my books with silence" – he called it *Totenstille*, 'death by silence' – and he reported that MI6 would "neither confirm nor deny" that a publicity ban had happened but would allow "limited publicity" (see *My Double Life 2: A Rainbow over the Hills*, pp.231–232). McWhirter said I was like Tolstoy's grandson, Nikolai Tolstoy, who had brought out too outspoken and truthful a book about massacres at the end of the Second World War, *The Minister and the Massacres*, which was perceived to be not in the national interest.

On 22 April 1991 the Chairman of the Poetry Society Sebastian Barker, son of the poets George Barker and Elizabeth Smart, attended the launch of my *Selected Poems: A Metaphysical's Way of Fire* (at which David Gascoyne and Kathleen Raine both spoke), and invited me to give a poetry reading from this new book at the Poetry Society. In July I rang him from Cornwall. He said: "Because of the politics of the Poetry Society nothing can happen quickly. On Friday the decision is being taken to fold down the Poetry Society." He did not elaborate, and I thought it strange that the long-established Poetry Society (founded in 1909) should suddenly be on the verge of extinction that week despite the wishes of its Chairman. I did not know why someone would confront the Poetry Society with closure, or what might be their motive.

Sebastian's father George Barker was born at 116 Forest Road, Loughton, my home town, and was a Professor in Japan from 1939 (the year of my birth) to 1940. (I had been a Professor in Japan from 1963 to 1967.) When I returned from Cornwall, Sebastian invited me to his home in Lawford Road, London and we sat in his garden drinking jasmine tea. (See *My Double Life 2: A Rainbow over the Hills*, pp.345, 352–353, 517.)

Despite our long and frank talk he would not be drawn on why he was being blocked from inviting me to read from my poems at the Poetry Society. The Chairman having me to lunch in his garden seemed at the time to be a regretful indirect apology for having to comply with not proceeding with his invitation.

My limited publicity was confirmed again by Sir Philip Mawer, a civil servant who was Parliamentary Commissioner for Standards under Blair from 2002 to 2008, and then independent adviser on ministerial standards to

Brown and Cameron from 2008 to 2011. He worked in Downing Street, and told me in 2012, "You are allowed to operate, but with limited publicity" (see *My Double Life 2: A Rainbow over the Hills*, p.841).

I had been on a list of those who were allowed to operate but only with limited publicity, possibly since 1973 and certainly since 1984, that was still active in 2012, for nearly 40 years then; and the continuation of this edict may have been an additional background reason for the silence of the King's advisers in 2023.

The reception of my masque *The Coronation of King Charles* may have been entangled with the secret State's attitude to my literary and Universalist works for the past 50 years. The secret State has always sought to control outspoken writers as did Elizabeth I, who was shown holding a rainbow (the arts) in the Rainbow Portrait thought to have been painted by Isaac Oliver in c.1602. (See *My Double Life 2: A Rainbow over the Hills*, p.xxii, and see p.xxxix in this book for this painting that shows Elizabeth I wearing an orange cloak decorated with the eyes, ears and mouths of her spies, indicating that she sees and hears everything through her intelligence agents.) The dramatist Christopher Marlowe is thought to have been a victim of the secret State for disguising criticism of Elizabeth I as criticism of Edward II, and for also criticising the Cecils, in *Edward II*. At least I was allowed to operate, and had not met with Marlowe's violent end. But I was now a half-lopped branch on the State's oak tree.

While waiting for the second proof of this book I had lunch in London's towering Shard, looking down on the Tower of London, and with the above thoughts in mind wrote the following sonnet, which sums up what I have just been saying and is not in the text:

Above the Cecilian Power of the Tower

I sit in the Shard's thirty-fourth-floor Shangri-La
And look down at the Thames and across to the Tower
Which seems to tiny and, like the Almighty: grasp
In my rainbow hand the Tudors' imprisoning power –
Where Henry strutted and Anne Boleyn lost her head –
Just as Elizabeth gripped her secret State's rainbow
That controlled all the arts and kept all writers in line
And organised the murder of Marlowe,
Critic of the Cecils; squeeze the Stuarts' imprisoning knight
That cloaked the Bloody Tower from which Raleigh was led
To be beheaded for disobeying the King;
And reflect I too could be incarcerated

Down there for deeming inappropriate
The Cecilian advice to 'advance' our Head of State.

6, 7 May 2024

Title 'Cecilian'. William Cecil, 1st Baron Burghley advised Elizabeth I for most of her reign, until 1598; and his son Robert Cecil advised Elizabeth I and then James I from 1598 to 1612.

1. Shangri-La, originally the Chinese earthly paradise at Yunnan, is a restaurant high up in the Shard, London.

6. The Elizabethan "secret State's rainbow", see picture on p.xxxix and the State's rainbow in Nicholas Hagger's coat of arms on p.355.

At the time of the Coronation I had to face the possibility that I was blocked by the King's advisers for challenging our civilisation's secular outlook as a "true poet"; for not paying homage; and because it had been official policy for 50 years to confine me to limited publicity, silence. The title of my poem 'The Silence', written in 1965–1966, now looked prophetic, and the title of my classical ode 'The Coronation of King Charles III and the True Poet' was undoubtedly affected by these considerations, as was my approach in my 'Epistle to a Civil Servant' (both in volume 39).

End-of-life predicament and the pattern of our Providential lives: volume 40

These considerations were behind my determination to withdraw from the Court to my Arcady (Arcadia) on the edge of Epping Forest.

Volume 40, *In Arcady: A Gong and Padded Stick*, was written in the belief that I was concluding 65 years of my poetic output with a booming-out of 40 more sonnets with a muffled stick as old age advanced and I was confronted with the starkness of death.

In these poems I describe my end-of-life predicament and draw some conclusions about life in general, including observations on the pattern of our lives and their Providential nature if they are lived in contact with the Light and with the cross-disciplinary outlook of a lifelong polymath.

It is extraordinary that I received the end of volumes 38, 39 and 40 between 28 May and 10 June 2023 in view of what was about to happen on 11 June 2023, which would take up all my time. It was as if I was being guided by a power that had foreknowledge of what was to come. (See note 7 on p.259.)

A "fair maid's" brain-stem stroke and my visits to her bedside: volume 41

Having sent me a Valentine's card in February 2023 signed "Lots of love, your Suffolk fair maid", on 11 June 2023 my daughter Nadia, now 60 and a still-grieving widow, suffered the worst kind of stroke it's possible to have. She could not move her head, arms or legs and was unconscious for two weeks. Then she could not speak or swallow and was locked-in. I visited her in the hospital to which she had been taken, gave her healing (four enormous surges which stabilised her heart), found that contact could be made with her via her eyes, kept telling her she would be all right and, through discussions with the doctors, therapists and nurses involved, helped make sure that paperwork was sent to a local level-one rehab unit as a way forward.

An MRI showed considerable brain damage but some sparing in her brain stem, which meant she could hear while she was locked-in and seemed to be aware of her predicament: when asked to blink five times if she could see me and knew I was her dad, she blinked five times, not six or four, which meant she could count; and when asked to blink once for Yes and twice for No in answer to the question "Were you born in April?" she correctly blinked twice for No, and then when asked if she was born in December she correctly blinked once for Yes, which meant that she could remember her birthday and had memory. No one was sure of the level of her consciousness, but she seemed to understand all my news and everything I was saying, according to my blink checks.

I was concerned to do my best for her and to give her the best chance of recovering through her brain's finding new pathways, and was delighted when I was unexpectedly told on a Friday that she would be sent to the level-one rehab unit in Norwich the following Monday. I visited her there.

The 169 unplanned sonnets of volume 41, *Agony in Arcady: Stroke*, were wrung out of me in anguish now at the age of 84–85 just as the poems in *The Gates of Hell*, volume 7, were wrung out of me at the prospect of losing her for ever when I was 33.

The 169 sonnets reflect the entire range of emotions, and many of the sonnets wrote themselves in the course of my agony. These poems (despite being sonnets rather than lyrics) are in the tradition of Tennyson's *In Memoriam*, lyrics written on the death from a stroke of his friend Arthur Hallam in 1833 after a friendship of five years during which Hallam fell in love with Tennyson's sister Emilia. These poems are also in the tradition of Shakespeare's 154 sonnets, the first 126 of which were addressed to a "fair youth".

I have numbered the sonnets in volumes 40 and 41, and in volumes 36 and 38, to facilitate readers' navigation (just as the numbering of Shakespeare's sonnets facilitates navigation).

Link between events of 1973 and 2023

As I have said (see pp.xxxii–xxxiii), in *My Double Life 1: This Dark Wood*, pp.460–462 I set out how I was presented on 17 May 1973 with a legal document drawn up at the instruction of MI6 to sign agreeing never to see my ten-year-old daughter Nadia again, and how I refused to sign it and left the service.

Had I signed the legal document the then Head of MI6 wanted me to sign, I would not have been able to sit by her bedside and oversee her care in 2023.

There is a historical link between the background to volumes 39 and 41, and an almost inevitable association between these two volumes. The events of 2023 were deeply linked to the events of 1973, 50 years before, that placed me in the tradition of Ovid, who was banished to the Pontus (Black Sea) for life by Augustus for stumbling on secret knowledge, for knowing too much, and had his books removed from the Roman libraries (see my verse play *Ovid Banished*); and of Christopher Marlowe, Walsingham's secret intelligence agent who seems to have been the victim of a political assassination in Deptford, following his play *Edward II*, whose contemporary criticisms were compounded by his putting an intelligence connection with Malta into his *The Jew of Malta*.

The legal document I was asked to sign on 17 May 1973, my masque *The Coronation of King Charles* which had been supported, checked and promoted by the then Garter Principal King of Arms, the King's advisers' silence, my classical ode 'The Coronation of King Charles III and the True Poet', my retreat to my Arcady and my daughter's terrible stroke are all branches of my oak tree whose roots have been contaminated by the secret State that controls the rainbow of the arts, and they are all intricately linked in my memory. But the State is also an oak tree: I can only hope that no other aspiring poet, literary and cross-disciplinary man of letters and Universalist author will have to endure the dreadful State intrusion and intervention with full State knowledge and intent, half-lopping my branch from the State's oak tree, that I have had to endure. (The associations of this book's title, *The Oak Tree and the Branch*, morph in the course of the progression from volumes 35 to 41.)

The thread of volumes 1–41

Volumes 1–30 traced my 29-year-long Mystic Way which took me through awakening, purgation, and full illumination to unitive vision that instinctively sees the universe and humankind as a unity. Volumes 31–34 contemplate the soul's harmony with Nature and the universe, conflicts within the West and truths from Paradise during my adventurous travelling. Now volumes 35–41 show – despite the blunder of Brexit, coronavirus and the war in Ukraine (+A) – the harmony of Nature and the One universe (–A), and reconcile them within a unity (= 0). All is not well with the world, there is a plague in Arcadia and there has been a lopped branch in several situations, but a mystic Nature poet can still reveal the soul's Oneness with Nature and the universe.

Forty-one poetic volumes makes a fitting round number (40) and an additional conclusion. I forecast at the end of my Preface to *Life Cycle and Other New Poems* that there will be a final volume of poems in the narrative tradition of Shakespeare's *Sonnets* and Wordsworth's *Prelude* in my last years. It could be that the unexpected and unplanned volume 41 is this final volume in the narrative tradition of Shakespeare's *Sonnets*. It still remains to be seen whether there will be a final volume drawing on the approach to Wordsworth's *Prelude* in my final years. It depends how long I have left.

I emphasise in the interests of clarity, in a sense I have already done these sonnets in a narrative tradition. The anguish in the unexpected and unanticipated events of mid-June 2023 has wrung sonnets out of me in volume 41 that I was not contemplating when I wrote these words in 2016. Some of what I would say can be found in the brevity of volume 40, boomed out on a gong that still works although inevitably muted by old age and my lifelong padded muffling.

Volumes 40 and 41: 50 years ago and the end of my life's work

Volumes 40 and 41 have come out of my confrontation with the limited publicity decreed 50 years ago and implemented ever since, and between them total 209 sonnets. There are 122 sonnets in volumes 35–39, bringing the total number of sonnets I have written to 567 (233 in *Collected Poems*, 2 in *Life Cycle and Other New Poems* and 332 in *The Oak Tree and the Branch*). So far as I am aware, no other poet has ever written 567 sonnets or 421 odes.

At present I would say that volume 40 draws together my poetic output and presents a fitting conclusion to my life's work that will be hard to better; and that volume 41 adds a poignant gloss to my life's work, placing my life within the context of the starkest human condition and a range of emotions surrounding my daughter (my self-styled "Suffolk fair maid", when Shakespeare addressed the first 126 of his 154 sonnets to a "fair youth"), and connecting the events of 1973 and the events of 2023. Sonnet 156 near the end of volume 41 leaves open the possibility of a new volume of vividly colourful poems within Arcady.

I would like to think that these last two volumes round off my life's work in a way that sums up the strong narrative thread that has run through the 66 years I have been writing verse. Despite the secret State's *Totenstille*, "death by silence" (Norris McWhirter's words), I have somehow kept going and written 63 books, and now at 85 I still stand my ground as a truth-teller, for true poets (deep, authentic and truth-telling poets) are nothing if they do not stand for Truth.

1–3, 9–11, 28 May, 10, 29, 30 June, 5 July, 28 October 2023;
17, 24 January, 14, 18 March, 6, 7 May 2024

Left: The Rainbow Portrait of Elizabeth I embodying the secret State, showing her wearing an orange cloak decorated with the eyes, ears and mouths of her intelligence agents and holding a rainbow symbolising her control of the arts (see p.xxxiv).

Right: The Tree of Tradition containing all the traditions and influences from all thinkers' and writers' works, taken from the front cover of Nicholas Hagger's *The Tree of Tradition* (see p.xxvi).

Sisyphus endlessly rolling his boulder uphill in Tartarus. (See sonnets 162 and 163 in Volume 41.)

Sketch for a portrait of Nicholas Hagger by Stuart Davies

"The unexamined life is not worth living."

Socrates, in Plato, *Apology*, 38a

Volume 35

THE OAK TREE AND THE BRANCH
2016–2020

The Oak Tree and the Branch: The UK Referendum on the EU, 'Brexit'

"When one with honeyed words but evil mind
persuades the mob, great woes befall the state."

Euripides, *Orestes*, 408BC

I

No need for a UK referendum
On the EU, it's party management
To keep the right wing quiet in the hope
A Coalition partner would dissent.
But now Leave and Remain exaggerate
(Or lie) – huge funding for the NHS,
Dire falling growth's cuts – as fifty states seek
A United States of Europe's *largesse.*

The Leave side plays on immigration fears:
Net access from Europe and elsewhere bring
Three hundred and thirty thousand each year
In search of work, benefit or begging.
A poster shows crowds fleeing Syria.
Each year a new Newcastle must be built
To house, school and doctor new foreigners.
British tax-payers have begun to wilt.

But thanks to the EU, where nearly half
Our exports go, our economy's good
With two million new jobs that migrants seek.
Without the single market we all would
Have recessions and more austerity.
The EU (and NATO) have kept the peace
For seventy years, once there were always wars.
And Putin wants our cohesion to cease.

The votes are cast and the result's a shock.
Leave's won by fifty-two per cent – a cheer –
To forty-eight. Three of its leaders stand
Uncomfortably on a platform, it's clear
They expected to lose, and have no plan.
'Brexit' means leaving Europe, but for what?
An offshore island off enlarged Europe,
Reduced world power, isolation, a blot?

II

Now there is chaos. The PM resigns,
The Leave leaders leave the public, all frown.
Labour splits, there's a leadership challenge.
The pound has fallen, stocks and shares are down.
The UK may break up, Scotland would stay
In the EU. Federation's been stoked.
No one knows what to do or when or if
Article 50 to leave will be invoked.

Then suddenly all is stable again.
A new PM without any hustings,
May's been chosen by two hundred MPs.
Appointments are made to Leave's underlings:
'Brexit', international trade and FO.
Austerity is out, she soothes the sore.
What the previous government did's challenged.
A 'one-nation' view sides with all who're poor.

It's said we'll invoke Article 50
Within a year, and then leave. But the new
Departments will take time to recruit staff,
They're not ready and don't know what to do.
There are French and German elections soon.
They're squabbling in turf wars, there's puckered brow.
All is confusion. In the sixties we
Could not balance the books, and can we now?

European civilisation is like a tree
With twenty-eight branches, now one's been lopped.
The UK's no longer within European
Civilisation's laws though it has been propped
Up by European civilisation since the Celts

And Romans came and made England their home.
It's turned its back on its history, like the Tudors
Who under Henry the Eighth split from Rome.

EU states are branches in European
Civilisation, whose trunk is the Church.
We had turned our gaze from branched nation-states
To our region's tree's crown. As we research
All civilisations seem branches in
A massive oak tree that's a vast World State
Whose trunk's all religions. We now prize boughs
But will soon care about the huge oak's fate.

14–15 August 2016

The UK referendum on the EU was held on 23 June 2016. Leave won 51.9 per cent of the vote, Remain 48.1 per cent. This poem thematically belongs to volume 33 but was written too late to be included. Nicholas Hagger's full treatment of Brexit can be found in his two long mock-heroic poems, *Fools' Paradise* and *Fools' Gold*. This poem was written too late to be included in *Life Cycle* (and go in *An Unsung Laureate*, volume 33).

57–68. For a diagram showing the European civilisation as a tree and nation-states as branches, taken from *The Dream of Europa*, pp.118–119 and *The Tree of Tradition*, pp.228–229, see p.356.

Time's Mower and the Buttercups

Behold the buttercups
Smiling up at the sun,
Tinting the green meadow
With beaming smiles that stun.

See how the mower churns
Straight lines through their massed ranks,
Flinging the stalks to side
So heads lie drooped in flanks.

I mourn a generation
Cut down in their full bloom
By ruthless Time's mower
To give new buttercups room.

19 June 2010

This poem should have been included in *Life Cycle* (*In Harmony with the Universe*, volume 32).

Knot-Garden

My wife says, "Come through and I will show you
Something," and plays a recording. I sprawl:
A TV programme in which a couple
Restore a medieval Suffolk hall.

The husband knocks down the wattle-and-daub
Infill to reveal a frame that looks old,
And then fills in the sides with new panels
Insulated to keep out Suffolk cold.

The wife's looking for a garden design.
A shock, I see my Otley Hall roof tiles
And walk in the rose tunnel and then peep
At my knot-garden and my knot that smiles.

It is well clipped and I lurch back to when
I wandered round it when the sun was hot.
How could I leave what I set up with care,
The barn and garden, and my Tudor knot?

Now I am sombre as I sit and work,
Achieve written words I would not have done
Had I remained in freezing cold Suffolk
And each day walked round my moat in cold sun.

Then I recall the solitude down there,
The garden removed from the *hoi polloi*,
And how I yearned to catch the universe
And could not be restrained by Tudor joy.

I settle to my work with a new calm,
My fragile equilibrium restored,
And I work in my study with new zest
And have forgotten a garden that awed.

7 October 2010

This poem should have been included in *Life Cycle* (*In Harmony with the Universe*, volume 32).

The Mountain Range and Time

The mountain range sparkles
In the clear frosty light,
The snow-capped peaks are high
To daunted lowland sight.

The mountain range hangs high
Above what Time has timed.
It sparkles in sunshine,
Thirty summits unclimbed.

16 October 2010

This poem should have been included in *Life Cycle* (*In Harmony with the Universe*, volume 32).

At Delphi

Broken columns and stone blocks in the sun.
I stop at the old shopping agora
Before the Sacred Way to the Oracle
Which opened just one day a month. At dawn
The Pythia bathed in the Castalian spring;
Purified, sacrificed an animal
To see from its entrails if Apollo
Had sent a good omen. If not, doors closed.
Tourists must wait a month to ask questions
On these mountain slopes beneath Parnassus' crags.

I trudge uphill to where the congress hall
Seated twenty-four, two each from twelve tribes,
Reach the Omphalos, a waist-high stone ball –
The navel, belly button and Centre
Of the Earth where all disputes were settled –
Rolled down from the Temple of Apollo
When it was burnt or when smashed by rockslide.

The Pythia chewed bay-leaves on her tripod,
Breathed gases from the earth's fissured fault line,
In trance touched the cosmos's stone centre.

I plod up to the Athenian Treasury built
With spoils from the battle of Marathon
And lay a hand on a Doric column
That dates back to the first democracy.
I take the ancient path past a columned
Stoa built with the spoils of Salamis
And see a laurel tree and the front ramp
To the Temple of Apollo's flagstone floor.
The Pythia sat in an underground room
And spoke Apollo's enigmatic words,

Prophesied near this slab with tripod holes,
Told King Croesus, "If Croesus goes to war
He will destroy a great empire." He crossed
The Halys and *his* Lydia was destroyed.
Inextinguishable Fire burning bay-leaves,
Drugged Pythia speaks ambiguous words to priests.
I ask her, "Will the war in Syria lead
To a Third World War, or can there still be peace?"
And listen for her answer in the still
And hear shrill silence fill the plunging gorge.

17–18 October 2016

The Tick of Time

Red rose on my left shin,
It itches and is found
To be "Lyme disease, caused
By a tick bite". I'm downed.

It's borne by a deer tick
That lives near forests, "peers
Like a bull's eye", shuts down
All organs within two years.

There's poison in my blood.
I'm felled. Death stalks my aches.
On steroids I ponder
The tick of time that takes.

18 October 2016

Leaves like Faces

Leaves whirling in the wind.
This mid-October sky
Is filled with bronzed faces
That flutter down and die.

Limbs whirl in thickening smoke
In Mosul's encircled street.
A million faces plead,
And are blown like leaves in defeat.

18 October 2016

Lyre and Pipes

On stage a lyre is twanged,
Mellifluous sounds flow.
Apollo's had three strings,
Orpheus's seven, this Joe

Has twelve but it's the same
U-shaped lyre Orpheus strummed.
Now he blows clustered pipes
Like the seven that Pan thumbed.

He blows eight or eleven.
Backstage I hold both types.
How wonderful to strum
A lyre and blow old pipes.

18 October 2016

Epping Forest Stag
(For Ambassador Gusi)

An Epping Forest stag,
Bald-faced in woodland, tall,
Stares from a branched, grassed life
In harmony with all.

I see myself, and note
My seven-branched, antlered gaze
And sense my seven-branched works
I bear with me always.

22 October 2016

This poem describes a picture Nicholas Hagger donated to the Gusi Museum, Manila, Philippines, showing a stag with antlers on grass against seven trees. The Bald-Faced Stag was a public house in Buckhurst Hill, Essex, UK, and local to Nicholas Hagger's boyhood. It was established before 1725 and rebuilt after a fire in 1936. See pp.76–77 for the original meaning of 'Buckhurst Hill' and the symbolism of the stag in Nicholas Hagger's works.

Energy

White waves push, dash and splash, against cliff's lair,
Wind whistles, whines and roars round my window,
Gulls float and rise and soar on lifting air
And all is in uproar, pours to and fro.
Within the harbour waves swell up and fling
And on the beach where cliffs fell, without pause
Waves tasting blood cascade and froth. Shaking,
The land quakes in the turmoil as wind roars.
A vast energy heaves the sea and falls
And swells into a pulsing surge on sand
And smashes into craggy cliffs and foams
And fountains over trembling harbour walls.
The sea crashes, pounds and batters the land
And the wild wind buffets and blows round homes.

30 April, 23 August 2017

Brexit Election

I HIDER

Election Day, sky grey as the campaign.
I walk among my roses and ponder.
May wants a landslide to strengthen her hand
For deals with the EU, a power transfer.
She wants to block free movement and control
Our borders, laws and trade, and walk away
From the single market and customs union –
And half our exports and income, and may.

I wander through clover and buttercups.
Her name, not her party's, is on her bus.
She's talked in slogans – 'Brexit means Brexit'
And 'strong and stable government' – at us
But's jerky and twitchy, not comfortable
In her skin, and lacks warmth like a robot.
She would not debate with other leaders,
She's a hider, while Corbyn chats a lot.

Carp nuzzle water lilies in the pond.
Her manifesto made pensioners foam:
No winter fuel for some, no triple lock
To keep pensions rising, and care at home
To be paid from their house after they've died.
She cobbled it up with her advice team.
Like a dictator, she does not consult
Her Cabinet, and gave Corbyn a theme.

I pinch rosemary and sniff my scented nails.
Seven weeks of campaigning's let Corbyn in.
All can see he's well-meaning and caring.
He is more comfortable in his own skin.
The people are tired of austerity.
He's bribed young voters with tuition fees.
He'll borrow, up the deficit. Why not
Pay for food banks for all and win with ease?

II HIDING

Night falls on the forest, birds call no more.
At last the Exit Poll at ten o'clock
On banners, TV screens and the towering side
Of London's BBC building, a shock:
Conservatives 314, the largest
Party, but no majority, a hung
Parliament. Stunned, pundits are sceptical.
Is May's hand with the EU now hamstrung?

I wake in dark and turn the radio on.
It's three-thirty, I listen for a score:
Labour 200, Tories 191.
I sleep and wake at five-thirty for more.
It's true, she has lost her majority.
She's had a hiding, she's solely to blame.
She has no mandate for a hard Brexit.
It's a mess, the EU's laughing at her shame.

Sunshine. News all morning, will she resign?
It's said the Irish DUP will want
To help but London has to be neutral
And can't have pacts with parties to Stormont.
She's driven to the Queen, returns to speak.
She's doing five more years, a victory speech
As if she'd won a landslide, she is in
Denial, deluded. All's changed, we screech.

I gaze across green fields in the warm sun.
Now her two advisers have both resigned.
They controlled all access from Ministers.
One wrote the care home plan that seemed unkind.
Now they are scapegoats for her shortcomings,
And she's too weak to block cries for their sack.
She called for sovereignty and democracy,
And anti-austerity answered back.

III HIDE-AND-SEEK

Paths through the roses make a Union flag.
A 'confidence-and-supply' deal's to be.
But the DUP are still bargaining,

She's sent out a press release too early:
A billion and a borderless Brexit.
And Scotland wants the single-market way.
Is 'no-deal' hard Brexit now dead at last?
Have voters saved our exports and the UK?

I sit and feel warm sunshine on my cheeks.
She is in office but is not in power.
She's told she has misjudged the public mood.
She's apologised for her mess, see her cower.
There's a new compromise in politics,
There'll now be hope, no more austerity.
There's been a catastrophic misjudgement.
She now clings to power with tenacity.

I stand beneath the cherry tree and muse.
The Queen's Speech is delayed, and there are fears
The Brussels talks are running out of time.
Three months have slipped by out of the two years
And we have not even started talking.
Our prospects are now looking very bleak.
We are leaving the EU, but for what?
Where is the hide-out of the deal we seek?

I fling brown pellets and the big carp rise.
The EU's challenged, and it's best to stay
Shielded from Putin, IS, migrants, Trump
Within the single market like Norway
And have some free movement, but we'll have lost
Our rebate and opt-outs, we'll be amiss.
The genius of our voting's steered between
The Left's Scylla and no-deal's Charybdis.

IV HIDEBOUND

Ten red-hot pokers burn the rockery.
Now the talks begin, and Davis gives in
To Barnier's timetable: divorce, then trade.
He's unprepared, no paperwork, can't win.
Seven thousand deals to strike in eighteen months,
Three hundred and fifty deals in the bank
Each month, a week of talks and three of deals.
A year has passed, and next month's deal's a blank.

A lone fox prowls along the garden fence.
Three million EU citizens can stay,
May's offer to the Council of Europe:
Under British law, not the ECJ.
EU leaders say it's not good enough,
And know the British Commons won't condone
A hard Brexit from the single market
As we can't afford to survive alone.

Bees nuzzle in the wafting lavender.
There's rancour at our plight, we will not cope,
Out there's a sombre mood of powerlessness,
No way forward, just drift, weakness, no hope.
No one believes that we can stand alone
As before Suez, our Empire has gone
And a minority government can
Do worse than stay in Europe – if still on.

Grey-necked jackdaws peck near the apple-trees.
Hidebound, May wanted to increase her power
And weakened it, and what is on offer
Will leave us poorer, and worse off (all glower),
No opt-out or rebate and so we might
As well not leave and keep our trade. There's spin
But we're in a mess, can't exist alone.
We need to reject the deal and stay in.

11, 13, 24 June, 1, 3, 8–9 July 2017

122. 'Hidebound', "narrow-minded, bigoted, constricted by tradition" (*Concise Oxford Dictionary*).

Within Dark Tunnels

I climb onto the gurney, a cannula
Is fitted – in my inside arm a bite –
In case I need sedating, which I won't.
I turn on my side, a scope with a light
Is pushed up into my intestines, I
Watch on the screen, travel up a tunnel

And pause to explore junctions. Near my heart
A white growth on the lining of my bowel.

"A polyp," says the surgeon. I watch as
A needle injects it, I feel no worse.
It swells into a balloon. A wire snare
Is pushed up near it by a Chinese nurse
Squatting on the floor. "Up a bit," he says,
"To the right, down, now." She lassoes and wrests
The blown-up polyp with the wire and snips,
Drags it out to send to a lab for tests.

The light travels up a new dark tunnel
And now behind my ribs on my right side
I see a round crater with a white crest –
"Another polyp" – and the needle slide.
The Chinese nurse lassoes it, drags it out.
I glide up another tunnel that's grooved,
Stop at yet another polyp and watch
It injected and lassoed, then removed.

I tour a mysterious darkened world
But no more larval polyps like white string
That can cause rectal bleeds and stomach pain,
No more tissue on the inside lining
Of my colon that can turn cancerous.
Reluctantly I leave my hidden deep
Where darkness returns as the camera leaves.
I marvel at soft-walled tunnels that sleep.

Within is all so organised, nothing
Is left to chance, each tunnel is a feed
In a well-ordered drain from my stomach
That breaks up food, distributes what I need
And processes the rest as waste, and this
System's in all humans and's running blind.
O how wonderful is the intricate
Waste disposal in me and all mankind.

24 June, 13 July 2017

Sea Stirred

Rain lashes at my painted window-panes
And runs down the glass as the sea rolls in
Long curling white breakers that break like stains
From the grey wrinkled waves that stir within
Mist that obscures the horizon – no, fog –
And blends with the vast greyness of the sky.
The sea has woken like a barking dog
That slumbered through the gusty storm's outcry
And now prowls past breakwaters to the beach
Beneath my window, sniffs prey and attacks.
I hear the wind whistle and whine and moan,
See the waves leap before its force and reach,
And all is energy that blows through cracks
Draughts as I sit holding my pen, alone.

16, 23 August 2017

White Crests: Motion and Stillness

A strong wind beats round my seaside house, raves
And gusts and buffets almost constantly.
I look across the bay, white crests of waves
Rise and then fall as far as eye can see.
Each choppy wave miles out, wind-whipped and raw,
Gives the green sea a restless, determined
Look, waves seem to be pressing towards shore
But dip and rise to the controlling wind.
Rushing winds and tides whose force seems diverse
And gulls that hover hindwards near the foam
Are moving and still forms of one presence
Which permeates the universe to nurse.
Amid motion I sit and watch at home,
Still, hovering on a One that's immense.

22–23 August 2017

Christmas Cherry
(A Metaphysical Poem to my Dutch PA)

I

I give you a Christmas cherry.
Forty-five orange cherries fizz
From leaves on a miniature tree.
Small flowers will become more berries.

It's on your desk to remind you
Of my forty-eight books, this tree.
You've assisted me on nineteen
During your ten years' work with me.

Or on this anniversary
Perhaps it pots forty-five years
You will work for me: ten now done
And thirty-five still to do. Cheers.

If from now each book takes two years
I'll start my last book when I reach
A hundred and ten, finish when
I'm a hundred and twelve. Don't screech.

Now I hear you have just counted
Thirty-five flowers and buds: a new
Crop of thirty-five more books with
Seventy more years' work from you.

Don't worry, I know a Nobel
Nominee who'll stem-cell us both
To live to two hundred with looks
Of thirty-five – *and* body growth.

The Christmas cherry cheers your desk,
Calls you to stay and look back on
The things we've done – and can still do.
It lives ten years, and then is gone.

II

Its ten-year life has just begun.
It represents the next ten years
Now that the last ten years have passed.
Please stay and put aside your fears.

Your native Holland calls to you
To leave anti-EU glares here.
This miniature tree's berries are
As poisonous as a Brexit sneer.

So stay, their toxin is not life-
Threatening. And my works reveal
The mix of beauty and despair
That there will be no Brexit deal.

The English used to welcome all
The persecuted and hungry.
Now you feel they're uncaring, bright
But toxic like Christmas cherry.

I know my books may seem toxic
To my unthinking countrymen,
But my works shine out truth to all
And truth seems tart and alien.

So stay, help me record the times
And catch their shine and bitter taste.
Your home is here, don't leave and let
This Christmas cherry go to waste.

26–27 October 2017

Title The Christmas cherry (*Solanum pseudocapsicum*) is a miniature tree with orange cherries that are mildly poisonous. Nicholas Hagger's Dutch PA, Ingrid Kirk, had worked with him for ten years, and the tenth anniversary was on 26 October 2017.

2. Orange is the national colour of Holland.

22. 'Nominee', Vincent Giampapa, who during the Gusi awards in Manila in November 2016 told Nicholas Hagger he was working on stem-cell arresting of aging that can enable 70-year-olds to have the quality of life of 20-year-olds and enable humans to live to 200 and have the looks and body development of 35.

48. 'Tart', acid, bitter.

A Vaseful of Flowers
(To my Dutch PA)

My card shows two vases, one small
With two flowers; one large with, serene,
A hundred and thirty-four flowers,
My bunch of works you put on screen.

The small vase holds the two of us,
The large vase works we'll do, it looks,
If we have years and energies
To finish eighty-six more books.

Listen, I have their seeds in mind.
I just need time, a hundred years,
And a clear head for them to grow
And your help that displays and cheers.

26–27 October 2017

Warm Sun on Cheeks: How the Universe Works

I lie on my sun-lounger with closed eyes
And feel the warmth of the sun on my cheeks,
And think of its photons that pass through me
And then of how it took millions of weeks
For each to be born as fused hydrogen
Atoms in the sun's core, rise and break through
To the sun's photosphere, then reach my cheeks
In rays in just eight minutes through sky's blue.

I think of how the sun that looks so calm,
An orange ball peeping through mist, at source
Is in fact a bubbling, boiling, seething
Hydrogen bomb, exploding with the force
Of a hundred billion hydrogen bombs
Each second, nuclear reactions that show
Its solar flares, leaping to massive heights,
Falling like hot rain on the fires below.

I think how each photon was created
Long before our ancestors left the plains
Of Africa, and took a million years
To escape from the sun's inner domains.
All human civilisation took place
While these photons that now bombard my cheeks
And pass through me were struggling to get out
To spend eight minutes reaching peaks and creeks.

Each photon began as a gamma ray
That escaped the density of the sun
As a ball of gas, that rose and then fell
As if the sun were raining, and is one
Of billions that were then sent racing out
Across the universe at light's great speed
To pass through my cheeks and then continue
For billions of light years, to just proceed.

One day's photons power the entire world's
Civilisation for twenty-seven years.
Light from our sun fuels the cosmos's life,
All life comes from the sun, whose light coheres.
Without light all humans would be nothing,
So is life an accident that's caused by
Incandescent heavings in the sun's flares?
Is there purpose in photons' hue and cry?

And does a similar process improve
And nourish our souls within body's flesh?
Does the Light which can only be perceived
By the soul in its corporeal mesh
Also bubble and boil and blast out rays
Of subtle Light to reach our meshed spirit
And constantly renew a spiritual
Network of humankind's souls when all lit?

As without, so within. With my two eyes
I see the physical sun that warms skin,
And with my inward eye behind closed lids
I see the spiritual sun that shines within.
Within the universe one law of light

Governs all bodies and keeps their minds wise
And brings all trees and plants to bud and fruit
And pulses all living things through their eyes.

I sunbathe in the sun within a shower
Of warm photons that keep my body fit
And fill my soul and its mind with wisdom.
At least, that's how it seems to my fed wit.
It seems I know how the universe works,
How light fosters beasts, insects, fish with fire
And trees and grass, water and air and earth,
And inspires all each second to aspire.

13 November, 16–17 December 2017; 17 February, 5 June 2018

A Dozen Jackdaws

I walk back from the cleaners to my car
Clutching a bedspread in a long round bag.
As I turn into the street where I've parked
A dozen jackdaws fly around me and nag.

Some perch on the roof of my old doctor's,
Two are on a streetlight, one in a tree.
As I walk on they take off and fly round
And settle again on new lights in glee.

I am alone in this street where I spent
My boyhood, and back home I put out bread
For a dozen jackdaws in my garden.
Are these those birds, have they followed my head?

I see them as watching me, their feeder,
And following my car when, quite at ease,
I drive and park to go to the cleaners,
They've got me watched from high-up roofs and trees.

I reach my car and still I am alone
And still the dozen black birds wheel about
And settle as if waiting for my food,
Joined to me as if by cords as they scout.

I get into my car and drive back home.
I look in my mirror, can't see them plead.
But all evening I am haunted by them.
Next morning I heap seed-bread where they feed.

And now a dozen jackdaws surround it
And in their pecking order take torn bread
And fly away, and I am sure they are
The dozen jackdaws that wheeled round my head.

30 November, 15–16 December 2017

Nesting-Box

A nesting-box on a tree
For a bat to nuzzle in.
In Japan ancestors
Come back and inn near kin.

My children, be aware
That when I've gone aloft
To drink tea with Shakespeare
And talk with Hughes, I'll oft-

-en fly down to this home
On the spreading oak tree,
Evict the bat and peer
For my lost family.

11 January, 17 February 2018

My Books Heaped like Raspberries

My books heaped like raspberries
To show my heartfelt thanks
For your decade's hard work
That gave them a camp's banks.

6 February 2018

Diving Birds

Offshore the distant sea birds are diving.
I pause my work and peer from my window here
And watch them wheel and, one by one, hurtle
Into the water, splash and disappear

And re-emerge with a fish from the shoal
That's drawn so many wheeling birds to arrive.
Birds of the air feed on the oceans' fish
With a perfected steep and fast nosedive.

I must have seen approaching fifty birds –
Gannets? Manx shearwaters? – from here gull-like,
Hurtle down with instinctive, intense force
And vanish in spray like a missile strike.

O birds wheeling slowly in the blue sky
Peering beneath the waves where you've all dropped,
You have stopped diving now, the shoal has gone
And I am pleased your killing has now stopped.

O Nature, what a cruel regime is yours,
Where no creature is safe, and all are prey
And prey on others, one selfish instinct
To gobble and gulp to live one more day.

15, 17 February 2018

Fifty-Nine Years Ago in the Hotel Miramar, Malaga

Fifty-nine years ago
I stood here with Hemingway
Near the end of the day.
His hair was white as snow.

Fifty-nine years ago
And now I have grown old,
White hair and feet gone cold.
Fifty-nine years like snow

Have melted and I know,
Look back on my bold youth
When, fearless, I sought truth
And time was a sideshow.

6, 12 April 2018

Among Grandchildren on Gibraltar

We stop at the border to Gibraltar's
Rock, cross the runway, pass the garage where
The SAS shot three IRA bombers,
Park for the cable-car, and rise to near
The summit, gaze down towards Malaga,
And Cadiz, the sweep of Spain's coastline, tell
Where Nelson's body after Trafalgar
Was carried ashore in a rum barrel.

A Barbary ape jumps on the rail to peer.
O grandchildren, all Europe is spread out
Beneath you like Spain, which can invade here
Any time and end British rule, and rout
A sway 'in perpetuity' ceded.
Look down for the cemetery where, faith-strict,
The dead Trafalgar seamen were buried,
See centuries of Anglo-Spanish conflict.

Grandchildren, you face a troubled era
As many nation-states compete in wars.
A chemical attack in Syria
Has given the US a bellicose cause
To fire missiles and rain thunderous blows
Against Russia and Iran, the allies
Of Assad's seven-year war to re-impose
Rule on all his state, which had shrunk in size.

The Skripals laid low by a nerve agent,
Diplomats expelled – a new Cold War sets
Nation against nation and at present
A Third World War's looming like Allied jets.
Now Syria's sliding out of control,

It feels we're back in the sixties before
The EU brought peace to Europe's torn soul.
Competing nation-states always bring war.

I see a hundred missiles targeting
Three sites linked to chemical weapons' stores.
They roar down in the pre-dawn dark, bringing
An Anglo-Franco-US message: pause
And dismantle all chemical warfare,
Chlorine gas was banned from the First World War.
But banned gas killed just half a thousand, while air
Barrel bombs have killed half a million – ban *them* by law.

The UN's failed to prevent seventy-two
Wars being fought worldwide in lands now torn,
And there are still nearly fifteen thousand nu-
-clear weapons. There were none when I was born.
O grandchildren, you face a troubled fate.
How good it would be if all hate could cease
So one benevolent and rock-like World State
Can ban war and nuclear bombs and bring peace.

I dream you may have a peaceful future
As citizens of a world government
That can build an Age of Peace and Culture,
Seize every terrorist and nerve agent,
All chemicals and bombs and *jihad* toads,
And preside over a pan-global state
That can build highways like Spanish toll-roads
And transform every backward country's fate.

Socrates said, "I am a citizen
Of Athens, Greece and the world." That's your stop.
O grandchildren, you'll be citizens then
Of Loughton, England, perhaps still Europe,
And the world, cosmopolitans at one
With humankind. And I entreat you now
To work for peace so under this warm sun
All schoolchildren have good lives and think 'Wow'.

The poet is not just a metric man
Who entertains some boozers with wordplay,

A hungry half-listened-to also-ran,
But a man of vision who points the way
To all who seek a higher truth for men
Than this ape we came from can know or rate.
And so I say to you, o grandchildren,
The way to truth is to dream a World State.

10, 12–14 April, 5 June 2018

Ancestral Tree

1

I sit with my grandfather by the fire.
He says, "We came from near Royston, and became
Lords of the Manor somewhere near Cambridge."
As we pick apples my father says the same.
Older, I find a Quaker graveyard with several
Tombstones with our name. Older still, at Bourn
I see in a mortuary chapel four
Grave slabs of our ancestors, much foot-worn.

I am invited to open a fête at
Bourn Hall, the house John Hagar the Fourth built
In 1602. I have a tour of the Hall.
The gutters proclaim 'HIF' beneath silt:
'Hagar Iohannes et Frances', but was
He really my forebear amid his sheep?
It's an IVF centre now, did they see me
As a potential benefactor for its upkeep?

I had two researchers track back my name
Through Grandpa's ancestors, but this new tree
Stopped in confusion at three men who could
Be in my family, no one could see
The way back. Now seventeen years later
An email's come, and my work's been approved
In Australia, and the man's missing link
Shows he's my cousin, seven times removed.

Inspired again I resume my ancestral tree
And, with the lords of the manor as my guide,

See a new link that can be laid before
The College of Arms to be verified.
I've my mother's tree but feel incomplete
Unless I test what my Grandpa told me,
And my father too. I know they'll be watching,
Very interested in what I put in my tree.

II

What is it that impels us to research,
Check baptisms and burials on websites
To take us back to where we need to be?
What is this yearning to belong to 'heights',
To an old family of sheep farmers who lived
Primitive lives and became lords somehow
To collect rents to supplement their income,
Rough people I would not converse with now?

It may go back to ancient memory,
To when we lived in caves, valued all who reared
Us, who'd been in our family and brought food,
All who'd helped shape our lives and should be revered.
We may have some atavistic desire
To recite our lineage and feel complete.
And so I am linked to lords on a tree
And am an apple as they were, fit to greet.

I sit and gaze up at my apple tree.
So many apples ripen in the sun,
My ancestors going back to Tudor times.
I'm rooted in ancient Tudor life, homespun.
Henry the Eighth passed a law that no one could own
More than two and a half thousand sheep on farm land
And fathers put their sons on different farms
So each could own two and a half thousand.

Putting the names in my tree I can sense
The struggles of those men centuries ago
To make a living and build a Hall for
Their descendants to live in and wield so
Great influence in their community, and keep
The local courts and rule with a mayor's stare.

And now I see, we make our trees to know
The power our forebears wielded, which we too share.

14–15 April 2018; revised 11 December 2022

A Split Cedar

A cedar's branch has sheared
And's held up by an oak.
It's propped against the trunk,
Could fall and crush and choke.

A man with knotted rope
Dangles from near the top
And chain-saws up the branch,
Lets himself gently drop.

Now the cedar is slim.
It stands tall with its crown
But a gash in its side
Is like a sobbing frown.

25 April, 30 May, 3 June 2018

Dove Supreme

A white dove with pink feet.
I tear two crusts of bread,
Chunks mound the bird table.
The dove pecks with bowed head.

Two jackdaws, two magpies
Swoop; the peaceful dove – what? –
Flaps its white wings and sees
Them off and scoffs the lot.

I strew two more slices.
The dove returns and lands,
Once more scoffs all the bread,
Gulps down each piece, then stands.

Amazing that the most
Peaceful of birds should fend
Off jackdaws and magpies,
And stand supreme at the end.

25 April, 30 May, 3 June 2018

Fountain: Newts

The fountain's been shorting,
The water's murky green
With tufts of blanket weed.
The newts cannot be seen.

John comes with a new pump.
Now water spurts and brims
Round the bowl to the pool
Where a baby newt swims.

O wonderful fountain
That brims over the bowl
And clears murk so we see
Newts wriggle in their Whole.

We too are like small newts
And wriggle to and fro
Beneath our trickling sky
In our clear Whole we know.

1, 30 May, 3 June 2018

The Setting Sun

A walk towards the setting sun
Down through the field to the wild flowers.
I turn and see my house couched in
Green Forest trees, outside time's hours.

I love green and orange sunsets,
I love the carp that wait for me

And speckled newts in the fountain
And the song thrush that pipes clearly.

I wander back through red roses
And lavender that makes me sigh
And now I gaze up at the bright
Full moon that hangs in the night sky.

The universe enfolds with love
And I rejoice in its harmony
And peep at all crawling creatures
From overjoyed eternity.

27, 28 June 2018

Like a Bee Crawling

Like a bee crawling on sprigs of lavender
I gathered nectar for works, and made a gold
Honeycomb out of my life which I now survey
For its lavender pattern now that I am old.

29 June 2018

The Deep

Snailfish live five miles down under great pressure
As if under fifty jumbo jets' tonnage.
They have transparent bodies and live in the canyon
Of underwater mountains, the mid-ocean ridge,
The gorge's floor torn by volcanic fire from the core.
Three-quarters of the earth's volcanic rents
Are in the deep, most of them on the ridge.
Gases come up through crevices, minerals set up vents
With as much life as tropical rain forests, half
A million animals crammed in a square metre,
A vent in the Atlantic's 'lost city'
Of sixty million turrets; their food bacteria
Hydrocarbons that are found in all living things. So,
Life may have begun round a vent four billion years ago.

29 June 2018

Siskins

Green birds flitting like butterflies
From the elm to the old oak tree,
A flock of forty, to and fro,
They're siskins, come to visit me.

I sit out in the evening sun
And watch their stuttering, fluttering flight.
O siskins, you can settle here
And hide in my leaves, out of sight.

Morning. All's still, no siskins flit.
The flock has flown to other trees.
But I recall how still I sat
As I watched you flutter and tease.

30 June 2018

Hovering Bird

How still the hovering bird
Hanging above the cliff
Impervious to the wind
That blows my hair to a quiff.

I sit on a seat and munch
My pasty by the bay
And watch the hovering bird
That's spying out its prey.

Now the still bird swoops down
And's gone beyond the quay,
And I sit on alone
With the wind and the boiling sea.

16 August 2018

A Deluge of Light

Engrossed in work I raise
My eyes to the calm sea.
A thousand splashing lights
Rain round a canoe and me.

In the bright midday glare,
A deluge of sunlight
Splashing round the canoe.
Glory for the gift of sight.

A cloud crosses the sun.
The storm of light has passed.
The sea is flat and drab.
I return to my work from the vast.

17 August 2018

A Harmony of Orange Lights

I gaze at the dark sea,
Lean on a stone wall and laze.
Waves wash gently to shore,
The moon's behind a haze.

Suddenly I'm aware
Of thirty lights flashing,
All orange on the dark
Horizon, each flaring.

Who are you way out there?
What ships or fishing-boats
Staking your territory
Like a dawn chorus of birds' throats.

Out on the dark night sea
A conversation jumps
Backwards and forwards, then back,
Unknown craft talking in clumps.

They say "Hello, I'm here"
And "Watch out, avoid me,
For your own safety" and:
"It's lonely on dark sea."

And through it all I see
The Eddystone Lighthouse share
Its white light six short times
And a seventh longer flare.

O lights dancing on black,
Warm orange flash-and-fade,
You exude a harmony
From your come-and-go parade.

20 August 2018

Fountain: Water Lilies

I sit in the sun and watch
The fountain spout and fill,
Overflow and trickle down
To a bowl with an iron grille

That shows, in lines and curls,
Twenty-five civilisations,
Including the European
Which has schism's separations.

And above the water-line
And the green blanket weed's blight
Seven perfect water lilies
Bask in the hot sunlight,

My seven main disciplines
I write my books in, each
Of whose iron lines and curls
Share their fifty-four ends: they reach

To the central stone fountain.
I look at my spouting

Inspiration held up by three
Graces, my Muses' spring,

And the civilisations and my
Lily-like disciplines rhyme
With my fifty-four iron-grille books
That will survive spouting time;

And all are within a rose
Garden where in twelve beds lurks
A Union Jack, the UK
In which I've spouted my works.

Now I am in a time
When the UK is to leave
The EU and follow
A Union-Jack future, and grieve.

26 August 2018

This poem was written as a Metaphysical conceit, an extended metaphor involving spiritual faculties and physical objects.

Sparrowhawk and Reality

I talk on the phone to Spain,
Absorbed in my word flow.
A fluttering, grey bird flies
Into my balcony window.

It hits the glass and falls.
Kestrel? It turns as I talk.
No, there in its glory, lines
On white, a sparrowhawk.

It flutters to the rail,
Turns its head, looks at me
And then flies to the oak.
I tell Spain what I see.

And now I am alert,
I'm looking outside, aware

Of my present reality
And Spain's a dream elsewhere.

11 September 2018

Ragged Tulip
(For Ian)

You are lying sick and in some pain
After an operation for bladder cancer.
It's not known how much they have got out,
There may have to be another.

I send you a card of a ragged tulip
And hope you'll recover and be out of pain,
Back into bloom and be in full voice
And fill an auditorium again.

But for now you are like a ragged tulip,
Your smiling well-being's been blown.
May your immune system now restore
You to the smile I have always known.

29 September 2018

We are like Trees

We are like trees in the autumn sun:
Tall, massive, branched limbs, stiff and slow,
Shedding poems like leaves, reflecting on
Our image in the water below.

We are like trees approaching winter
When there are no more poems to shed from on high,
And our branches are gnarled and bare,
Our trunk and arms that now reach to the sky.

We are like solid, enduring trees.
It's unthinkable we can disappear,
Be removed from the ground so it can't be seen
Where our roots were, no trace or tear.

We are like trees in late autumn,
We still have our leaves, and we look golden
And russet in our fall's colours,
Majestic in our turning, and stubborn.

29 September 2018

In Front of the Fireplace

I sit again where I sat the entrance
Exam for Oxford in front of a lit fire.
Last year the fire was warm on my back, this year
The fire is laid unlit, which I don't admire.

And that late mid-December afternoon
The light was dingy in this dining-hall,
I peered but could hardly read what I had written,
Squinting in the gloom and then sensing a call.

I wrote hard to become one of the four
Out of a hundred who would be admitted
To a future that would bring me sixty books
Once I'd embraced a destiny revealed in my head.

30 September 2018

6. Original version: "The light was dingy in this dining-hall tomb,".
8. Original version: "Squinting myopically in the gloom."
12. 'A destiny'. For the destiny see 'Being like a Puddle' (pp.37–38).

Magical Moonlight

4am, I go to the bathroom.
Magical moonlight paints the floor.
I look through a window, a pale
Green glow in the garden and on the door.

I am back in Cornwall, one evening
I walked by the sea, the beach was lit
In a lovely glow that was bright enough
To see where a breakwater's been split.

O moonlight, I love you and I love
The moon that fixes an eye on me
And do I see a raised eyebrow?
O moonlight, glow across the sea.

28 October 2018

Oak Tree

An oak tree in autumn,
Two thousand leaves on the lawn
And still the oak tree's leafed,
There are more leaves to be shorn.

Like an oak tree I stand
Gnarled and seven-branched, and spread
Two thousand poems beneath,
And still more poems to shed.

O oak tree and poet,
You obey the same law that chimes
With the universe and shed
Your style of truth many times.

I am within Nature,
I speak with tongue of trees.
I shed my leafy works
And will lie in a field beyond breeze.

15 November 2018

Plasters and Bandages (A Far Memory)

I stick a plaster on my right thumb
To cover a crack below the nail
And another on a left finger,
A slit in the skin the cold's left frail.

And suddenly I remember
A fat bandage around my thumb

Frayed at the edges and stained with blood
Seeping through the bandage rounds, all numb.

And all my fingers were bandaged,
I had bandages on both hands
And on my head, round my forehead,
I a young man fighting in foreign lands.

A memory from a bandaged life
In the First World War. I can hear the drums,
When I was wounded on head and hands
And had fat bandages round my thumbs.

The memory has passed and I am back
In this current life, eighty next year,
And I'll soon slip away from my skin
And may come again in a different veneer.

28 November 2018

20. 'Veneer', "thin covering" (*Concise Oxford Dictionary*).

Blown Spume

A howling gale, the swelling sea spouts up
The harbour wall, the wind takes the blown spume.
I battle with the wind to pack the car.
The wind tugs my hair, blows into my front room
And rattles lampshades even up the stairs.
I am like the gulls soaring against wind
And rising, blown off course, as I clutch bags
In each hand, pick a way down steps, disciplined,
And stagger to my car boot as if loading
Waist-deep in water, and now there's lashing rain
That soaks my body-warmer as I wind
The rusty chain round granite stone, lock chain
And leave the house to brave the wind-blown foam
And head inland for shelter and drive home.

18 December 2018

Being like a Puddle

I bring a card and say how pleased I am
She's not got cancer, hear about the testing
That has left her with pain from biopsies
And an inserted stent to carry bleeding
Away before it clots near her kidney.
I sit in a room with a Christmas tree's blinking
Lights, sink into a cushion with a stag
And she says she controlled pain with her breathing.

She asks about my experience of the East,
And how I think when I meditate. I sigh
And say, "I sit cross-legged with cupped hands
And empty mind of thoughts, the ego's 'I'
And rational, social planning, shopping lists
And cheques to write and what's on TV that night,
And work, and am still like a stone, and just
My rising and falling breaths, and the Light.

"I close my eyes and with ego shut down
The soul comes into its own, and reflects
Like a puddle, and in due course the clouds
Break and a sun shines through and soon connects
And is reflected in my puddle-soul.
It has great energy, like the daytime sun,
And it fills my body with healing and keeps
Me free from sickness, at one with the One.

"Until the seventeenth century, there were no doctors
Or drugs or medicines save for picked plants.
But the Church knew this ghostly Light banished
Disease and kept the soul healthy with chants,
And so when a priest said, 'Let us pray,' all bowed
Heads and became like a stone, being, still,
Not in process or becoming amid sounds
Like a television's or a fly buzzing.

"The Church was the guardian of the Light
And brought it down at prayer time to fill all
The congregation with an inner health.

But today, it's forgotten the Light's call
Or what it's there for, and an Archbishop,
Enthroned in robes of Fire, did not understand
The fire on his cope. And the monarch's forgotten
How Charles the Second's healing touch brought hope.

"The Church and King and Metaphysical
Poets all knew the Light preserved, but now
There are outer images in the media,
Sounds of thumping music that are lowbrow
And no inward stillness. And so the true poet
Is misunderstood amid outer television
And all he can do is write his vision down
In poems to preserve the tradition.

"So when I sit still with cupped hands and close
My eyes, I become a stone and a puddle-soul
And absorb the white radiance of the Light
That shines into my reflecting soul, makes whole
And's channelled through my flesh to make skin glow,
And know it's the primeval Light, my source
That unifies the universe and fills
And heals all creation with its energising force."

22 December 2018; revised 11 December 2022

Soul like a Puddle

As I fill up the car
In the garage in the dry,
Raindrops on a puddle,
Each splash obscures the sky.

So it is in my life:
When I look out from my soul
As from a still puddle
I clearly see the Whole

But when my soul is troubled
With drops from a busy world

My way of looking's circles
As in a puddle that's swirled.

10 February 2019

Hearts like a Shout

I open your Valentine's card.
Little red hearts fall out
On the papers on my desk,
Tiny red hearts like a shout.

O my wonderful daughter
Who has time to think of your dad,
Thank you for the two-score hearts
That have made sure I'm not feeling sad.

14 February 2019

Orange Sun

An orange sun slides behind the Spanish hills
That surround distant Barcelona, like a kite.
From my ship's balcony I see a green dusk,
A dark sea and a black feather of night.

How full of sunny energy was my life
When I met Hemingway somewhere out there,
Towards those darkening hills and feathered sky,
And now the sea's turned black in the twilit air.

12 May 2019

Farewell to my Europe

I FAREWELL TO ITALY
I sit on this ship's balcony and reflect
At eighty on the places I sought out
In the Mediterranean when a callow youth,
Which I have just revisited as a kind

Of 'hello again' to old friends, and a kind
Of farewell to my classical heritage.
I am a European, and Europe's
Monuments meant much to me as a boy
When I was steeped in ancient history,
They inspired me as I sought and found my way,
And still draw now I have achieved my goals.
I am with an American company on
The *Norwegian Star*, but nearly missed my ship
As I was put on a wrong bus to the port
And nearly loaded on the *Norwegian Epic*,
A ship like an enormous block of flats
That takes more than four thousand passengers,
And had to return to reach Tarragona.
We were the last to board, and I thought back
Sixty years to when, in Barcelona,
I read an anthology of the Metaphysical
Poets while hitchhiking round Spain, outwardly
Unconcerned about the next place we would reach
But inwardly travelling in one direction.
I had heard my calling on a school field seat.
I knew I had to steep myself within
The poetic tradition, and had just left the Law,
A move opposed by my well-meaning parents,
But now I know I made the right decision.
  Now I relive my voyage of farewell
In a succession of haunting images.
The *Star* sails to Cannes, where my second son
Will arrive this night for the film festival,
And we are driven up to Cap d'Antibes –
And I look down at Antibes' Citadel
And terracotta roofs where Graham Greene
Lived in his eighties in a 'modest' house
And then gaze across towards Cap Ferrat
Where Maugham, also a spy, spent many years,
Two whose books I have enjoyed in the past,
And later linger in Saint-Paul-de-Vence,
A medieval village. I'm back in
My return from Libya, burdened with care,
In a personal and political nightmare,
And drive from Cannes to Monaco and then
On to Rapallo and sit with Ezra Pound,

A monument with discerning eyes, nearest
To Dante's, eighty-five, and share with him
My plan to write an epic – now fulfilled –
On the Second World War in the tradition
Of Homer, Virgil, Dante and Milton.
Pound said, "If you can see it you can do it."
I 'did' it in thirty months, and Ted Hughes saw
All four volumes come out and wrote me cards.
And I've written fourteen hundred stories,
Having followed Greene and Maugham into secret work.
I see my path through life like a road up a hill
That is clear when viewed from the top, eighty-year-height.
The next day I wake up in Livorno,
Near where Shelley drowned in this sparkling sea,
Near the beach where Byron burned his body
And cut out his poet's heart. I think of how
He conceived his 'Ode to the West Wind' in a wood
Near Florence where we're driven, '*per* Careggi',
And I think of the days I spent in Cosimo
Medici's villa, absorbing Ficino,
Who presided over the Renaissance.
We walk down narrow streets to the Duomo,
Santa Maria del Fiore, the lily,
And beyond Ghiberti's Gate of Paradise
In Florence's Piazza della Signoria
Perseus holds up the head of Medusa
Which will turn you to stone if you don't look away
Within three seconds. I think of my early poem
'Medusa', in which I warn myself of a force –
The Law – that would turn me to stone if I did not
Turn my soul away and avoid its destructive gaze.
This time I can't say farewell to Dante's house
Or the place by the Arno where he met Beatrice,
I peer up the Arno, beyond the Ponte Vecchio
And think how I stood here twenty-six years ago.
We drive on to Pisa and walk to the Leaning Tower
And I think of Galileo, who used it in
His experiments on the law of gravity,
And think of the last time I saw it, when
On the Lung'Arno, alongside the Arno,
In a small river bar beneath a bridge
Near the station roundabout, I had a vision

Of two works completed within ten years,
My epic *Overlord* (forty-one thousand lines
Of blank verse) and three hundred and seventeen
Classical odes, the first 'four-book' odes penned
Since Horace, all finished ten years later.
I achieved my bulk by glimpsing a challenging task
And bringing it into being, as with these two works.
I cannot complain about what the Muses inspired
Me to write – two epics, four books of odes,
And *The Gates of Hell*, Metaphysical love poems;
The bulk of Homer, Virgil, Horace and Ovid,
All bubbling into my consciousness like a spring
From the beyond, a Muse's gushing within.
Like Ovid I knew too much and was walled round
With silence by the deep State of the day,
Which exiled me as surely as Ovid was banished.
I cannot help it if powers beyond my control
Curtailed the dissemination of my works,
Which had to find their way by word of mouth.
  I bid farewell to my beloved Rome.
The boat docked late, so our tour's been cancelled.
I've hired a minibus, driver speaks no English.
I've foregone my ticket to the Sistine chapel.
But, put out in rain, I realised we once stayed
In a fifteenth-century palace a short walk
From St Peter's Square, where I saw the Pope,
John Paul the Sixth, preside over a mass.
I walk through rain to take a lingering look
At those few days when I got inside Rome,
Found the grave of one whose name was writ in water.
Now a museum to Leonardo's genius.
Sheltering from rain I see from models in wood
His inventions – glider, parachute, helicopter,
Armoured car and multi-barrelled cannon,
Spoon-shaped catapult, double flute, stereoscope,
Projector, surfboard float, lifebuoy, cog-wheel,
Ball-bearing, chain drive, hand-cranked and self-propelled cart
And bicycle, all from his Universalist
Imagination that also evoked past scenes:
The Madonna, the Last Supper and Vitruvian man.
I cannot look again on the Apennine Way
Where sixty-two years ago I saw catacombs.

Within the Pantheon I again marvel
At what Agrippa began, Augustus's friend,
The two-thousand-year-old dome, all one piece.
I later see that the bottom three levels
Of the Colosseum have Doric, Ionic
And Corinthian columns, carved and installed
While Vesuvius was burying Pompeii.
  And now I wake in Naples, and look out
From this balcony on which I've been scribbling
And see Capri, and think how we both walked
From the main square to Tiberius's villa.
I see Vesuvius, a third of its 79 size,
And recall falling off it sixty-two years ago,
And grazing my arms. Its ash is still in my skin.
We drive up to Posillipo's hilly ridge
And look down on the Bay of Naples and Sorrento,
Cloudy Vesuvius and Capri's Tiberian rock,
And on the other side at Pozzuoli
And the Phlegraean Fields; sadly, Baiae and Cumae
Are out of sight, and I cannot say farewell
To places I researched and discovered:
Virgil's tomb in the *columbarium*
(Moved from the Castel dell'Ovo near where I sit
On this balcony) and the ruined towns
Beneath Vesuvius which show how the Romans
Lived their everyday lives and met their needs.
I have loved so many ruins in Italy
That gave the world the great Roman Empire
And then the Renaissance, and, an old man,
I admire the Italian continuity
And great old fragments that inspired my work.
It is a wrench to say goodbye to these.
In this warm sun, I, who face my extinction,
Feel so well, and the words flow from my pen.
I feel I could live for ever, and not have
To bid farewell to my favourite Italian haunts.
  The ship passes Capri as it heads towards Greece,
And I scan for the villa where Tiberius
Ruled for ten years and where we walked eighteen
Years ago, found the leap where he threw his enemies,
Saw rocks he knew – it all crowds back. Goodbye.
  Somewhere out in the dark is Paestum, where

I nearly died in the Temple of Hera
Sixty-two years ago, violently ill
In my sleeping-bag before Hera's altar.
I returned to thank the goddess for saving me
(Although Hoppit still insists that was his doing).
I nod to Paestum, come in and go to sleep.
I wake as we enter the Straits of Messina
And recall a time when I saw the great whirlpool
Odysseus saw between Scylla and Charybdis,
When sixty-two years ago I travelled
By train on a pilgrims' ticket (six pounds
Return) from Naples to Syracuse to see
The Weeping Madonna, the statue that shed tears.
And later over breakfast I look out
At white Etna rising into the sky,
And I recall how off Catania
Sixty-two years ago, in a small boat
With Lorenzo singing 'Santa Lucia',
Etna spewed red lava before me, erupting
Into the twilit sky as in 79
Did Vesuvius, but on a smaller scale.
Etna, I'd bussed as far as I could go
Earlier that day, and I have seen you since,
From the Villa Paradiso's bedroom window
Nineteen years ago when I drove round Sicily.
Etna, hail and farewell, a Roman salute:
Ave atque vale, old friend and permanent
Fixture and reference point in my memories
I am sad to see recede as we sail for Greece.
I sit at the ship's back and look down at our wake
And now Etna's below the horizon,
A memory that will soon be as distant
As the memory of long ago when it erupted,
And the Romans and Italy's fine places
Have receded over my memory's horizon.

II FAREWELL TO GREECE

And Greece, so much to say farewell to.
We enter Santorini's caldera
Where a 'Minoan settlement' was destroyed
By a huge eruption where I now sit,
More than three thousand six hundred years ago.

Twenty-three years ago I visited
Akrotiri and wrote of the Admiral's house,
And now again I walk in this Greek Pompeii
And see the signs of advanced civilisation:
Toilets, clay pipes, a clay bath, jars, slate floors,
Doors and windows with wooden lintels, and now,
At last, the Admiral's house by the public square
(Which was triangular), 'West House', but where
Is the wonderful painting of his fleet of ships,
The naval expedition setting sail?
I found it in the Athens National
Archaeological Museum, it's come back to me.
I bid farewell to the Admiral at his house,
Which slides into a memory like his ships
As the cable-car swings us down to the tender.
As the *Star* pulls out of the caldera, which recedes,
The Admiral still haunts me, he has no name
And the prehistoric city has no name –
Akrotiri is a nearby medieval town –
And is not Atlantis, which Plato placed
Beyond the Pillars of Hercules (Gibraltar
And Tunis), beneath the Atlantic Ocean.
My mysterious Admiral was master of the fleet
In a Cycladic and Minoan settlement.
Farewell my Admiral but you still haunt me.
  I wake in Athens on Sunday morning
And tour deserted streets and find the slopes
To the Acropolis, and stand and gaze
At the Parthenon and Erechtheion
Which I drew in dark evenings when sixteen,
Lingering over the six caryatids,
In awe of the Athenians who stopped the Persians,
Like defeating mighty China from the East,
And of temples they built during their long war
With Sparta, like this small temple to wingless
Athenian Nike, so, having no wings
She would always be on hand to bring victory.
I bid farewell to the sixth century BC
And its monuments which meant so much to me
While I wanted to be an archaeologist,
And I later drive past the ruins of Plato's
Academy, and recall my excitement

When I found where Plato wrote of Socrates,
Now under grass and trees and fallen stones,
And where Aristotle taught, Alexander's mentor.
I say farewell to all these worthy souls.
As the ship pulls away I gaze at Phaleron Bay
Where the Persian fleet arrived, and we later pass
Aegina, where our two boys swam along the coast.
I say goodbye to so many familiar hills
With a heavy heart, for I have loved them all.
I wake in Mykonos and take a boat
To Delos, the birth place of Apollo.
Sixty-one years ago on the waterfront,
Having walked there from the stone house I'd rented
For twelve pence a night (and a donkey that brayed)
I ordered breakfast (bread, butter, honey)
But never ate it – a boatman called, "Delos."
I boarded, paid and landed on lava.
The boatman would not wait, so I returned with him.
Now sixty-one years later I see what I missed:
Three ruined temples to Apollo and round
The oldest, five Athenian treasuries,
Holding talents paid by the Cyclades,
Silver protection money so Athens
Would defend them against the mighty Persians.
Only strewn marble blocks survive that bank.
In 454 the treasuries were moved
To Athens and funded the Parthenon
And other buildings on the Acropolis.
Hermes' head's on a pillar, an old friend.
I stand and soak in what fascinated me
At sixteen, how Athens funded its empire.
But what I sought sixty-one years ago has gone.
Back on Mykonos I can't find the café
Four paces from the water's edge, all's changed.
The Mykonos of my memory has gone,
There's a wide promenade between cafés and sea,
And I say farewell to a place that is no more.
Argostoli in Cephalonia.
I recall being driven to Ithaca
Twenty-four years ago and visiting
The Palace of Odysseus, who Homer
Says was "King of the Cephallenians",

Passing under a stone bust to Lord Byron
In Vathy on the way back and seeing
The sixteenth-century Saint Gerasimos
In a monastery, dead four hundred years
But perfectly preserved with swarthy skin,
His body shown just one day every year.
I discuss the saint with our guide, Gerasimos,
His namesake, in a lingering farewell.
Now I pass the house in Metaxata
Where Byron stayed in 1823
Before fighting the Turks at Messolonghi
And dying of fever. In 1815,
At the Congress of Vienna, a British
Protectorate over the Ionian Islands
Was set up, and Byron called upon Greeks
To liberate themselves from Ottoman rule
And he recruited several hundred Greeks
(Mostly Albanians) to his private army
As freedom fighters, he said from his own money
But he was surely Government-funded
And acted, like T.E. Lawrence later,
In a seemingly personal capacity
While advancing British foreign policy.
I bid farewell to Byron's Romantic fight –
He carved his name on a Sounion column
To defy the Turks – and as our ship ploughs on
I see distant Ithaca and bow my head.

III FAREWELL TO DIVIDED EUROPE

My eightieth birthday. I sit and watch
The sea slide calmly beneath my balcony
In Kotor's mountainous Illyrian bay
And all my classical odes jostle to greet me
And all round me crowd faces I once knew,
All smiling from beyond – my family
And friends who are no more, a host I loved
Who've gathered round my chair to beam at me.
And among them Roman and Greek faces
Who are set to welcome me when I join them.
  In the Serbian-Orthodox monastery
In Cetinje, Montenegro, a monk
Unlocks St Peter's coffin and shows me

John the Baptist's right hand, the two fingers
That baptised Christ intact, a dark brown hide
Beside a fragment of the cross, relics
Brought by the monks at Malta and lodged there,
And this unexpected and special favour
On my eightieth birthday makes it seem
The faces include the Baptist and Our Lord.
But in my ship's cabin in the afternoon
I open cards from those still in this life,
My loving family and those near me,
And reflect on how fortunate I have been.
  Now in Dubrovnik, I recall how I
Ran out of money on my way back from Greece
Fifty-nine years ago, and took my last
Ten pounds to a ticket-seller in Skopje
Who took pity as one humankind member
To another and gave me a bus ticket
To Dubrovnik and a boat ticket to Rijeka,
From where I could use my return train ticket,
A kindness that still haunts me in the fortress.
I see pictures of the Serbian bombing
Twenty-eight years ago, and where shrapnel
Gouged the Cathedral walls, and we drive through
Villages with bombed houses from that time.
Croatia joined the EU for lasting peace
Which the EU has brought to post-war Europe,
And as I sip fire-water (local brandy)
In the country home of the Glavic family
I think of Balkan nation-states waiting
To join the EU and live in new-found peace,
Montenegro in six years' time and Croatia
With full currency union in two years.
Today is 'European elections' day
And all the minor states of old Europe
Are voting to improve their conditions.
Only my nation-state is trying to leave.
O how sad that Europe's doing wonderful things,
Raising the standard of roads and economies,
And the UK's heading for isolation,
Torn apart by savage division and conflict,
Seeking to leave the EU without a deal,
And increase tensions with its member-states,

And is imploding into powerlessness.
I will soon bid fond farewell to Venice
(Its waterfront loggias and the lion of Mark),
Which dwindled from great power to backwater.
I, the poet of British decline since
The nineteen-sixties, more than fifty years,
Shake my head as the fire-water fires my throat
And I long for a united humankind
In a democratic World State that will end war.

14–27 May 2019

Kestrel

Outside by the sea near Hayley Island
A kestrel hovers, still on the wind, watching,
Then dives and stops for one more searching look,
Then swoops and flies off with a vole, flapping.

In Russia, alert, aware, I survey
The men who'll lead me to talk war with Putin,
And dive, then hover, then swoop and carry
Signed books to give him after I've gone, and begin.

O kestrel, you are back again, I see
You hover and study the same terrain,
Then peer and finally turn away and fly.
Your prey's slipped away like mine, I know your strain.

10 June 2019

A Great Illusion

I

May's been forced to retire by her right wing
And after a beauty contest between
Her would-be-successors, two candidates
Have spoken at fourteen hustings that have been
All round the country and now it's the last one
At London's Excel Centre, and it's not clear
If either should be PM. One blusters and jokes,
The other's managerial, neither has the vision to steer.

Both have been forced to support a 'No Deal'
Even though it would be disastrous for jobs,
As the hundred and sixty thousand Tory
Voters are uppermost in their minds and 'gobs',
And not the general electorate out there.
Party considerations must come first –
Looming recession, an unemployment rise,
National woes can be ignored as a cloudburst.

News breaks. Boris Johnson's plan for 'No Deal'
Is to postpone the Queen's Speech until 'consent'
November and send the MPs home for the last
Two weeks in October, so Parliament
Has no time to discuss 'No Deal''s dangers.
He wanted to leave the EU to restore
The sovereignty of the UK Parliament,
And it's not allowed to discuss 'No Deal' any more.

I muse on history as the car glides there.
Before 1872 'hustings' averred
A platform where candidates for Parliaments
Addressed electors. It's an Old-Norse word
Meaning 'house of assembly', and then passed
Into Old English, it's a primitive, not new,
Democratic concept but effective
As electors hear what candidates will do.

I sit near the front among two thousand.
The audience is relaxed, doesn't seem in awe.
It does not look or feel as though we are
In the biggest crisis since the Second World War
Into which the new PM will be plunged.
Faces don't look anxious, no one is tense.
Have I misjudged the seriousness of our plight
Or are they ignorant, unaware, without sense?

Cameras train on a screen, I see MPs
Walk by. At last we start, Chairman speaks now.
Johnson goes first, introduced by Liz Truss.
He talks of getting Brexit done, not how.
His left hand's in his pocket, his right hand waves.

He talks like a Messiah, he wants his grin
To revitalise the Party and take back
The Brexit Party's vote and trounce Corbyn.

From time to time there's loud applause, some rise
And clap in a half-done standing ovation.
I see Parris in the row behind me.
He's wearing green and doesn't rise or, stubborn,
Applaud, like me he is an observer.
It's all about Party, not our country.
Johnson says he'll renegotiate the deal
Although the EU says this cannot be.

Johnson holds up a smoked kipper sent from
A business in the Isle of Man and strikes a blow:
An EU regulation now requires
It must be sent with a plastic ice pillow,
Which is senseless and increases costs – a gaffe.
For the Isle of Man's no more in the EU than India,
And it's a British regulation that ice
Must protect kippers from transmitting listeria.

He's ended and now sits with the Chairman
And answers random questions from the hall.
They're all on social issues – mental health,
Care homes, welfare – not about Brexit at all.
Again I feel the absence of crisis,
The chosen questioners are all diverse with spin,
Showing the Party's liberal and tolerant.
Johnson leaves the stage, Hunt waves his way in.

Hunt is more fluent and lists his policies.
He's more managerial, a safe pair of hands.
He understands business and making profit.
His tax cuts are business-friendly and suit brands.
You couldn't put Johnson in charge of a school –
It would go bankrupt – but you could make Hunt Head.
He lacks charisma and does not inspire.
Both back 'No Deal', I can't vote for what either said.

II

Next day a shock. A Commons vote is called
To block the next PM from suspending
Parliament to force through a 'No-Deal' Brexit, it must
Be convened to discuss Northern Ireland's working
For five days. It's carried by forty-one,
And Johnson has been warned not to be a proroguer
Of Parliament to get 'No Deal', so how will he
Get the UK out by the thirty-first of October?

The maths don't change because Johnson's now PM,
All's still paralysed. We were told with an earnest frown
Brexit will strengthen Parliament's sovereignty,
Not that it must be dictatorially shut down.
And the Government's majority's still only three.
Johnson's said he won't extend, and 'No Deal''s closed.
So will Article 50 now be revoked?
There's a new PM but everything's still exposed.

An early general election is planned
As Johnson's majority's three, a concern.
It could be *after* delivering Brexit
So the Brexit Party voters will return;
And if someone else will reduce the Tory vote
It must come while Corbyn's still Labour leader.
The election may have to be called next week
If Johnson's to deliver Brexit by the end of October.

The choice has whittled down: support Johnson,
Get low taxes and a booming economy,
Or if Tory rebels topple their leader –
If he's taken down by a minority
On a no-confidence vote – have socialist Corbyn:
Wealth tax, high taxes to pay for his 300 billion
Programme of high-spending nationalisation
And promised private-school abolition.

The President of the European Commission's
Said though the Withdrawal Agreement can't in any
Way be changed, there can nevertheless be
A long extension to Article 50.

The Brexit Secretary's told Barnier
The Agreement's dead and the backstop's nowt
And must be scrapped, and 'No Deal' looms once more.
And now only an election's the way out.

Hundreds of economists all mention
'No Deal' will bring recession and borrowing
Of 30 billion a year. There will be a shock
To the UK economy that will be lasting.
The hustings have been a Great Illusion,
With truth regarded like the smoked kipper – wrong.
There may be an election next week and neither
Would be Prime Minister for very long.

17 July 2019

Triathlon

The seaside triathlon's finished.
Applauding crowds, loud microphone,
Runners running, bent, exhausted,
All noise and energy, and groan.

Now all is still, and on calm sea
Ten thousand lights splash and repeat
As if the sea, not to be outdone,
Is showing how it too can compete.

27 July 2019

Wildness

The rain is lashing on the panes tonight,
The wind whistles, in my window I'm in awe.
The sea's breakers creep in under white foam
In five, now six tiers, heading towards the shore.
The harbour wall endures, having withstood
Two hundred and twenty years of battering storms,
And I, bent over my work, pause and look
As in the dusk Nature is raw and swarms.

The sea thrusts towards me with a wildness,
Heading for my position, relentlessly well
Rolling shorewards beneath my wet window,
And I sit like a hermit in my cell,
My eyes on the writing I have been doing, warm,
And feel at one with the advancing sea and storm.

29 July 2019

A Squall

A squall beside the sea,
Rain hoods and umbrellas blow,
A slanting rain from inland,
People huddle and go.

The sea's emerald, now silver.
Nature's mood's protean,
And the squall is the surface
Flux of the changeless One.

30 July 2019

Destiny at the G7

I

The G7 leaders breakfast in Biarritz
At a long table, three dozen looking grey.
Trump speaks, all listen, then I watch Johnson
Say he wants red tape lifted so the UK
Can export lamb and pork to the US.
There's a special relationship in sight
Between two blusterers who manage truth
To put their own deeds into a good light.

Yesterday Tusk, standing at the podium,
Said he hoped Johnson wouldn't come to be known
As "Mr No Deal" to which Johnson snorted
That the EU would be known as "No Deal" alone
If they did not remove the dead backstop
From the Withdrawal Agreement, without doubt.

The ERG have said they will not vote
For the Agreement, backstop in or out.

The papers are full of the future plans.
The EU's to be told the UK won't pay
Thirty of the thirty-nine billion it 'owes'.
Parliament may be prorogued five weeks, they say,
And there may be a General Election on
October the seventeenth, the Tories are ahead.
There's talk of a deal possible, but what will happen
Depends on what the EU does, it's said.

So the UK faces a change of course
From the EU to an offshore island
That some believe will have global clout as
An Atlantic bridge between the EU and
The US, but others believe will be
A vassal state in the US's view.
A country's destiny is its global role
And the UK must choose between the old world and new.

But in the case of the UK it's back
To how it was in the 1960s
When it coped alone, but had a deficit.
It's back to borders, less trade and bridges.
I think of the planting of America
From the UK, and now all's in reverse.
Will the UK become its fifty-first state?
This PM's optimistic, couldn't be worse.

II

I think of the Europe that I have known,
The French D-Day beaches, and the German
War places, and my beloved Greece, the fifth-
Century ruins of the Peloponnese beckon,
And the islands, and the Roman Empire.
I grew up with a bond to old Europe
Through classical antiquities and war,
And am sad to be leaving Europe at a gallop.

I found all civilisations pass through the same
Stages, that as they decline include union –

The USSR, and the European Union now.
The EU Johnson so wants to welsh on
Is the current stage of the European
Civilisation the nation-states of gold-mine
Europe have now entered, and so the UK
Cannot leave and do better, only decline.

25 August 2019

A Life Draws to a Close
(For Ian)

The sea is hushed, its waves
Edge gently to shore, each breath
Moves slowly, like sleeping
Before approaching death.

And I think of the hospital drips
And swollen skin that won't mend,
The kidneys that have failed,
As a life draws to an end.

O gentle sea, calm ward,
It is sad when life's near night
And the soul rises from flesh
And floats up the tunnel to Light.

31 July 2019

Breakers

The waves surge in from an olive-green sea,
The breakers' white surf struggles towards shore.
The night's storm's left the beach well-washed, with a line
Of seaweed on the water's edge, the roar
Where the wind blusters and blows is endless.
The horizon's misty where sea meets sky.
A lone gull heads towards it, battered by air.
On the wall near my window the ivy blows high,
All Nature has been in uproar all the night
And I too have been buffeted awake

And have lain in bed in the dark while the wind blew,
My being attuned to the invisible window-quake
Coming at me with force I mirrored though blind
As breakers from my deep tore into my mind.

9 August 2019

Full Moon and Reality

A full moon over sea,
Eyebrows, nose and mouth fledge,
And a shimmering yellow line
Near the calm water's edge.

Up there's round reality,
Below is a shimmering line
That distorts the round face
Into an illusion, a spine.

And I think how the round Light
Shines down onto my calm soul
Which mirrors a shimmering line
That's not the source of the Whole.

12 August 2019

2. 'Fledge', "grow feathers" (*Concise Oxford Dictionary*), and so 'form, take shape'.
3. 'Shimmering yellow line', moonglade (the bright elongated reflection of the moonlight on the dark sea).

Our Expanding Universe

Astronomers have now reached an impasse
On how fast the universe is expanding
And flying apart, they have made different
Estimates and may be forced to rethink
Their ideas about time and space. No more
Do they feel they understand the universe.
It's all a conundrum that's mysterious.
Our greatest minds are baffled by what's known.

Before expansion debates there was the discovery
Of dark matter, believed to be made up
Of undetected particles whose strong
Gravitational pull explains why galaxies
Do not fly apart; and of dark energy,
Which is accelerating at the rate
At which the cosmos is expanding. And now
There's a third bafflement to think through.

A century ago, Hubble found the greater
The distance between two galaxies, the faster
They are moving apart, like raisins in
A loaf when the dough rises and expands.
The speed of the universe's expansion,
The Hubble constant, has a precise value,
Much sought-for yet unknown, which would explain
The cosmos's origin, age and fate.

Astronomers seeking this value have probed
The behaviour of galaxies near ours,
The Milky Way, to see how fast they are
Speeding from each other; and the rippling
Pattern of light, cosmic background radiation,
That formed after the Big Bang 13.8
Billions years ago, tracked from satellites
In space. Till recently, the estimates were close.

But now the discrepancy has widened,
The lower Hubble estimate has got lower,
The higher higher. One measures how fast
The universe is expanding today,
The other predicts from the physics of the early
Universe. A Hubble constant of 70
Would mean the universe is expanding at
70 kilometres per second per megaparsec.

One megaparsec's 3.3 million
Light years, when a galaxy's that distant from us
It will move 70 kilometres (43.5
Miles) per second faster from us as a result
Of the expansion of the universe.

Changing the Hubble constant from 67.4
To 73.5 would cut the universe's age
From 13.8 to 12.7 billion years.

The trouble is, some very old stars have
Estimated ages of 12 billion years,
Leaving too little time for them to form.
Measurement error is not a cause for
The differences in Hubble constant values,
So perhaps a new class of subatomic
Particles travel close to the speed of light,
Dark radiation that includes neutrinos.

Or perhaps there was a dark-energy
Episode not long after the Big Bang,
Or perhaps the particles that make up dark
Matter interact more strongly with normal
Matter than previously assumed. Both would
Have an impact on the Hubble constant.
O wonderful cosmos we find ourselves in,
And wonderful minds that so nearly understand it.

3 November 2019

Feeding Time

I break up two slices of bread
And throw the bits onto the end
Of my long terrace, watched by crows
And jackdaws perched on the roof's bend.

One's on the tall lightning-conductor.
I wave him down, go in and sit.
A dozen black birds flutter and swarm
And peck, some several bits, then flit.

A large raven with an injured leg
Limps up and pecks with its leg in the air
And looks forlornly at me and its mate.
Ravens are always seen in a pair.

More come. I move, they fly. They're not
Like trusting Galapagos birds that are nice
And settled on my wrist, at one
With humans as in Paradise.

In this fallen world, even those who feed
Are treated warily and feared.
I stay still behind my long window
Until the terrace end's been cleared.

O what it is to be a bird
And perch on a rooftop and wait
And wait till the untrusted giver gives,
But fly off if he moves to the 'bait',

Untrusted by creatures of time,
Who've lived in the moment for years and shone,
Fattened themselves on charity's bread,
Feeding in time until they're gone.

I am feeding creatures of time
And so I'm feeding Time itself,
Some of the creatures that perpetuate
Time by feeding from humans' food shelf.

9 November 2019

The Message of the Fireworks

I stand by the school oak tree in the dark.
Rockets shoot up, explosions are loud
And white and green palm trees fill the sky.
Children wear lights, I stand in a crowd.

We're celebrating Bonfire Night, the failed
Plot to blow up our British Parliament,
Which has blocked our national independence,
And is now prorogued, closed, to discontent.

Some see our Guy Fawkes as Johnson,
We're living under a chaotic regime.

If we're independent we'll be worse off.
We can't stay in the EU, it's out of steam.

There's an election and both leaders
Are terrible, each in his own way.
"What's best is a hung Parliament so both leaders
Can wreak havoc" – that's what the fireworks say.

10 November 2019

Autumn

The mists have come, the leaves have turned,
The maple's orange by the gate.
I feel a chill in the autumn air,
Winter's looming, snow won't be late.

The path is muddy to the gate.
Mice come to the loft for warmth, and lurk.
The crows and jackdaws wait for bread
And I am buried in my work.

I proofread and make notes, cut off
From what the season's doing outside
While all creatures are watching the sky.
I must leave my work and be sharp-eyed.

17 November 2019

Falling Apart: Atrophy in Cerebellum, Vocal Cords (A Fragment)

My doctor refers me to the consultant
Who sent me for an MRI more than
Two years ago, which found I've atrophy
In my cerebellum; moderate, not severe.
Now he asks me to walk across the room.
Eighty, feet apart I walk easily.
Then he asks me to walk in a straight line.
Two steps and I've lost my balance and step sideways.

Six steps and I've stepped sideways three times.
I've lost the ability to walk in a straight line.
He refers me for a new MRI scan
To see how far my deterioration's gone.
The back of my head is atrophying.
There is nothing I can do to walk straight.
The freedom with which as a youth I walked
And ran effortlessly has been taken away. I'm old.

I'm falling apart. Only two days ago
I was found to have a gap between the lips
Of my vocal cords. I will now tend to be hoarse,
Speak with a thin voice, my clear speech has gone.
I have to go for muscle-strengthening advice.
The body is a wonderfully-balanced
Piece of precise engineering, but when
Time's nearly up, it begins to fall apart.

30 November 2019

Hail

Hailstones lash my window,
I peer through the twilight.
Round blocks of ice on my sill,
By the Roundhouse a lake in the night.

I shiver in winter cold
And from the distant dark
I hear the ocean breathing
Of the in-out waves, hark.

Hail, hail, you brought me out
Of my deep writing trance
So I could see your ice
And hear the sea's panting dance.

14 December 2019

Shoreline

Wave upon wave curls and foams white to shore,
Six waves make their way to where they will end,
Stirred by the storm that lashed rain on my pane
And's now calmed, leaving sedate waves that trend
And edge shorewards like minutes in an hour
Or days within a week or months in a year.
All's olive-green and white and a near mist
As time foams like decades, to make an end here,
And now I see the crests of eight decades
Full of busy surfing as they push to reach
Shore, and, watching, I wonder why my decades
Will end when they reach shallows on the beach
And contrast the magnificent crests out there
And the still water on a shoreline that's bare.

15 January 2020

Abednego

I said, "Bed time, Abednego,"
And I was back as a small boy
And my mother, hands out by the fire,
Says, "To bed, Abednego." O joy

At her teaching me of *Daniel* 3,
Shadrach, Meshach and Abednego,
Punning on "to bed you go". I see
How she taught me what I should know.

30 January 2020

1, 3–4. Nicholas Hagger's mother used to say, bent by the fire, "Bed time, Abednego."

Another Sparrowhawk

Is that a still long-tailed tit on
A ball of feed in the bird feeder?
I see a speckled sparrowhawk
With wing bars swoop from the juniper.

The still bird leaves its camouflage,
They dance mid-air, four times the hawk
Tries to seize it and then flies off.
The bird sensed it and did not squawk.

30 January 2020

Snakes

Biggest storm for seven years.
Wind gusts round the house, I stir
For down my window-panes
Fifty long snakes slither.

They snake from top to bottom,
I watch spellbound, a boy
Again in the war, watching rain.
O snakes, you've brought me joy.

9 February 2020

Poems written in Jordan, Egypt and Turkey

Promised Land

I stand where Moses stood and look across
The Dead Sea to Qumran and Jerusalem
And the River Jordan's valley green as moss,
And the oasis of Jericho, and Bethlehem
And the mountains from Hebron to Nablus, so fair,
Then I turn to where the hills of Amman throng,
And now a wind gets up and blows my hair
And I know that like Moses I have not long.
But just as Moses saw the Promised Land
And then died somewhere here on Mount Nebo,
So I too see a Promised Land entice
With a shimmering world peace beyond my right hand
And countries like these hills that are aglow
In a harmony that gleams a Paradise.

1 March, 2–3 September 2020

Bedouin Tent

I stand in the long Bedouin tent with sandstone seats
Where Lawrence sat and later O'Toole to dine,
And talk with a Bedouin whose grandfather
Blew up a Turkish train on the Hejaz line
With Lawrence and then stole the Turkish gold
It was carrying and distributed it to spend
To the villagers as payment and reward
For their revolt, which would bring to an end
The 500-year-old Ottoman rule.
He has nine brothers, I have just met two.
His grandfather died a hundred years ago
And I feel connected to him and what he knew
As I sit in his long dark Bedouin tent
And drink tea where Lawrence did amid dissent.

5 March 2020

All-Looking Among Bedouins

I sit near a fire and smell the scented smoke
As a family of Bedouins serve me tea,
And now feed me on sand-baked chicken and rice.
The sun's set, in the failing dusk each palm tree

Has a clear silhouette, and a singer twangs
A rababel. I sit like Dushara, the all-looking
Chief god of the Nabataeans in the Petra Siq,
Shown as two eyes and a nose, and all-knowing.

5 March 2020

Three-Tiered Fountain

I sit by an Arab fountain.
From the top water overflows
To a small bowl, then a large bowl,
Then the fountain's base and repose.

⌜ So it is with the spring of my
Inspiration, which bubbles and, swirled,
Splashes down into my soul,
Then my mind, then the wider world.

5 March 2020

1. In the foyer of the Mövenpick Hotel, Petra, Jordan.

Sunset: Ra

I wait on a rocky height near Wadi Rum
For the sun to slide behind the mountain, Ra's barque.
I sit with the awe of an Arabian man
And watch Ra dip, and the air's now chill and dark.

5 March 2020

Ramesses the Second's Concubine

I go into the Cairo mummies room
And immediately see Ramesses the Second
Lying on his back, his hands above his face,
His fingers spread as if he's looking at them,
Hooked nose unlike the nose in his statues,
Curly-white hair dyed yellow in embalming,
Brown skin. He's eighty, the age that I am now.
And I think how I was regressed and saw myself
In a line of women in the Ramesseum
When Ramesses stood in a golden crown
Uniting Upper and Lower Egypt
And picked me out, so I was the Chosen One
And felt a surge of joy, and honoured pride.
I thought I was a temple maiden, but they
Remained virgins and retained their purity.
The line must have been a line of concubines,
And I this hooked-nosed man's chosen concubine.

16 March 2020

1–2. Nicholas Hagger visited the Egyptian Museum of Antiquities and saw Ramesses II on 10 March 2020.

Jellyfish

As a jellyfish in the sea
Puts out a trailing tentacle
And hooks a seaweed strand
To stop its sinking wobble,

So this human in air
Puts out a trailing arm to clutch
The rail as he wobbles down
The ship that's rolling too much.

Mid-March 2020; 10 December 2022

In the Roman Theatre at Aspendos

I sit in the theatre at Aspendos,
The best-preserved Roman theatre on the turquoise coast.
A dozen sparrows chirp from the third tier,
And I marvel at how much has been preserved,
The sixty arches and fine acoustics,
And I am back in the second century
Amid twelve thousand Roman citizens,
And see in my mind the wooden canopy
Above the actors who played Plautus here,
And share the silence beneath the centuries
Since then with the magnificent chirping of the sparrows.

13 March 2020

Volume 36

THE TAPESTRY
2016–2023

The Tapestry is in three parts which reflect the algebraic formula encapsulating the wisdom of the East that Nicholas Hagger discovered in Japan in 1965, and that is in all his works: +A + –A = 0.

Part One:
Tapestry, the New World and the One

1
My Tapestry

A tapestry tells a story, as does
The Bayeux Tapestry, cloth embroidered by
English designers soon after the Norman Conquest,
With Harold holding the arrow in his eye,
From an English, not a Norman perspective
Though commissioned by the House of Normandy;
And as does the New World Tapestry on the founding
Of the US. The story on my tapestry
Is of the birth of my long destiny's
Journey from childhood war to mystic peace,
To know the One and dream a better world
In a split Europe in which Brexit and war cease,
Rooted in past glories, a dream to shape in my mind
A reunited world and humankind.

16, 20–21 April 2023

2
The Bayeux Tapestry

The Bayeux Tapestry, seventy-metre-long
Strip of linen with fifty-eight scenes, compressed,
Which I saw in the company of D-Day veterans,

Shows events leading up to the Norman Conquest
Spearheaded by William, Duke of Normandy,
At Hastings, where Harold died during his loss.
I am rooted in Waltham Abbey, whose third church
Was built by Harold, who prayed at its true cross
Before the battle and was by repute buried
Under its altar, now a churchyard grave, his home;
Also in my Bruges family, and in Fairmead
Where I live near the Tudor split from Rome.
On my tapestry's embroidered a modern split,
A Europe which the dismal UK quit.

16, 20–21 April 2023

7. 'Third church'. Harold built the third church at Waltham Abbey in 1060, and it was demolished and rebuilt in 1090.

12. Henry VIII's split from Rome began in the time of Anne Boleyn in the late 1520s and early 1530s, and continued in the 1540s in Henry VIII's third hunting lodge (known locally as Elizabeth I's hunting lodge); at nearby Copped Hall, where Henry VIII heard a gun fire at the Tower of London signalling that Anne Boleyn had been beheaded; and at nearby Waltham Abbey.

3
New World Tapestry

On the long kitchen table at Otley
Hall where it's thought the Jamestown voyage was planned
Is carefully spread the New World Tapestry,
A phase in the settling of the new land,
Stitched embroidery larger than Bayeux's pitch
On the Norman Conquest. For Gosnold's role,
Heads bent round my needle, I add a stitch
And think of Fates bent round my infant soul:
How Clotho wove the thread that got me born,
Which Lachesis embellished with events,
Threads that would decide what would be unfurled;
Atropos will cut the threads I have drawn.
I see a tapestry of incidents
In my mind's journey to a bright new world.

18, 21 August 2016; 4 June 2023

1–3. A section of the two-hundred-and-sixty-seven-foot-long New World Tapestry was brought to Otley Hall on Friday 12 June 1998.

5. 'Pitch', "a salesman's advertising or selling approach" (*Concise Oxford Dictionary*).

6. 'Gosnold's role'. Bartholomew Gosnold was no.2 in Admiral Newport's voyage of three ships to Jamestown, the crew having been recruited at the Gosnold family's Otley Hall.

12. 'Drawn', "pulled, closed, attracted" (*Concise Oxford Dictionary*).

4
Berlin: City of the One

You sent a shudder through me as a child
For you were where my destruction was planned,
A place of evil where reason was wild.
You had to be blasted to rubble, and
Now seventy years on you are a tranquil
City with a thousand bridges, the free
Hub of Europe. I wander through your still
Quaint Christmas markets in what used to be
East Berlin and in jostling crowds I cease,
Sip *Glühwein*, buy gingerbread men and search
For shells, recall what fire-bombings have done
And marvel that you are now so at peace.
I pass where a mosque, synagogue and church
Will share one site in your city of the One.

4, 12 December 2015

5
Berlin Wall

And I think of another time when East
And West were separated by this wall
I stand before, a mural like a beast:
Brezhnev and Honecker kiss and appal.
I see a grim, bare concrete wall deface
A street near Checkpoint Charlie, twelve feet high,
And recall on the Spree three giants embrace
As East and West, back under one rule, cry
With joy. I grasp today's date and, apart,

That I've lived forty-six years with my wall,
Fragments of which survive across my heart.
Though I'm now unified I still know all
Those years ago I was walled out, and so
I now survey its ruins with sorrow.

4, 12 December 2015

6
Brexit Blunder

Now another wall's gone up around our coast,
Borders are back after forty-seven years without,
And passport-checking, and the end of free passage.
The UK's a nation-state with less clout.
We've come out of European civilisation,
Which we've been involved in since the Roman time
And since Augustine and the Church of Rome,
With wars every thirty years during our prime.
Now we're past our best, less trade with our neighbours
That's lost over four per cent of GDP,
And are having to trade with far-away countries,
Many of our doctors and nurses are across the sea.
Interdependence is out, nationalism's back
And so prices are up, our economy's under attack.

21, 23 April 2023

2. 'Forty-seven years without'. 1973–2020.

7
New World

I look across the darkened sea, half-blind.
The new world I foresee is borderless
With an electorate of humankind,
A lower house for all nations' progress
Based on the UN's General Assembly;
A Senate and part-federal world government
That can end war and confiscate surely
All nuclear weapons, disarm world dissent.
So many in the last century saw this –

Churchill, Truman, Einstein, Gandhi, Russell,
Eisenhower, Gorbachev – and now just me
Among Western authors of the abyss.
I'm to be given an award, but just foretell
A better world for all humanity.

18–19, 21 August 2016

13. 'Award'. Nicholas Hagger had heard that he had been awarded the Gusi Peace Prize 2016 for Literature.

8
Peace: Grandchildren, Aleppo

I take two of my grandchildren to the beach
And walk with them to the rocks by the caves.
They scramble on boulders, net for shrimps, reach
Then leave the sitting gulls and walk through waves
Holding their shoes till sand gives way to stones.
I look up at the cliffs and rock pipits
And across to harbour walls built with groans
In the seventeen-nineties, know peace that flits.
But then on TV I see Aleppo.
The regime's bombed a street, a boy as small
As my younger grandson is carried out (looks crease),
Blood down his face, and sits still – no tears show –
With such composure, and I know that *all*
Humankind needs a universal peace.

18–19, 21 August 2016; 4 June 2023

9
Distant Lights

Over supper I say, "Brexit is pause,
They haven't recruited the staff they need."
And you say, "I could help them draft their laws,
From home. I've worked in Luxembourg, indeed
For the European Commission, I'm a jobbing
Solicitor with drafting skills." "You'll see,"
I say, "Parliament needs ten years' drafting,
Changing each law. You should tell our MP."

Later I stand above dark sea and peer
At distant lights along the horizon
That flash and pulse from lighthouses and ships
Halfway to Europe we've cut loose from here.
I see each light as in a networked one
That includes all humans like radar blips.

18–19, 21 August 2016

3–5. Nicholas Hagger's daughter-in-law Kate Hagger had worked for the European Commission's Publications Department and expressed an interest in helping to redraft UK laws on 18 August 2016.

10
Bridge

I walk over the harbour bridge – ropes stun –
That lets ships through, tilting into the sea.
My shadow strides with me in August sun
As I cross from old age to my youth's quay
And am back in my younger self that found
The universe was One, what I should do
And did not flinch from millions of words bound
That I must write to achieve and accrue.
And back in my young self I ponder when
I first glimpsed the world's unity, the All,
And history's, find what my inner child saw.
I glimpse my early memories, and then
I'm in my high chair, war map on the wall.
Could I have known the One when I was four?

19, 21 August 2016

1. The harbour bridge is in Charlestown, Cornwall. It has two rope rails.
4. 'Youth's quay'. Nicholas Hagger sat on the beach near the Pier House quay in the early 1970s. He occupied the Harbour-Master's House in 'old age's quay' from 1987.

11
Bomb

I stand before the house I lived in for
Two years before D-Day, dreading the dark

And whine of the V-1 doodle-bug bombs, not roar.
I look up at the room I slept in – hark,
I'm counting from the cut-out up to ten
And hear the distant crash that means I live.
Lying in bed in the blacked-out night then
I knew that war is wrong and primitive.
One night the windows blew out from a bomb
That fell on the cricket field: boom and crack;
At the gate, going to the post, I saw,
With my father in the dark, an awesome
Flash light the house bright as day. We turned back.
I stand where the gate stood and think of war.

19, 21 August 2016; 4 June 2023

1, 9–13. The bomb fell in March 1944 and blew out the windows of 52 Brooklyn Avenue, Loughton, Essex.

12
NATO

I stand by Porthleven pier and observe
The surfy sea push incessantly in
As wind blows through my hair and lungs with verve
And I am one with winds and tides and skin.
And I think of Russia's hostile hardball,
And NATO's collective defence – and its saw
That an attack on one ally's on all.
I think of Corbyn not wanting a war,
Saying he would not help NATO allies,
Calling for NATO to be closed, saying
He would ask Russia not to fight, to cease
War as talk's better. The surging surf sighs.
I want to end war but see NATO bring
A balance of power that can preserve peace.

20–21 August 2016; 4 June 2023

5. 'Hardball', "uncompromising methods or dealings, especially in politics" (*Concise Oxford Dictionary*).
6. 'Saw' (noun), "maxim" (*Concise Oxford Dictionary*).

Part Two:
The Tapestry Room: Tudor Living and the One

1
The Tapestry Room in Henry the Eighth's Second Hunting Lodge

Henry the Eighth's Egham hunting lodge in gloom.
From its Great Hall, the receptionist's taken me
Upstairs to Anne Boleyn's personal Drawing-Room
Where Henry courted her six years secretly,
And unlocks the door. I see huge tapestries
On either side of the Adam-and-Eve fireplace:
A hunting scene and a forest. Behind the bed is
Another of people, a gift – I study each face.
Is there one thread, like Actaeon disturbing
Diana bathing and turned into a stag, to be
Killed by his own hounds? They're not revealing,
But I know a door's been unlocked to a tapestry
That hangs in my soul and tells of my destiny,
Of another hunt that's put antlers on me.

22 May, 1 June 2021

Title 'Second Hunting Lodge'. In these sonnets Henry VIII's first hunting lodge was Poteles in King's Avenue, Buckhurst Hill, Essex – the name Buckhurst Hill originally combined the word 'hill' and the old terms for a wood ('hurst') and male deer or stag ('buck'); his second hunting lodge was Great Fosters in Egham, Surrey; and his third hunting lodge, built between 1540 and 1543, was on the outskirts of Chingford and is known as Queen Elizabeth's hunting lodge because she rode a white charger up the stairs to celebrate the victory over the Spanish Armada in 1588. In the 1540s Henry VIII processed there while staying at his first hunting lodge, Poteles, crossing its 300-acre deer park known as Fairmead ("fair meadow"). See further references to the three hunting lodges on p.98 ('Tudor Deer-Hunting'), pp.180–182 ('In Fairmead in Arcadia'), pp.201–203 ('Rose Garden like a Union Flag'), pp.257–258 ('Death') and p.263 ('Postponing'). Ladycross, in Beaulieu, Hants, the first main hunting lodge built by William the Conqueror in 1079 for hunting in the New Forest, was used by Henry VIII. In the 17th century it was in a bad state of repair and was torn down and replaced by the current stone building.

1. 'The Tapestry Room'. Great Fosters, near Egham, Surrey and near Windsor, was Henry VIII's hunting lodge while he was courting Anne Boleyn between 1526 and their secret wedding in 1532. The three tapestries in The

Tapestry Room there are described as early 17th-century Flemish tapestries. The stag is Nicholas Hagger's trademark (reflecting his roots in Buckhurst Hill, see title note above), one seven-branched antler symbolising the seven disciplines in which he has written, and the other seven-branched antler symbolising the seven genres within English Literature in which he has written. Nicholas Hagger stayed at Great Fosters, a Tudor building in Egham, Surrey on 22–23 May 2021.

12–13. 'A door's been unlocked.../...and tells of my destiny', see sonnets 13, 16, 17, 23 and 25 in volume 40, *In Arcady: A Gong and Padded Stick*.

14. 'Another hunt', see the title to Part Three.

2
Tapestries in the Soul

I go over the scene in my mind's gloom.
From the Great Hall where Henry dined I stroll
Up to the Drawing-Room known as 'The Tapestry Room'
And the tapestries that are hidden in my soul.
Two huge tapestries hang either side of the chimney,
One hides a door to a secret stair from the chamber
Above down to 'The Anne Boleyn Room' with flabby
Emblems on the ceiling: a falcon holding a sceptre,
A Tudor rose, lion passant, fleur-de-lis,
Arched crown. Now I sit by the Great-Hall fire's warm glow
Where Henry sat and know I can hang my wee
Tapestries-in-words that will tell the sequential flow
Of my hunt through knowledge and disciplines to find
The Oneness of the universe and humankind.

22 May 2021; revised 7 January 2023

7. 'Flabby', "hanging down, limp, flaccid" (*Concise Oxford Dictionary*). Also obese, oversized.

13–14. 'Hunt', see the title to Part Three.

3
Roots in Bruges

Looking at these Flemish tapestries I think
Of my family's origins in Flanders,
When Carolus Haggar in 1366
Took his Bruges family to Chelmsford as sheep-farmers,

Perhaps fleeing the plague epidemic
In the Low Countries, and so the sheep could roam
The Hagars went to Bourn and became lords
Of four manors and built their English home,
Bourn Hall, with their H on the guttering,
And their arms: three Flemish lions, with a raised paw, sure.
It is now a fertility clinic.
When I opened Bourn's Millennial Fête a tour
Was laid on of Bourn Hall's ancient rooms, and I see
My Bruges roots in their four manors: my four-school Oak Tree.

23 April 2023

10. The Flemish (now Belgian) lion was on the coat of arms of the Counts of Flanders, and three Flemish (now Belgian) lions are on Nicholas Hagger's coat of arms, see p.355.

12. Nicholas Hagger opened the Bourn Fête on 1 July 2000 as a descendant of the Hagars and Carolus Haggar. After opening the fête Nicholas Hagger was asked to buy Bourn Hall.

14. 'Oak Tree'. Nicholas Hagger owned The Oak-Tree Group of Schools (four schools); hence the two oak trees on his coat of arms along with three Flemish (now Belgian) lions passant.

4
A Tapestry on the Fall of the West

I wander by the Saxon moat and muse
On whether Anne put her ex Henry Percy's prize
Emblems – sphere, boar, key, scimitar – as clues
In her Drawing-Room ceiling for status in Henry's eyes,
And the secret stair in the fireplace's side that led down
To her bedroom below and her own ceiling
Emblems: falcon, rose, lion, fleur-de-lis and crown.
And I see Henry in a yew walk, standing
At the Abbot of Waltham's Copped Hall, listening, fat,
For the cannon that signalled Anne had been beheaded.
Now I sit by the Great Hall's hearth where Henry sat
And I know I can hang a word tapestry in my head
To tell how I witnessed the fall of the West
In scenes from my life, which my experiences attest.

24 May, 1 June 2021

1. The Saxon moat at Great Fosters is ADc.500.

2–7. It seems that all the ceiling emblems at Great Fosters in Anne Boleyn's room on the drawing-room were added by Anne's daughter Queen Elizabeth I in 1598 (see Part Two, no.18, 'Swan, Delving', note on p.87.)

5. The door to the secret stair is in the left side of the fireplace in the Tapestry Room.

8–10. Henry VIII discussed divorcing Anne Boleyn with the Abbot of Waltham Abbey and eventually confiscated Copped Hall on 23 March 1540, and Mary I and Elizabeth I both lived there as virtual prisoners at different times. Legend has it that Henry VIII was at Copped Hall on the day of Anne Boleyn's execution, 19 May 1536, and heard cannons signal Anne Boleyn's death.

5
What my Tapestries Won't Show

Now by this Saxon moat I ask the Whole:
What do my tapestries show in each picture
That adorns the walls of my Drawing-Room soul?
Not hunting Actaeon stumbling on Diana
Bathing with her nymphs and, changed to a stag, hunted
By his own hounds and killed; nor Venus's clutches
To stop Adonis being gored till dead
By a wild boar; nor the Bayeux Tapestry's
War and conquest; nor the shield of Achilles.
No, a modern theme of the rise and fall of the West,
The founding of America amid Jamestown's trees
Planned at Otley Hall, and my knot-garden quest
And Coopersale Hall where Elizabeth planted a tree.
I sit by a Saxon moat amid local history.

24 May 2021; revised 7 January 2023

6
Connaught House's Knot-Garden

I walk and unravel my Connaught-House knot
That's central to twenty-five civilisations
And shows how they grew in the other beds and shot
Up from a single white point into nations
(A ping-pong ball of Light on a thin stake).
And as the beds show, all are equalling,

Ex-empires are level with ex-colonies' take
And now is a time when the West is tottering,
And about to fall, as the East begins to heave
Upwards into a levelled-down World State's confines.
That is the theme of this tapestry I weave
With weft and warp, across and downward lines,
On the fall of the West and the shrinking of the UK
Back to England's borders in Henry the Eighth's day.

25 May 2021

7
Achilles' Shield

Tapestries have pictures – of Achilles' shield's dents
Or Actaeon turned to a stag and hunted down,
Classical myths – or else narrate events:
The Norman Conquest, founding of Jamestown,
Or Operation Overlord. But my compressed
Long tapestry is not on a myth or event
But on the long decline and fall of the West
And the rise of one multipolar government.
I too face a fall as, now at eighty-two,
I face my coming death and will be dust
But take comfort from the New World Order due
After the virus, which will always be robust:
The coming order that's my legacy,
Which I have brought in, but will not live to see.

25 May 2021; revised 8 January 2023

8
England as in Henry the Eighth's Day

I sit in my knot-garden whose box curves mirror
One of six endless knots Elizabeth drew
On the 1544 prayer-book cover
She gave her stepmother Katherine Parr, and view
Fairmead, Henry's new hunting-lodge park, and detect
An echo, for we're now in a Henry time
With an obese leader who's had six 'wives' and, unchecked,

Has broken from Rome and left Europe in its prime,
Believing a new empire is at his call,
Without having seen my seven-foot-long chart
And its law of civilisations' rise and fall
In which isolation caused by a choice to depart
Hastens a nation's parabolic decline.
I study my knot's infinity design.

25 May 2021

14. 'Infinity design', an 8 on its side: ∞. Two infinity signs together, one north-south, the other east-west, form Elizabeth I's 1544 knot in Fairmead's Connaught House.

9
What Wyatt Saw

Wyatt, via whom with Surrey I inherit
This sonnet form from Renaissance Italy,
Knew Anne Boleyn and was rumoured to have had an affair
With her before she was chosen by Henry,
And wrote she wore "*Noli me tangere* ('Don't
Touch me'), for Caesar's I am" round her neck after then;
And 'stole' from her pocket her HA ring on a chain
And teasingly showed Henry while they played bowls – men!
Arrested years later, from his room in the Tower
He saw five men, each led to the block alone,
Beheaded two days before Anne, and wrote
"*Circa Regna tonat*", 'thunder rolls round the throne'.
O Wyatt, your sonnets are full of Anne, and showed
Me a tradition and influence I have followed.

17, 23 April 2023

1. Sir Thomas Wyatt (1503–1542) was a poet and diplomat who introduced the sonnet into English literature. He was rumoured to have had an affair with Anne Boleyn before she was chosen by Henry VIII. The Earl of Surrey (1516/17–1547) was one of the founders of English Renaissance poetry and developed the Shakespearean form of the sonnet.

5–6. "*Noli me tangere*, for Caesar's I am" comes from Wyatt's sonnet 'Whoso list to hunt, I know where is a hind'. Wyatt refers to Anne Boleyn as a "deer" (perhaps punning on 'dear'). George Wyatt, the poet Sir Thomas Wyatt's grandson, told the story that when Wyatt was entertaining Anne Boleyn with his poetry while she did her needlework he noticed a ring on a chain seemingly inscribed with these words "*Noli me tangere*" from Wyatt's sonnet hanging from her pocket, and snatched it from her and kept it as a trophy. "*Noli me tangere*" ('Don't touch me') may be associated with Christ's words to Mary Magdalene after the resurrection, see the *King James Version* of the *Bible*: "Jesus saith to her [Mary Magdalene], Touch me not; for I am not ascended to my Father."

7. "HA" stands for Henry and Anne. It was unwise of Wyatt to show this ring to Henry VIII during a game of bowls as it may have led to Wyatt's later imprisonment in the Tower in May 1536 for adultery with Anne Boleyn.

10. The five men included Anne Boleyn's brother George.

12. "*Circa Regna tonat*" comes from Wyatt's sonnet '*Innocentia Veritas Viat Fides Circumdederunt Me Inimici Mei*'.

10
Henry the Eighth's Copped Hall

I stand before Copped Hall, whose pediment
Shows Light and Shadow, ancient light and dark,
And ponder how Henry came here to present
His divorce from Anne to the Abbot – his clerk –
Of Waltham Abbey, and how he confiscated
Copped Hall and the Abbey, and installed his heirs,
First Mary, then Elizabeth who planted
These holm-oaks, and another that still shares
Domesday Book's Coopersale Hall, where, Providentially,
I founded a new school whose badge avers
Its 1561 royal pedigree.
I now own this local link to the Tudors,
And now live near here, where Henry hunted
In the grounds of a new hunting lodge he founded.

2 June 2021

9. Nicholas Hagger founded Coopersale Hall School in 1988 and it opened in April 1889. The badge on the pupils' blazers shows the holm-oak Elizabeth I is said to have planted in 1561 at the same time as she planted the holm-oaks at nearby Copped Hall.

10. 'Aver', "assert, affirm" (*Concise Oxford Dictionary*).

14. 'A new hunting lodge', the one built in 1540–1543, now known as Queen Elizabeth's hunting lodge.

11
Henry's Third Hunting Lodge

I stand in my knot-garden and look beyond
The wire fence where a stag's antlers were trapped
To King Henry the Eighth's third hunting lodge,
Which he built in this Fairmead, 'fair meadow', where, rapt,
All watched deer and stags roam in a hunting scene.
I reflect my endless knot was disinterred
From the tapestry manuscript book the young Queen
Elizabeth designed and embroidered
With blue-silk-and-tapestry stitches that awe
And gave to her stepmother, Katherine Parr (a quilt) –
Henry's sixth wife, in 1544 –
One year after the new hunting lodge was built.
And I am linked with Henry's Copped-Hall shrine
And his third hunting lodge through this knot's design.

2 June 2021

6–10. Elizabeth I was eleven when she embroidered the tapestry cover of her manuscript book for Katherine Parr in 1544. See 'England as in Henry the Eighth's Day', lines 1–4 (pp.80–81), for how Nicholas Hagger's endless knot mirrored Elizabeth I's 1544 endless knot.

10. 'Quilt', "covering made of padding enclosed between layers of cloth, and kept in place by cross lines of stitching" (*Concise Oxford Dictionary*).

12
Otley Hall's Knot-Garden

I think of Otley Hall, where I first planted
A knot-garden with Sylvia Landsberg's flair:
A Tudor gabled house, with wattle-and-daub-spread
Walls and candle burns and a creaking stair.
My bedroom was in the old dining-hall,
Where came the Earl of Essex, Southampton too,
And the Earl of Oxford and Bacon (I recall),
And Bartholomew Gosnold, who picked the crew
For his voyages to Martha's Vineyard and Jamestown
In the beamed and panelled Great Hall adjoining

The linenfold panelling Wolsey brought down
From Hampton Court: 1520s' swanking.
In my box knot-garden feel the One flow
Through the central knot to where civilisations grow.

2 June 2021

3. 'Wattle-and-daub-spread', "interlaced rods and split rods or twigs plastered with mud" (*Concise Oxford Dictionary*).

7. The Earl of Oxford. The 17th Earl of Oxford Edward de Vere, who some regard as Shakespeare.
'I recall' mischievously suggests that Nicholas Hagger had a far memory of that Tudor time and could speak from direct experience of the guests at Otley Hall.

11. 'Linenfold', "a carved or moulded ornament representing a fold or scroll of linen" (*Concise Oxford Dictionary*).

14. Otley Hall's knot-garden contained 25 herb-beds, one for each of Nicholas Hagger's 25 civilisations as set out in *The Fire and the Stones* and *The Rise and Fall of Civilizations*.

13
Knot-Garden: The One at a Glance

Crowds come in coachloads to gaze at my knot-
Garden in Otley Hall's medieval grounds, where
A symbol of the One in the universe, a spot,
A small white ball, is suspended in mid-air,
The pre-Big-Bang single point, then four loops, dense,
Of crossing eights, infinity lips that pout
Nothingness, Non-Being, Being and Existence,
Interwoven and then radiating out
Into twenty-five floral beds with every
Medieval flower (pansies, peonies and pinks),
The world's twenty-five civilisations in symmetry
In a variety of colourful petals and chinks
Where bees buzz in the lavender and dance
And the whole of Creation is taken in at a glance.

2 June 2021

12. 'Chink', "an unintended crack that admits light; a narrow opening, a slit" (*Concise Oxford Dictionary*).

14
Seckford's Head

In Tudor Suffolk, under Seckford Hall's
Tall chimneys, crenulations and Flemish
Gables, I sit near the Great Hall's panelled walls
Where Sir Thomas Seckford, Elizabeth the First's stylish,
Bearded Master of the Court of Requests held court
Before the hearth with ten heads of 'the staff'
In two rows carved in wood, his in the central port
Of the bottom row, judging from a lithograph
Showing him in the old Great Hall, in the gloom
On the wall near the bar – staring, intense.
The Queen in a stone statue outside our room
Holds sceptre and orb, justice's instruments,
And I walk in the grounds amid quacks and caws,
At one with Tudor living out of doors.

20 July 2021; revised 8 January 2023

15
Muse's Slave

You say over dinner, casually, with mirthful freedom,
Taunting in your kind eyes, "I've not worked out
Where on the spectrum that includes autism
And Asperger's your fanaticism is." I pout:
"You're referring to my inspiration, inspired thought.
I go to a place, enter into its spirit,
Evoke Elizabeth the First's visit to hold court,
Feel where she sat, put her in a sonnet
That obsesses me till it's done, move on unvexed
And don't look at it again, like Maugham have no interest
In my earlier works, only in the next.
My Muse and the angels send me words they've compressed,
Which I transcribe, their amanuensis, engrave.
My 'fanaticism' is being my Muse's slave."

20 July 2021; revised 8 January 2023

16
The Fall of the West

I see a tapestry of the fall of the West:
China in red and its hundred and forty blue
Belt-and-Road-Initiative colonies and conquest
Of all continents; and, isolated, askew,
The US and Europe looking fragile despite
Their nuclear weapons and nine hundred bases that split.
I see China with a trade surplus and might,
And a once unipolar US with a deficit,
I see power tilting east and the Pentagon
Fund research to slow down China's progress,
I see an American lab make a bio-weapon
That can keep the West from sinking in its own mess.
And I know this tapestry has a truthful look
As I'm looking at the cover of my own book.

9 February 2022; revised 13–14 January 2023

14. The cover of Nicholas Hagger's *The Fall of the West*.

17
Nothing's Changed: All Fools

This is where I came in eighty-three years ago:
Rockets and ruined cities, and rubble,
Decades of infrastructure gone, and trillions to go
To rebuild what's been lost, and all's trouble,
And driving troops forward to their certain death.
Now it's Ukraine, and how are things better?
Rockets and mortars, debris and snuffed breath,
People with nothing sobbing beneath shells' whir.
Decades to rebuild, and who's going to pay?
And, lied to by all his generals, Putin
Urging troops onwards to 'glory', to become clay.
It's All Fools' Day, when people are taken in.
Nothing's changed, and hopes of a better world
Have been blown apart like bits of a body hurled.

11.40am, 1 April 2022; revised 14 January 2023

18
Swan, Delving

I sit in the sun with daisies round my feet
Back at Great Fosters and gaze at the floating swan
Whose neck's delving in this Saxon moat near my seat
And look back at the house where Elizabeth's arms on
The porch lintel proclaims '1598' in gloom.
Here she delved back to when at this second hunting lodge Henry
Met her mother Anne Boleyn in the Drawing-Room.
(My bedroom tonight) when she was betrothed to Percy
And crept with her down the secret stair, wheezing,
To the chapel, next to Anne's bedroom where
She put Anne's royal insignia on the ceiling,
And on the Drawing-Room ceiling the armillary sphere,
Boar, crowned key and scimitar of Percy.
Still the swan delves deep like a historian who's busy.

14 May 2022; revised 14–15 January 2023

2–13. At Great Fosters, Henry VIII's second hunting lodge, Elizabeth I remembered her mother Anne Boleyn, who was betrothed to Henry Percy when Henry VIII met her, by decorating the ceilings of Anne's room with her royal insignia and of the Drawing-Room with Percy's insignia, in 1598.
3. The moat at Great Fosters goes back to ADc.500.
8. Percy. Henry Percy, Earl of Northumberland.

19
Devout Anne Boleyn

This chapel.... Anne agreed to marry Henry
In 1527, aware Mary,
Her sister, had had a three-year affair with him
And was cast aside. Anne was a devout lady,
Had a book of hours (prayers, psalms and scriptures
To be read at set hours each day) printed
In Paris that year, and did not consummate
Her relationship with Henry till they were wed
'Unofficially' in Dover in November
1532 – hence this chapel; and then secretly
In Whitehall Palace in January when pregnant.

And she took her book of hours devoutly
To her death, gave it to a lady-in-waiting,
Before the swordsman struck off her head for her King.

14 May 2022

1. 'This chapel'. See line 10 of the previous sonnet, 'Swan, Delving'.
3. Mary's affair with Henry VIII lasted three years from 1522 to 1525.
8–11. Anne Boleyn's secret 'unofficial' wedding to Henry VIII in Dover was given as 14 November 1532 by chronicler Edward Hall. She was married in a secret ceremony at Whitehall Palace on 25 January 1533.

20
Glorification

So now my delving's found what happened here.
Anne, betrothed to Percy, was courted by grand
Henry in this room where I write this, and Percy (o dear)
Was forced to give her up as his father had planned
That he should Mary Talbot, and in distress
In 1535 (so Anne would participate),
Now Northumberland, separated and childless,
He made the King his heir and left his estate
To Henry and Anne's child Elizabeth, the King's heir,
Who in gratitude put his emblems on this ceiling
And Anne's royal emblems down the secret stair
In the room reached by dignified creeping.
So the Queen glorified Anne's tawdry meetings and mirth,
And made this place a monument to her own birth.

14 May 2022; revised 15 January 2023

1. 'My delving's found what happened here.' Anne Boleyn and Henry VIII met in 1522 when she was a lady-in-waiting to Catherine of Aragon, and by 1526 Henry was infatuated with her. They met for seven years before they were married. Henry separated from Catherine of Aragon in July 1531. Anne Boleyn and Henry married on 25 January 1533. Catherine of Aragon's marriage was annulled on 23 May 1533. Elizabeth I was born on 7 September 1533. Anne Boleyn was beheaded on 19 May 1536 before she could benefit from Percy's bequest, but Elizabeth benefited from it – hence the emblems of Percy and Anne on the ceilings of a hunting lodge (Great Fosters) that became a monument to Elizabeth I's birth.

21
Tapestries: Actaeon

I sit on in Great Fosters' Tapestry Room
And gaze at the three tapestries that have pride
Of place on the walls, to either side of the stone
Fireplace (which shows Eve born from Adam's side,
Serpents twisting away from an angel,
Adam ploughing and Eve nursing Abel) –
Both hunting scenes, that show a ferocious kill:
Three men jabbing pikes at an animal,
And a hound biting a deer's neck to its death.
And a third tapestry on the wall behind my bed
Shows a Flemish Prodigal Son being welcomed
Back by his mother and brother who thought him dead
And circle their hands and make a formal bow.
I've been a Prodigal and Actaeon, and am a stag now.

14 May 2022; revised 22 January 2023

14. Ovid in *Metamorphoses* describes how Actaeon saw Diana bathing on Mount Cithaeron and was turned into a deer with dappled hide and antlers, a stag, and was later killed by some of his own fifty hounds (see pictures on p.354). At the time of this visit to Great Fosters on 13 May 2022 Nicholas Hagger had seen the divine Light (including experiences of the oval cloud) 114 times (see p.xxviii for the basis of this calculation, omitting the eight 2023 experiences) during and after his 29-year-long Mystic Way which ended in unitive vision in 1993, and filled with secret knowledge (including the Light, which is as divine as, or more divine than, Diana) had turned into a stag, which is on his coat of arms (see the antlered stag at the top of his crest on p.355, one of the seven-branched antlers symbolising the seven disciplines in which he has written, the other seven-branched antler symbolising the seven sub-genres within literature in which he has written). In 'Actaeon's Fate' (below) he muses that he will be killed as a result of some of his more-than-50 books.

22
Actaeon's Fate

I look at Actaeon living normally,
Hunting until one day he stumbled on
A naked goddess, knowledge forbidden.
There was a need to silence Actaeon.

Turned into a stag, was he too condemned to be
A Muse's slave, write in seven disciplines
And in the seven genres of literature,
Seven barbs on each antler that rule my word spins?
Was his work also suppressed so that the truth
Of how he had seen his West would not be spread?
That's where I've reached, banished for telling it as it is.
Now I wait to be torn to pieces and left for dead
By some of my books which will hound me like Actaeon's hounds,
An Actaeon-stag awaiting a fate that confounds.

22 January 2023; revised 25 January 2023

5. See pictures on p.354.
13. 'By some of my books', as a result of some of the poet's books. 'By' in the sense of 'as a result of'.
14. 'Confound', "throw into perplexity and confusion" (*Concise Oxford Dictionary*).

23
Clarity

In this Tapestry Room all is now clear.
There's a secret door behind the tapestry
To the left of the fireplace, I can feel its outline.
It was covered in the seventeenth century.
The tapestries are of Flemish hunting scenes,
Emphasising the hunting-lodge theme, much later;
And the ceilings here and in Anne's room were redone
By Queen Elizabeth to honour her mother.
The wooden panelling over the stone hearth
Saying *Ratio, Veritas, Victoria*
(Reason, Truth, Victory) was here in Henry's day.
This room had Elizabeth's holy memorabilia.
She stamped family emblems on its ceiling,
And this hunting lodge held for her a deep meaning.

14 May 2022

24
The Return of the Prodigal

I look again at the scene above my bed,
A tapestry my Renaissance mind, achurn
That it's lived before, informs is a new telling
In Flemish terms of the Prodigal Son's return,
Kneeling, showing his shoes' soles worn bare from
His journey to far lands, and his right arm,
Fingers out, ready for a hello bow,
His father bemused, his mother with open arms calm
And his brother's right arm raised for an elaborate bow.
A group stand nonplussed, and in a distant meadow
Are fatted calves, one of which will be sacrificed.
I once lived during the Tudor time and know
How Renaissance minds drew on Biblical parables
And looked for a fatted calf among animals.

14–15 May 2022

2. 'Achurn' (neologism), "churning over, reflecting". For the use of 'a' before a word, compare aslake, asweat (see Nicholas Hagger, 'The Expatriate', 1963, "Aslake for sleep, asweat for dawn to creep").

25
Decius Mus's Sacrifice

Five tapestries in Kilkenny Castle
Show consul Decius Mus (after dreaming
That Rome would defeat the invading Latins
If a consul sacrificed himself) holding
A statue of Mars holding one of Victory;
Telling Manlius, his fellow consul, a beast-
Like leader of Rome's army, of his plan;
Then bowing his head before the high priest,
Marcus Valerius, and reciting a prayer;
Then being speared in his neck as his horse falls under fire;
Then lying dead on a couch. Rubens designed
Them, his theme of self-sacrifice for the empire
Has been to men in centuries of wars a cause.
O Jupiter, may there be no more wars.

4 August 2022

1. 'Five tapestries in Kilkenny Castle'. There were ten tapestries in all in Kilkenny Castle, Ireland. Five are stored there and five (referred to in the poem) are on display. Decius Mus had a dream that Rome would be saved if a consul sacrificed himself. The ten tapestries were made in Paris in 1660 and were used as rugs before being rescued by Frank Kavanagh for Hugh Butler, then owner of Kilkenny Castle.

Part Three: Tapestry, Hunt to Find the Oneness of the Universe and of all Humankind

1 Wonderment

A store's insect cushion called out to me.
It caught my eye from far: a dragonfly,
A swallow-tail, a beetle and a bee.
They could be at my back when, desk-bound, I
Write of my harmony with living things.
I bought the cushion, brought it in a bag,
Now it's ready to support my musings.
I look again at the four heads and flag
One hatches from ponds, one from pupa's squeeze,
One frequents soil and one nuzzles flowers.
I love all butterflies, smile with assent.
I love all crawling wings and honey-bees
That sip nectar from glorious lavenders.
The One fills me with endless wonderment.

20–21 August 2016; 4 June 2023

8. 'Flag', note (verb).

2 Oneness

The North Downs golf-course grass near Merrow's high.
In the rough beneath the first tee I lay
Amid sedge and wild flowers under blue sky,
Alone on a baking hot summer's day.
Azure blues and meadow browns fluttered near.

I suddenly grasped everything around
Me was alive, it buzzed and sawed so clear.
Time stopped and I had a sense on the ground
Of the Oneness of the universe at
Fifteen. I'd sensed it at seven – it still jars,
Among grasshoppers that sawed on the flat
Heath 'the Stubbles', and under brilliant stars
On a frosty night in a friend's garden –
But never as profoundly One as then.

21 August 2016; 4 June 2023

3
Conviction

Then there was that March morning, my answer's.
I had been on tenterhooks, wished to leave
Law for Literature, and found my father's
Letter before breakfast. Driven to achieve,
I took it to the college lake and, bent
On the stone seat near the arched gate, tense knees,
I read that my choice now had his consent.
I looked up at the lake and saw the trees
And trace of cloud on the still reflected,
And the weeping willows, and I blended in
And sensed I *was* the lake and the lake – worse –
Was in me, and I'd *always* existed.
I grew in stature, great power filled my skin
And poured conviction from the universe.

22 August 2016; 4 June 2023

9. The 'still', the lake's surface.
11–12. 'The lake – worse –/Was in me'. Even more extremely, the lake had flooded into the poet.

4
Purpose

And then the day before I left England.
I walked up to the Strawberry Hill Pond,
By the fallen tree gazed at the island

And, bruised by my father's death, the beyond,
And suddenly I became immensely
Aware of trees, mallards, water-boatmen
Skating on the still surface by the tree
And sensed the purpose in the scheme again,
Instinctively knew everything – all food,
Each creature – is within a plan, the Whole,
Whose purpose is deduced – like a symbol –
From all its forms but contrives to elude
Our rational understanding. And my soul
Was filled from a warm vital principle.

22 August 2016; 4 June 2023

4. 'Father's death'. Nicholas Hagger's father died on 15 October 1963.

5
Rock

Past like the wind, thirty-four years have blown,
Time ever rolls like the waves' shoreward boom.
Nothing stands still yet still I hear the moan
Of the wind that Hallowe'en round your room,
The plaintive howling at the window-sill
As you sank back from life into your sleep
And released your last breath, now stone still till
Strewn ashes on a mist's lawn where I creep.
That many years I have been an orphan,
I've made my way and stood on my own feet
And have done well, yet though I'm an old man
I still see that evening as a rock seat
Above the waves I look down on, and climb.
Love is like a staunch rock in flowing time.

2–3 November 2016; 4 June 2023

1. 'Past' (adj.), "gone by in time and no longer existing" (*Concise Oxford Dictionary*); also 'passed'.
4. Nicholas Hagger's mother died on 1 November 1982.

6
A Tapestry of a New World Order: A Coming Golden Age

Oneness. I went before the world's philosophers
And brought in the One as a supranational state,
Universal State of the Earth, which if
Copied supranationally by the UN would create
A democratic partly-federal World State
That would usher in a universal peace.
The tapestry's not about the New World
In America, but a New World Order's lease
In which the four Great Powers (the US, the EU,
Russia and China) form a multipolar world and get
Together, and head off a Third World War.
My tapestry's about a world that has not yet
Come into being, peaceful allies in a cage,
East and west, no war, and a new Golden Age.

4, 5 June 2023

7
Tapestry of Oneness and Peace

But it is also an Age in which the One's supreme.
All my early experiences of the One
Have shown the unity of the universe
And how the Oneness reflects itself like the sun
Politically in the oneness of all humankind.
The earth looks so peaceful from outer space,
An astronaut sees continents side by side
And it's inconceivable they're racked by wars that displace
When all around suggests a Oneness between
The earth and the moon, the planets and stars, and each mind.
The tapestry catches this structure round the earth
And the Oneness of the universe and humankind.
And it shows the emergence of a one-world state
That can end wars and bring hope in place of hate.

4, 5 June 2023

8. 'Racked', tortured, torn.

8
A Tudor Outlook

I saw a tapestry of incidents
In my mind's journey to a bright new world
Like the New World Tapestry spread out on
Otley Hall's long kitchen table, unfurled:
A tapestry of woven events that made
A life. But then the world turned dark (Brexit-black,
Covid and then Ukraine), and I was diverted
Into other works. Yet I was still drawn back
Into the Tudor time I seem to recall,
The Tudor outlook of a Renaissance man.
And now I am old, at eighty-three I have
The events to weave a tapestry and plan,
But am handicapped by my shortage of time
And the endless dark events waiting to chime.

22 August 2022

9
Bayeux Tapestry Revisited

I walked round the Norman Bayeux tapestry,
And saw Duke William cross to a new land
And replace Harold, its erstwhile ruler,
And glimpsed the pattern of my life, a Grand-
Tour journey from a longing to see the world
And absorb all books to opening to the Light,
Receiving new powers over thirty years,
Seeing the universe as a recondite
Unity, with all contradictions unified
In the One behind it all, and I, a spry
Duke William, am crowned in my new land, see
My old self with an arrow in his eye
Lying dead beneath my shadow, which I've become,
And buried at Waltham Abbey near my new home.

22 August 2022

1. Nicholas Hagger visited the Bayeux Tapestry on 13 April 1976.
8. 'Recondite', "abstruse; out of the way; little known" (*Concise Oxford Dictionary*).

10
Past Lives

I look back on the tapestry of my life
And see the Otley Hall knot-garden I
Replicated in Essex in the Fairmead of Henry's
Third hunting lodge, and now relive my
Excitement I felt in the Otley kitchen
As a real tapestry unfurled on its table, rushes
As I image bits of my life stitched out in yards
As in Henry's second hunting lodge's tapestries.
I see bits echoing places from long ago.
Is my excitement in my pilgrim soul, my core
That has lived many times before, in Roman times
And as a Tudor, and has seeds for many lives more,
A recycled soul in new outward form, unseen?
Are tapestries echoes of what we have once been?

22 August 2022

5–6. Nicholas Hagger saw a section of the 274-foot-long New World Tapestry spread out on the kitchen table at Otley Hall on Friday 12 June 1998 ('New World Tapestry', see pp.70–71).

10–12. 'Core', "central parts of various fruits, containing the seeds" (*Concise Oxford Dictionary*). Nicholas Hagger focuses on the destiny of his core – his destiny – in volume 40, *In Arcady: A Gong and Padded Stick*.

11
A Deer in Arcady

A deer's near our lawn, it's come in from the fields
Of Fairmead, Henry the Eighth's hunting-ground.
It would have been hunted from 1543,
Now it's gone to ground in bushes, I hear a sound.
I go and clap, now it breaks out past me
And rushes at a gate and bounds, sullen,
To our far corner, and I see it turn
And race up a path to our knot-garden.
It's a scene familiar for five hundred years.
LiDAR pictures of round huts beneath our field
Taken from the air may be Tudor deer pens
And not where Anglo-Saxons lived and mealed.

I stand in the ancient deer park amid flowers
In Arcady, and hunt a deer like my ancestors.

16, 20 May 2023

10. LiDAR images show land without grass or trees. See Nicholas Hagger, *A View of Epping Forest*, p.287 for a LiDAR image of faint circles beneath his main field in what used to be Fairmead deer park.

14. 'Arcady', Arcadia.

12
Tudor Deer-Hunting

Henry the Eighth stayed at his royal palace
Near Buckhurst Hill station, where ruins were found
In Silberrad's father's garden, and processed
On a track to the hunting lodge he'd completed around
1543, across what is now
Buckhurst Hill's top cricket ground next to Braeside
And through the Forest down to Connaught House
And across Fairmead deer park, and watched with pride
As archers hunted deer in the King's party,
And fed on their kill, a feast of venison.
Then all paraded back across Arcady
To the local palace, and next day went on
Back to London, having had a day of fun,
Of rustic delight in the bucolic sun.

17, 20 May 2023

1–2. See note on pp.76–77 for Henry VIII's three hunting lodges and the original meaning of 'Buckhurst Hill'.

3. Silberrad. John Silberrad was a QC who lived at Dryads Hall, Loughton, his father's home. His father Oswald Silberrad, was an industrial chemist who researched into explosives and after the Boer War discovered that TNT could be used as a detonator. He lived near Buckhurst Hill station on the site of Henry VIII's first royal hunting lodge, Poteles, in King's Avenue and John Silberrad showed Nicholas Hagger its foundations under his garden. John Silberrad has a building at the University of Essex named after him.

4–5. Henry VIII's third hunting lodge, built between 1540 and 1543, is 2.4 miles from where Poteles used to be, the other side of Fairmead deer park (see pp.76–77), and is now known as Queen Elizabeth's hunting lodge because she rode a horse up its stairs to celebrate the victory over the Spanish Armada in 1588.

13
Tapestry that Draws on the Tradition and Reveals Oneness

In Great Fosters I 'saw' a tapestry
That would tell of my hunt to find the Oneness (in my quest)
Of the universe and of all humankind,
And would tell of how I saw the fall of the West,
And having described the cover of my book
I now take stock in my wonderful Arcady
Of my overall tapestry that shows my search
For Oneness as the West retreats quietly
And falls into a multipolar arrangement.
All my contacts with tapestries have shaped
This overall tapestry covering a table
That draws on the tradition of tapestries draped
To reveal universal aspects of living's process
That are rooted in the past and proclaim Oneness.

6 June 2023

12. 'Drape', "hang, cover loosely" (*Concise Oxford Dictionary*), here 'draped', 'hung loosely'.

Volume 37

A PLAGUE IN ARCADIA: ONENESS WITH NATURE AND THE UNIVERSE

2020–2023

Poems Influenced by Coronavirus

Solitude

I sit alone and breathe my confined air.
One cough or sneeze can violently shower
A hundred thousand most contagious germs
At speeds up to a hundred miles per hour,
Bioaerosol droplets the width of a hair
That can remain suspended in the air and cloy
For seconds or weeks and can penetrate
Deep into lungs and infect and destroy.
I sit apart from ferocious invasions,
Bunkered at my desk, linked to the world by a screen,
And subsist, survive, and in the oak tree beneath
Light freezing rain watch two large jackdaws preen.
I sit alone, content not to be gasping
As my immune system grasps this viral thing.

30 March 2020; revised 16 December 2022

6. 'Cloy', "satiate or sicken" (*Concise Oxford Dictionary*).

Rejoicing Amid a Deadly Virus

I sit and look out at a still Forest.
The blue sky's empty, no planes drone or whine.
The budding trees in March are tipped with green
And the long field glows verdant in the warm sunshine.
All Nature's taken on a brilliant hue,
Now there's no pollution from air and road,
And I'm content to sit and isolate
From a deadly virus that cannot be slowed.

Time was when it would have been a bubonic plague
And social distancing would have kept me alive.
At eighty, I'm one of the vulnerable
Who must see all as lepers – to survive –
Who should wear a bell round their necks and call, "Unclean",
But I rejoice at the vivid grass and green.

30 March 2020; revised 25 December 2022

4. 'Verdant', "green, fresh-coloured" (*Concise Oxford Dictionary*).

'Old People's Home'

I sit in my 'old people's home', and can't
Go out except for one walk a day and back.
I'm over seventy and in the vulnerable group
And am imprisoned to escape a virus attack.
It's all round us, it's blowing in the air
Like invisible dandelion fluff in the wind, or burs.
It's lurking on surfaces – my post-box,
The gate, perhaps even the newspapers
I collect from a box outside my gate, and leaf.
And outside there's a glorious summer's day,
Blue sky and last night a pink supermoon.
But like the plague dodgers of the past in their way –
Shakespeare and Milton – I must stay in and thrive,
And write my next work and hope to stay alive.

7 April 2020

Virus

A blue-sky day, the buds are flecks,
The grass is brilliant green,
Birds flit in early-morning sun,
All Nature has a sheen.

But think, like pollen in hay fever
A dreadful virus spreads,
And I am cooped indoors to escape
Its tentacle-like threads.

10 April 2020

Romantic Isolation

Romantic poets walked alone,
Isolated and free.
Now I do too as I isolate
From a virus that can kill me.

10 April 2020

Pink Supermoon

I peer out for a pink
Supermoon in the night sky.
The moon has an oval halo
Like a pupil in an oval eye.

The bloodshot moon peers down
Onto our darkened loam,
And's surprised there are so few lights.
The virus keeps all at home.

10 April 2020

Bees in the Rosemary

I sit in the sun and watch bees sip
Nectar from the potted rosemary.
I watch two crawling ants, and live
Through insects' urgent mentality.

O how good it is that I can feel
For these tiny creatures that go
About their business when I'm busy,
And don't ignore their right to stow.

11 April 2020

8. 'Stow', "pack (goods etc.) tidily and compactly; fill (a receptacle) with articles compactly arranged" (*Concise Oxford Dictionary*).

A Cluttering of Jackdaws

I walk down the field for exercise
As I isolate, still virus-free,
In brilliant sunshine, and two jackdaws
Fly down and peck sharp-eyed near me.

I reach the far gateway and turn.
O look – I count – there are now, I pause,
Sixty-two jackdaws pecking the grass,
A 'cluttering' of grey-black jackdaws.

I walk back towards my distant house.
They watch, grey-necked, black-capped, with edge
And I realise they feel safe near me:
When I'm here the fox won't leave its hedge.

11 April 2020

10. 'Edge', "sharpness; incisiveness, excitement" (*Concise Oxford Dictionary*).

Thinking Jackdaw

The potted flowers are watered.
A jackdaw hops, bends round.
Its black beak's along the puddle,
It's sideways along the ground.

One side of its face is wet,
But it's hoovered up a drink.
O jackdaw how clever you are
To drink sideways like that – to think.

13 April 2020

Coronavirus: A *Memento Mori*

I look at the skull of an Indian woman
That sits in my alcoves, she died in her prime.
It's a *memento mori*, a reminder
That I will die, and am living on borrowed time.
Coronavirus is a reminder

Of mortality that death will demean
We know not when, as surely as if we are
On a list for the Place de la Concorde's guillotine.
I walk to the second field in my garden,
The virus is on surfaces and in the air,
And my shadow as I walk away from the sun
Is my ghost, my death confronting me with its stare
To transcend my mortality and all inner strife.
A *memento mori* calls to a love of life.

20 April 2020; revised 26 December 2022

Title '*Memento mori*', "a warning or reminder of death" (*Concise Oxford Dictionary*).
6. 'Demean', "lower… dignity" (*Concise Oxford Dictionary*).

Drooping Daisies

A dozen bellis daisies
Have dropped their yellow heads
Like children looking down,
In the rain loved by flower-beds.

O daisies, do not droop.
It will soon stop, this rain.
The sun will soon come out
And you'll raise your heads again.

28 April 2020

Dragonfly

My hair is like an overgrown garden.
As I sat out in warm sunshine at four
A dragonfly flew down and settled on it.
I did not move, I posed as grass and straw.
My grandchildren saw and thought it amusing.
I said like Francis of Assisi I attract
Nature to sit on parts of me in this time
Of isolating from the virus, it's a fact.
We cannot cut our hair unless we stand
And wield scissors in a mirror, or let a spouse.
We live without services as the Romans did,

We live like Victorians, not straying from the house,
And have rediscovered relating to Nature's skies
And simple things, like hosting dragonflies.

30 April 2020

Cuckoo

A fat cuckoo with an open mouth
Being fed by a smaller bird which drops
Food it has found within its throat,
A slave to its demands and strops.

I gaze at your picture and wonder if
That's how you see me every day and night
And if you feel tied to feeding me,
And empathise with that small bird's plight.

1 May 2020

Sea and Rocks

A craggy cliff of Cornish rock
And a tranquil sparkling sea below.
They complement each other: hard
Rock and heartful soft waves that flow.

It's a beautiful picture that shows your soul,
Your watery softness kind to crabs,
And the relentless, determined
Rock-like solidness of my carved slabs.

1 May 2020

Smiling Buttercups

As I walk up the sloping lawn,
I tread warily between
A hundred buttercups, all
Smiling in the sun, at the green.

O buttercups you've grown so
Quickly since the lawn was mown,
Enjoy your time in the sun,
Till your smiles are cropped and thrown.

18 May 2020

Two Potted Geraniums and a Blind Down

Your card shows two potted geraniums
By open Venetian blinds, one down, one up,
On either side of a window, and beneath
And on a wall, creepered, growing flowers cup.

I see the back says 'Catching the sunshine'
And I know instinctively that you see me
As beaming on you as you cope with a blind down,
Precariously perching and caring miserably.

You said you couldn't find a proper card
During lockdown, but it's chosen with thought
To show in a down blind a life ending,
In a careless image carefully chosen and bought.

25 May 2020

Lesser Stitchwort

As I stride in isolation
Down the sloping field like Mars
Buttercups, purple vetch
And lesser stitchwort like stars.

As I trudge back up the slope,
Tread carefully, don't crush
Each smiling buttercup
And stitchwort's starry blush.

26 May 2020

Small Tortoiseshell

I walk to the second field
And look where the brambles cling:
A small tortoiseshell at rest,
Its wings spread, dazzling.

It flies off in the sunshine
And rapidly returns
And settles on a nettle
And folds its wings to ferns.

O tortoiseshell, you love
This sunshine as I do
And you're not stung by the nettle.
As I walk back the sky's blue.

29 May 2020

Buttercup: Provinces and Disciplines

As I walk in solitude,
A hermit in dazzling green,
I see the buttercups smile
From their five petals and preen.

And now I remember
The Arch of Hadrian stun
In Jerash, and its flower
With six petals, each one

A Roman province – surely
A five-petalled buttercup for
Its petals are just the same,
Hadrian added one more?

O smiling buttercup,
Did an Emperor put on his arches
Your image for his empire?
Now you're *my* five provinces:

Literature, mystic Light,
History, philosophy,
International politics,
My five main disciplines, see?

29 May 2020

Stars

I walk in the burgeoning grounds.
The laburnum and lilac are gone,
And wisteria and rhododendrons.
Now foxgloves and peonies come on.

It's not lavender time yet,
The roses are coming to bloom.
But oh, by my feet, tiny stars,
Give ten-petalled stitchwort room.

The lesser stitchwort's too small
To see unless you peer low
But in this transitional time
Their stars are the stars of the show.

30 May 2020

Meadow Brown and Purple Clover

It's the last day of spring,
Summer's already here.
I walk down the sloping field,
A meadow brown is near.

I bend and examine
The two spots on its wings.
And purple clover, I count
A five-pointed leaf that clings.

And I am back as a boy
Amid flowers and butterflies,

As alone as I was then
On the Stubbles under Nature's skies.

I straighten and trudge up the slope
To the distant house, alone
In this lockdown solitude,
Humbled by what Nature has shown.

31 May 2020

Goldfinches

You say you've goldfinches
In your estuary garden
And have just bought niger seed
So they will come often.

And I think of when I returned
From Iran and saw three
Goldfinches in my garden,
And my heart leapt with glee.

They have not been since then,
What, thirteen years ago,
But I still think of three goldfinches
That left my heart aglow.

1 June 2020

Buttercup

Behold, the buttercup,
Five petals filled with sun.
It's lived and grown till the mower's
Trimmed the lawn, and it's been undone.

And now, no buttercup.
Flowers bloom, then are no more.
We all bloom and then go
Back under the earth, it's a law.

3 June 2020

Blackberry Brambles

I stand by blackberry brambles and watch
As meadow browns cavort and settle and meet
And skip off into the meadow and return,
Full of joy in this blue-sky summer heat.

I watch as azure blues dance round my feet.
I feel I'm being watched, and turn and see
A staring fox that sidles into a hedge
And a dozen butterflies dance in pairs round me.

23 June 2020

Swallows

It's windy, I pick up spears
Blown from the palm I can reach,
Then walk to the back lawn.
Green parakeets fly down and screech.

They hurtle round my head
And squeal a fond hello
As I fill their nut feeders,
Provide their food in the snow.

I feed the fish, the carp
Barge the goldfish aside
And gobble the granules.
Now the goldfish is satisfied.

I walk in the main field.
Two resting muntjac deer
Get up and jump through the fence
And lie low, disappear.

But look, swooping swallows.
They're back, four hurtle round me,
They skim the freshly-cut grass,
Saying hello from last year, free.

And I remember going out
On my balcony and they darted,
Saying hello again,
In all directions round my head.

Hello, swallows, hello,
You're the same ones, I can see,
And hello parakeets.
We're all in harmony.

27 June 2020

Swallow, Companion

I walk again, the field is still.
Swallows, have you all gone?
But joyfully a swallow swoops
And darts and flies head-on,

And swerves playfully, it's playing
With me. I wave, it flies
And's lost in trees but comes again.
O swallow, you surprise.

You're keeping me company on my walk,
You're delighting in being back.
And I love your darting and swerving
As you feign an attack.

28 June 2020

Treading Round Flowers

As I walked through my meadow,
"Don't tread on us," begged the flowers.
I trod round white clover,
Buttercups' and stitchworts' bowers,

I trod round purple vetch
And tipped grasses that meet,

I walked so carefully
My eyes were fixed on my feet.

At last I was across,
Then I remembered, my swallow
Had not flown out to greet me
And swoop over my meadow.

6 July 2020

4. 'Bower', "a secluded place enclosed by foliage, (*poetic*) an inner room, a boudoir" (*Concise Oxford Dictionary*).

Clover

Now I see that my lawn
And meadow's a clover field.
When our mower high-cuts
Clover's everywhere revealed.

I have lived in clover
Without realising. I'm so
Blessed to live in clover
But know it will soon fade and go.

9 July 2020

A Swallow's Circle

I meander in the meadow
With Tony, and before long
I say, "I call, 'Swallows,
Where are you?' in a singsong."

And at once, from behind the trees,
Four swallows dart and skim
Low round the green meadow
And fly over the hedge's brim.

But one returns and swoops
And describes a circle round us,

A perfect circle, saying,
"Hello again, no fuss."

It's left Tony quite stunned,
As it flies away up above,
That birds can interact
With humans with such love.

24 July 2020

Sky on Fire

As I took a cardboard box
To the bins by the gate, I turned.
The whole sky was on fire,
Every deep red cloud burned.

I returned and looked round the back:
A fire in the oak tree ahead,
And its flames crackled and blazed.
A red sun turned the sky red.

31 July 2020

Wistful Orange Moon

I sit in my window by the sea,
After months of the virus attune
Myself, after dark, to its serene calm,
And o, the man in the moon.

With an orange face, eyes, nose and mouth,
And a long orange causeway
Across the water to my house,
He's watching as I work today.

I mirror his half-profile face,
His lopsided, mournful stare
And feel a joy rise in my heart
That he looks wistfully on my lair.

3 August 2020

Sheep Huddled

I walk for the papers,
Sheep in the Cornish lane
Are standing, some sitting
In the field, sensing rain.

On the way back they're huddled
On the ground in a swarm,
Some by a hedge and some
Under trees, sensing a storm.

O sheep, I walk without
An umbrella or raincoat,
And you know the weather
Better than humans who emote.

5 August 2020

Lights in the Dark

I walk by the night sea,
A dozen lights flash-douse
From the horizon, boats
And the Eddystone Lighthouse.

The lights flash in the dark,
Warning all that they're there.
I look at the surging sea
And am glad I'm where I stare.

5 August 2020

Splashes of Light

The hottest day of the year.
I sit and gaze at the sea.
Ten thousand water splashes,
A shower of light to the quay.

The sea's a giant puddle,
It's dancing with splashing light.
My soul, too, is a puddle
That is splashing bright white.

O sea and my white soul,
Which I see bright when I darken
To sleep, enjoy your splashes
Before those clouds blacken.

A shadow across the sea,
All trace of a shower has gone.
And in my soul's a dark,
No more is the Light that shone.

8 August 2020

Fluttering Moth

I sit in my window,
The sea booms in the dark.
Two moths drawn by my light
Flutter, then settle and park.

O moths, you're drawn to my light
Just as I am drawn to the glow
That hides within inner dark,
Flutter at the Light I know

On the window-pane of my soul
And settle and bask in the sun
That shines out at midnight,
My day's lifelong work done.

9 August 2020

Sunlight Rains

Sunlight rains on the sea
Which jumps round the fishing-boat,

A shower of leaping water
As the sun pours light round my throat.

I sit and feel at peace,
Present in the moment, raw,
Then turn back to my blank page
And wait for words to pour.

10 August 2020

Honey-Bee

I sit and look at the sea.
By my knee, tiny white flowers
And a honey-bee hovers
And sips and nuzzles and scours.

O bee, please be careful
For humans have sneezed from this seat
And the virus may be where you sip.
Stay alert while you eat.

10 August 2020

4. 'Scour', "search thoroughly" (*Concise English Dictionary*).

Sparrow

A sparrow in the garden,
It flew in from the sea.
It's a black-bibbed house sparrow,
And I am filled with glee.

And I am taken back
To the sparrows under the eaves
Of my childhood home, chirping,
Flitting in the pear tree's leaves.

The sparrows disappeared
Like grasshoppers, for years.

And how good to see a sparrow
By the sea, I fight back tears.

12 August 2020

A Speedy Swallow Pities a Slow Human

Why does the human walk to the end
Of the meadow, turn and return, trudging?
He doesn't seem to have an aim,
He's wasting his energy wandering.

We swallows hurtle on the wind,
And skim to catch insects, our need.
We wheel and zoom and eat on the wing.
We speed to an end, so we can feed.

How slowly the human plods up the slope,
We could reach his gate in a few seconds' whirr.
Humans waste time and are pitifully slow.
We swallows are lords of the air, superior.

26 August 2020

10. 'Whirr', "continuous softly clicking sound as of a bird's wings" (*Concise Oxford Dictionary*).

Elm

My new elm's shaped like a flame,
In breeze its edges flicker
With pale green, not dark green,
As if on fire in its centre.

My birthday-present elm
Is full of energy,
No trace of Dutch-elm disease
As it waves merrily.

29 August 2020

Goldfinch on a Flowerpot

I gaze out of the window
And start, on a flowerpot
Next to the lavender
Is a goldfinch – what?

The last time I saw
A goldfinch in the garden
Was the day I returned from Iran
Thirteen years ago, I'm back then.

O goldfinch, an untouched feeder
Hangs on the cherry-tree
Full of your niger seed,
And now you've come back to me.

29 August 2020

A Tilted Head

I see you in your composed widowhood,
I see you sure of yourself within and wise,
But then a troubled look, and as you tilt
Your head and widen your made-up eyes
I see with shock your mother in her youth,
The same expression I saw on her face
And her beauty, even though I'm told you're like me.
O my daughter, I wish I could cure your life of all trace
Of the uncertainty you can see ahead,
Caring for your mother, moving for survival's sake
And not sure where the next phase of your life
After this Covid will take you, and I ache
For the tranquillity I would like to bequeath
To you, but cannot so long as I continue to breathe.

5 September 2020

Second Childhood

When you were a toddler I took you for a walk
Each day, first down to Edogawa bridge – we'd sneeze –
In Tokyo to look at the canal,
I held your hand, you little by my knees –
Once I picked you up when we saw a crowd
And I saw a body brought up from the canal's stains,
And when you asked "What is it?" I said, "A dolly" –
And later along Tripoli's sandy lanes,
And now I'm over eighty the roles are reversed,
You walk effortlessly and observe the sloes near the wood,
On a hedge, and pink flowers on blackberry brambles,
And I'm being walked by you, in my second childhood.
And so it is: small daughters depending
On fathers who depend on them in their shuffling.

7 September 2020

Crow and Water Lilies

Crow, standing on the fountain's rim,
Jet-black and large as a raven,
You're like a harbinger of Death
Above the water lilies' fountain.

Crow, fly away, I'm awaiting
My scan result, and am watching
Water gush down my three Graces
And pour life down on the basking

Yellow water lilies and tiny fish.
They love the sun, they don't want a pool
Under the shadow cast by Death.
They shudder, your dark presence is like a ghoul.

8 September 2020

Dandelion Clock Nearly Blown by the Wind

A dandelion with fluff
Most blown away by wind,
A dandelion clock blown
And not much left behind.

I look at my own clock,
Nearly blown away into air.
I have a little left
And rejoice in being here.

13 September 2020

Sowing by the Moon

The ancient civilisations sowed by the moon,
A full moon means high tide, wet ground, good toil,
And carrot seeds sown then have good juices
And the vegetables draw minerals from the soil
Such as calcium, which nourish humans.
All life was lived in harmony with Nature then,
With the moon, the sea and the soil, and there was peace
As an eighty-year-old went into his garden
Every morning soon after dawn and noticed new shoots
And was part of the rhythm of growing leaves
And of the process of growing vegetables,
With a good wife wanting nothing but golden sheaves;
And was content to be at one with the vast
Universe that still supplies what made things grow in the past.

Undated (between 13 September and 10 October 2020)

Flashing Lights Across the Sea

I gazed across the dark sea
At Jupiter, stars and ten lights
That flashed and died and flashed:
Ships' greetings and warnings in nights.

But then in the chilly air
A cloud obscured the sparkling stars
And a wind brought light rain
And I turned and walked past the cars.

O lights, my heart responds
To your flashes and flickers of love like a bomb
That greets my human eyes
Though I can't see where they're from.

10 October 2020

Cormorant

A calm sea with wind ripples,
Only my cormorant's spree –
Bobbing, its long neck diving,
Resurfacing out to sea.

Spellbound I watch as it dives,
I gaze as it bobs again.
Oh no, it's flying away,
Black wings flapping close to the main.

My cormorant has gone,
There's a wide expanse of blue.
All's still, but no sign of life.
Cormorant, I'll look out for you.

13 October 2020

Flaming Elm

I saunter down the lawn
And lo! The elm's yellow.
It flickers like a fire
In the sun's October glow.

Not long ago I carried
It in one hand, and now

It's rooted and a glory
Flames out, twice my height somehow.

And now I see the trees
In the Forest beyond, still not brown,
Are also leaping fires
With a life-force that won't die down.

25 October 2020

Veiled Mist

An autumn mist, and all is grey.
I see the silhouettes of trees,
All's still and lifeless, all is dank.
A jackdaw peers with a 'Feed me please'.

Lockdown, the first of many days
When I'm a prisoner of my home.
The future hangs like a veiled mist
And I peer back at the jackdaw that can still roam.

5 November 2020

Sparrowhawk Still

Sparrowhawk in the oak tree
Swoops down on a great tit
At my bird feeder, which flies.
Sparrowhawk wheels back to sit.

Two jackdaws make passes
But sparrowhawk does not budge,
Sits still as a dead branch
In this November sun, to judge.

Now great tits come for nuts.
Sparrowhawk is still, watching.
O be careful, little birds.
Death's camouflaged and waiting.

19 November 2020

Crepuscular

I'm late for my daily walk
In this Covid-plaguey time.
It's twilight in the field,
The shades of night are sublime.

No sign of life, no bats,
No birds in November gloom brood.
I saunter in blissful
Crepuscular solitude.

I am the grass and the sky
In the gathering dark's pout.
All creatures have gone to roost,
Only this human's about.

22 November 2020

Shadow on the Sea

I stand by the sea wall,
Gaze up at the starlit arc,
And then at the flashing lights
From ships and rocks in the dark.

From the street light behind me
My shadow's behind waves' bars,
Stretching out towards the lights.
My head's among the stars.

It's a dark night, no moon.
I am alone: it's me,
The stars, interacting lights,
And my shadow on the sea.

10 December 2020

Clouds like a Spider's Web

The night's clouds radiate
In a criss-crossed spider's web
And the bright half-moon crouches
In its heart like a spider at ebb.

I stand beneath the black tide
On my dark balcony,
And see the universe
As a criss-crossed unity.

Out in the dark I sense
One radiating cloud
Round my centred head reach
All shadowy shapes in this shroud.

8 January 2021

Plague

In 1350 people went to Salisbury
Cathedral to pray for deliverance from the Black Death.
Now they queue to be vaccinated against
Our plague, Covid-19, which steals our breath

And has killed eighty-seven thousand people
And is rampant with new mutations, variants
That overwhelm the immune system and still
All hope of a speedy deliverance,

But in our secular time we no more believe
That praying to God will exempt our bondage
Of infection from queuing in corridors
To gasp to death from oxygen shortage.

I see a husband hold his aged wife's hand
As masked she lies, eyes closed, at her life's end, vague,

And regardless what we believe we are now used
To twelve hundred deaths a day from this new plague.

And Death's become real to us, he loiters
At the end of lanes, at the foot of stairs,
Waiting to reap us as we cough and sweat
And succumb to an early departure from our prayers.

16 January 2021

Flocks

I walk during lockdown.
A flock of birds against cloud,
Flying west in a long line
With M-shaped wings, in a crowd.

And now another flock
Heading west from cold air.
I can't tell what the birds are,
They're like gulls but are dark, they look rare.

They fly slowly as if they know
They've a long flight ahead.
O birds, what made you so sure
Where you're going's better than whence you fled?

28–29 January 2021

Sparrowhawk Not Welcome

It's the national bird count.
A lot of small birds cluster.
Suddenly they all vanish.
A sparrowhawk's on their feeder.

Sparrowhawk, you are splendid
With your barred orange chest and your mount,
But go, you're not welcome.
There are now no birds to count.

5 February 2021

Sparrowhawk's Claws

I glance at my balcony.
O no, a sparrowhawk
Has a blue tit in its claws,
On its back, and is pecking its squawk.

I rise and open my door.
The sparrowhawk flies off and soars,
Magnificent orange and bars,
Clutching the blue tit in its claws.

O blue tit, all you did wrong
Was feed at my feeder,
And as you pecked a nut
Death loomed like a sparrowhawk's blur.

9 February 2021

Moth

A moth huddles on my window.
The snow's drifting down, it clings.
The fields and trees are white.
My moth shelters with outspread wings.

O moth, it may be cold
But all's good in the One
And spring will soon be here,
And then you'll be warm in sun.

9 February 2021

Fox

I walk down my snowy lawn.
In the field two foxes stare.
One slinks through the fence to next door,
One stands its ground to scare.

O fox, this isn't your field,
But you are welcome to stand.
So don't stare me out as if
I'm a trespasser on my own land.

12 February 2021

Icicle

An icicle by my window,
Tapering spike of iced light.
It hangs from the gutter,
Memorial to a cold night.

O icicle, frozen
Drips of water in air that's fine,
Now the sun is out, your life
Is as transient as mine.

13 February 2021

Buttercups

Midsummer June's buttercups
Have turned to face the sun.
They smile above the small stitchworts,
A thousand having fun.

Now the mower's cut their heads.
They lie like piles of tears.
Don't cry, buttercups, your stems will flower
Again with youthful spheres.

15 February 2021

Ladybird

Ladybird, I see you
Crawl near the white rose's stem,

A red fire in the warm sun,
Each black spot like a gem.

Ladybird, I too am
A fire with black spots from the One
As I crawl past a chestnut
With white candles lit by the sun.

15 February 2021

This poem was written while walking.

Sun on Sea

A murky rainy day.
The wintry trees are bare,
The lawn is free from snow,
Grey clouds hang low everywhere.

I go to the webcam
That shows my seaside home.
A lovely sunny day,
The sun's sparkling in the foam.

I wish I were in Cornwall
Now there's spring weather there,
And not here in Essex where
There's a chill in the wet air.

18 February 2021

Moon like Cheese

A Snow Moon in the sky,
The nearest the moon gets
To the earth in its year's phases,
Glows red as the sun sets.

Its light passes through particles
In our lower atmosphere,

It's called 'Snow' because it's the time
Of snowfall in Nature's year.

A Blood Moon in the sky
Three months later – in May
During a lunar eclipse –
See its light's refracted display.

O moon, your tides control
Human minds and the seas,
And you vary your look
Like a now white, now red cheese.

1 March 2021

Cherry

Easter Monday morning,
And minute flakes of snow
Drift down to the green grass
And a cherry tree aglow.

This sunny afternoon
I walk past the hedgerows
White with glorious may
And lo! The cherry tree glows.

5 April 2021

Blossom like Frost

I walk across the field.
May blooms on all sides stun,
Hang white like recent frost.
Blossom melts in the sun.

The second field, and more
Blossom like frost shouts, "Yes."
O wonderful Nature that's white
In spring, clad in winter dress.

10 April 2021

Sparkling Sea and Gulls

Spring sunshine, from my window,
Breathing in sea air, a shock –
On a sparkling sea gulls scream
And flock around a rock.

Something has died, and lies
On a rock in this calm sea
And they are all feeding
In a life-perpetuating spree.

14 April 2021

Daisies, Stars

A freezing Arctic night.
The daisies are all closed.
They shiver in the frost.
The stars are feeling frozed.

Across the bay the lights
Of lighthouses flicker
And ships flash out and fade.
The stars twinkle and shiver.

O daisies, think of the stars.
Like your petalled buds, they fold;
And think of the distant lights –
All share your Arctic cold.

15 April 2021

4. 'Frozed', "extremely frozen by bitter cold" (neologism).

Herring Gull

A freezing Arctic chill.
I eat my fish and chips
Sitting on the harbour wall.
A herring gull stares at my lips.

O herring gull, you can't
Have what's above my chin.
Go down and join the gulls
Screaming at what the sea's washed in.

15 April 2021

Sparkling Sea, Sneeze

A gentle high tide and the sea
Sparkles and dazzles in the sun,
And screwing up my eyes I sneeze
In heartfelt appreciation.

A thousand jumping, dancing lights
Beneath my window, and, undone,
Dazzled, I sneeze again and again,
Each sneeze a sparkle to the One.

16 April 2021

Smiling Night

I walk under the stars.
The moon is on its back over the bay,
It's smiling down the night.
I smile at the Milky Way.

The sea is fairly calm.
The lights on the dark's horizon
All wink at me in turn.
The universe is at one.

17 April 2021

Two Foxes

A warm sunny teatime.
I listen to birds at the field's edge.

A fox watches intently,
Then gets up and heads for the hedge.

I stand in the bottom field
And aware of being watched, see
Another fox staring.
It too heads for a hedge to flee.

O foxes, I am sorry
To disturb your paws-out, Sphinx-like rest,
But humans share Nature.
Please rest assured, you're each my guest.

23 April 2021

Death Staring, Waiting

I wake with a painful shoulder and a blood leak
In my arm, can't raise my right hand, go again
To my gym and walk, cycle, treadle, pull weights.
I still can't raise my right arm, my shoulder's in pain
And may have been infected by a wound
On the back of my hand, from a marble worktop's stay.
My GP can't see me and says I should go
To A&E for a blood test and X-ray
As I may have sepsis from my earlier wound.
Sepsis can be fatal in twelve hours, I go back.
Two hours slide by, thirty wait to be called.
A man in a ghost mask and hood, dressed in black,
Death, sits and stares at me. This is how it will be
When we die, we'll wait to be called in such company.

6 May 2021; 28–29 December 2022

6. 'Stay', "prop or support" (*Concise Oxford Dictionary*).

Last Call to the Afterlife

I've had a blood test, an X-ray and been seen
By a consultant, and have been told I
Have fluid in a septic shoulder joint.
I've waited for the bone people to try

And take a fluid sample to see if I've got
Sepsis, bursitis, or a shoulder that's frozen.
A consultant in scrubs examines me and barks,
"There's no fluid, and there's no infection.
You've a torn muscle and calcification.
You'll have an MRI and then I'll know
The way forward, you'll have painkillers till then."
So I haven't after all got sepsis, though
A doctor and consultant thought I had, it's not rife.
I'm not awaiting my last call to the afterlife.

6 May 2021; 28–29 December 2022

Owls Hooting

"Tu-whit, tu-whoo!" hoots an owl,
A tawny owl that's wise,
"To be a wit and to woo,
That's how young men should rise."

"Whoo-whoo," hoots back an owl,
A barn owl that sees what's true,
"Who are you, who? Seek Truth.
That's the path young men should pursue."

25 May 2021

Moon

A round large yellow moon,
A supermoon in eclipse,
And a shimmering yellow causeway
Across the sea's wrinkled dips.

A huge round yellow moon
Golden above the sea,
That sends its shimmering light
Across the waves to me.

26–27 May 2021

Downpour from the Sun

The sea is dazzling,
A thousand leaping lights
Sparkle waves to the horizon's
Mist with their jumping whites.

The sea is hallooing,
Splashing flashed lights that glint
In a downpour from the sun
As drenched, I shelter and squint.

30 May 2021

Stitchwort Stars

The meadow has been cut,
I walk through tufted green,
See fallen buttercups.
Yellow vetch can't be seen.

I walk and see clusters
Of tiny stitchwort stars.
The buttercups towered above them
And looked down on them as scars.

But now the mighty have fallen
And the tiny stitchworts survived.
Nature's a great leveller,
O stitchworts grow, you've thrived.

16 June 2021

Swallows Back

I walk in the long meadow,
Birds hurtle and dart and skim.
Four swallows, the four from last year,
Are back. Swallows! I brim.

I call as they dart round me
And keep me company
As I walk through the long grass,
And swerve and dive, so free.

O swallows, my long-lost friends,
It's good to see you again.
And each of the four hurtles
A Hello round my mane.

5 July 2021

Bee in the Lavender

I go out into the dusk,
The lavender's still, see.
But one bumble-bee works
From sprig to sprig, thoroughly.

O bee, it's time you flew home,
Your work is done for the day,
Yet still you hover and settle
On each mauve sprig and spray.

Now I sit in my room
And work on each insight,
And hover and settle and hover,
Thorough in what I write.

But I'm thinking of the bee
That is still outside in the dark
Foraging for nectar
As I forage for truth's trade mark.

18 July 2021

Sparkling Sea

The sparkling sea again,
A thousand splashes of light

As the sun beats on the waves
And paddlers gasp at the sight,

Transfixed at the jumping sea
As open-mouthed fish leap
And gulp the splashing food
The sun has strewn on the deep.

4 August 2021; revised 10 December 2022

Sea Storm and Mind

Rain runs and washes down the window-panes,
The sea outside has long white surf-lined waves,
Wind beats round my seaside cliff-edge house and strains,
The angry air lashes, sea foams and raves.
A mist veils the horizon and a lone
Storm petrel flaps wings low over waves and fast,
And I am at the epicentre, on my own,
Of an elemental froth and gusting blast.
A gull soars by, floats on the wind near me.
Otherwise it's my eyes, drenched windows of course,
Hissing rain, lashing wind and turbulent sea
As air and water dance to one gusting force,
One surge that drives both sea and wind, and sorts,
And also drives my mind and its surging thoughts.

5 August 2021

The Evening Star is Bright

The evening star is bright
And's now hidden in cloud.
A mist round the headland,
The lighthouse light's in shroud.

I stand in cloudy dark,
More rain is on the way.
And what used to be bright
Has vanished, like the day.

7 August 2021

Fallen Leaves

I tremble like a leaf
In a late-autumn gale,
I still cling to my tree but know
I can't last long, I'm frail.

A lawn of fallen leaves
Like a generation gone
From a virus in the air,
And my time will soon come, I'm wan.

9 August 2021

8. 'Wan', "pale, exhausted, worn; (of a star or its light) partly obscured, faint" (*Concise Oxford Dictionary*).

Shooting Star

I gaze across the sea.
Jupiter is very bright,
I peer into the stars.
The dog days are here tonight.

And where is the meteor shower?
Suddenly an orange trail,
A shooting star from the west's
Sped across the sky in a gale.

And now it's night again
And no more hurtling rocks,
Meteorites burning out. I turn
And go back in to clocks.

But deaf in my curtained room,
I am out among stars, though blind:
Aware of more meteorites
And a universe in my mind.

9 August 2021

4. 'Dog days', "the hottest period of the year (reckoned in antiquity from the heliacal rising of the dog-star)"; 'dog-star', "the chief star of the constellation Canis Major or Minor, especially Sirius" (*Concise Oxford Dictionary*).

A Calm Sea

A calm sea and a mist.
No waves, it's like a lake,
Reflections from the masts
Of two boats shimmer and flake.

And I too am in calm,
At eighty-two at peace
And no turbulence disturbs
My reflections on my decease.

12 August 2021

Moth Drawn by Light

Moths still on my window,
Drawn by my bright desk light.
They've flown on the sea wind,
Swept from stone crannies, this night.

And like a wind-borne moth
I too am drawn by Light:
Still, look at my oval cloud's
Satiny downy white.

12 August 2021

7. 'Oval cloud'. See volume 38, *An Oval Cloud.*

Pecking and Picking

Dozens of blue tits peck
At the bird feeders and fly
Out with a nut and return
To the towering hedge nearby.

And dozens queue outside
A store and train themselves
To wait their turn to pick
Their seed from its emptying shelves.

2 October 2021

Soul Sings

In its eighties soul sings,
Bits of music invade
And soul sings along to them,
Hosannaing as they're played.

In its eighties moments sing,
Absorb and tremble the soul:
The beauty of the earth
And the order within the Whole.

11 October 2021

Shimmering Gold

The evening star in the sky.
I peer over the sea wall,
Look left to the headland
And lo! a round moon ball

And shimmering gold across
The lapping waves near the shore.
I stand spellbound in the dark
At the moon and a causeway of ore.

21 October 2021

Rock Pipit

My rock pipit's on the wall.
I see its yellow streaks
It looks at me and flies down
To a foot from my foot and peeks.

It's tame, I wonder if it's
Recognised me though wild:
A hot day last summer,
When it perched on the wall and smiled.

22 October 2021

Between Moon and Star

I stand at the wall between
A bright moon and a bright star,
The evening star on the hill.
Both call to me from afar.

Beneath, the night sea laps.
A causeway of shimmering white.
And beneath the star, in the dark
I reconcile dark and light.

24 October 2021

The Power of the Sea

Another storm at sea.
Rain on my window-pane.
Surging waves crash against
The sea wall again and again.

Will the digger that's been shoring up
The cliff before it caves
In be swept out to sea
By the power within the waves?

24 October 2021

Nuthatch

My nuthatch is back, sloping
Downwards on the bird feeder
That's bulging with fat nuts.
It pecks with a swagger.

Its pink chest is gleaming
In the early sunshine.
In its upside-down world
Looking down from the top is fine.

9 November 2021

Squelching Heart

My heart is squelching round the room
As I lie on a couch and start,
Stripped to my waist, in electrodes,
As a probe's moved round my heart.

The squelching's like plodding through mud:
My trudge to extinction.
And any time it could fall silent –
O heart, keep squelching on.

10 November 2021

Fox Sniffing

Look, a fox is sniffing
Under the bird feeder,
Unaware I'm watching
As I give my breakfast a stir.

He's following a scent
That may lead him to prey,
And I spoon a mouthful
Of oat food for this day.

17 November 2021

Carrion Crow

A sleek black carrion crow
Is pecking among the leaves
Outside the test centre
And eyes between my sleeves.

A positive lateral flow
And now a test to confirm
I have the dreaded plague.
Its staring makes me squirm.

O crow, Death's harbinger,
Strutting around my breath,
Fly off, don't menace me
With my impending death.

19 November 2021

Black Crow and Plague Victim

I sit and stare at the black crow that waits
As a plague victim stared in another time,
And as a leper stares out at barred gates
I ring my bell and shout 'Unclean', in mime.
It stares on, waiting for my decline, I guess.
I know it should be mild but I could be
Snuffed out within a week, my works a mess.
I set myself to finish them all in three
Years, archive them for scholars who will pore
Over my scribbles, understand and know
Why I have written each line, what I saw.
I will not give in to this stalking crow
That wants me to lay down my pen and be gone
With a final blot, and become carrion.

19 November 2021

Blood-Red Sun

A blood-red sun rising
Above the peaceful sea.
I watch from my window:
Blood and tranquillity.

And now a golden sun
Dazzles with its blinding round.
The sea washes in, I squint
And all disquiet has drowned.

16 December 2021

Surging Waves like a Virus

Waves surge in, crested with white foam, and fall,
Line after line of frothing curls roll, biff
And grate the shingle, whop the harbour wall
And fling up spray from below the rocky cliff.
Wave after wave of relentless surging sea
Drawing energy from last night's full moon
Which hung in the night sky, round, yellowy.
I watch the cascading sea from my room and swoon.
But I also think of the virus, and of how
Like a moon it propels waves of variants,
Delta (which I had) reaching shore, and now
Omicron's frothing foam and dominance.
And I inhale drifting spray with each breath,
Which may reach my lungs and swamp me to my death.

18 December 2021

3. 'Whop', "(variant of [intransitive] 'wap') to strike with heavy blows" (*The Shorter Oxford English Dictionary*).

Reddening Sun

We turn off to Cornwall in February,
O look, yellow furze, gorse, winter's over.
I drive through lanes and sense the coming spring.
There will soon be buttercups and clover.

Cornwall! where the sea pounds and washes to shore
And a wind from the Channel clears all city chests,
And all slow down and are blown by a sea breeze
And faces glow red in a reddening sun that guests.

11 February 2022

Storm

The sea slowly foams in, wave after wave,
Mist to the horizon, window's lashed by rain.
Crest beyond crest until sea blends with murk
And a gusting echoing moan of wind in pain.

Each wave gathers and stately rolls to shore,
From crest to sliding foam white net of surf.
The universe's on a roar and Nature cowers,
No birds or sheep on the steep green hillside turf
Across the harbour whose calm waters are whipped
As rain blows in like misty flakes of snow.
All's cold, I shiver in my dressing-gown
As, at one with the surging sea in my window,
I watch the roaring wind in the mist coerce,
At one with the mighty power of the universe.

13 February 2022

After the Storm

After the tree-felling storm,
The surging house-high waves,
Staccato of lashing hail,
Wind tearing roofs as it raves,

This calm night under the moon,
In the frost planets wink.
I gulp in Cornish air
And yawn as far lights blink

Across the bay to the cliffs
Of the headland, a lighthouse's flare,
And far out answering lights say
"All's well with us" here and there.

18 February 2022

War and Spring

Bombed apartments, ruin
And rubble everywhere
Filling our screens for hours,
Full war is very near.

White cherry blossom on blue,
Parakeets hang and sway,

Sun's warm on cheeks, spring's here
And war seems far away.

26 March 2022

Waiting on a Clot

I've had my CT scan and my blood test.
I sit in the spaced waiting-room in the Same
Day Emergency Care hospital unit,
And now await the calling of my name
So a doctor can explain what I have got.
I'm supposed to have a blood clot in my lungs
Which could at any moment go to my heart
As my blood test showed D-dimer (that bungs)
Was positive and high, suggesting a clot.
I've had iodine pumped into my veins
So the scanner can see if there's a blockage
Indicating where the clot has reached and reigns.
And any moment it could go to my heart
Leaving my last works unfinished, and no restart.

30 March 2022

8. D-dimer is a protein fragment from a dissolving blood clot.

On a Precipice

I haven't told my children I'm on the edge
Of a precipice above a dark abyss,
That mortality has crept up on me.
I thought I'd be at eighty-five in bliss.
I must get on and finish all projects
For I'm still short of being eighty-three,
So I can make a tidy withdrawal
When the time comes and leave my legacy
In good order, and no unfinished works.
But a pain in the bottom of my lungs has cast doubt,
It's barged into my plan, and this may mean
My days are numbered, as I'll soon find out.

And I'm standing on the edge of Beachy Head
Waiting to hear if I'll be plunged into the dark, and dead.

30 March 2022

Reprieve

The young doctor calls me in, would I explain
What happened to me. I go through it again on her rack.
She says, "We haven't found any evidence
Of a clot, but there's fluid in the sac
Round your heart, which is making your heart struggle
And can be dangerous if it's not treated for the frail.
It's called pericarditis." "That's what I said,"
I say, handing her my printed-out email.
She looks in amazement, and says, "Your diagnosis
Was completely right – better than the GP's.
We'll give you something to bring the fluid down.
You've had a virus (Covid?) that's caused this disease."
So my mortality's recalled, I've been reprieved.
I'm still alive, I'm not saying farewell, I'm relieved.

30 March 2022

Game (or Gammy) Heart

Again I sit and wait to hear my fate.
My heart rate's high, even when I sit back,
My poor game heart's impeded from outside
All round it, squashed by its pericardial sac,
Compressed, so it has to beat twice as fast
To maintain control of my bodily
Functions while I sit at peace, hands as if I'm
Meditating, Buddha-like, half-slit eyes. Gamely
My heart pounds on, pushing my blood (still coping
With being swamped by iodine) to go
To the far end of my arteries and back,
Pumping non-stop instead of on auto.
Will I breathe sea air next week as planned in Cornwall,
Or when I'm called will they keep me in hospital?

1 April 2022

Title, 3. 'Game', "spirited, eager, willing; [pronounced 'gammy'] lame, crippled" (*Concise Oxford Dictionary*).

Leaning Daisies

Lo for the tilting daisies
That lean towards the sun.
I smile on a street corner
And the sun winks back in fun.

Fluid's squashing my heart,
I sense the coming night
That will stop its beating,
But the sun makes things all right.

1 April 2022

Daffodils

The daffodils look down
Beneath the setting sun.
Are you sleeping, daffodils?
Twilight's not yet begun.

The daffodils are sad
As nightfall's drawing near,
But remember, daffodils,
When you beamed at the sun's warmth here.

1 April 2022

Wagtail

A wagtail on my lawn
Amid dandelions and daisies.
It's still and wags its tail,
In the sea-breeze rejoices.

Elsewhere someone's dying
At ninety-six from a fall.
It's still and watching me
As if I'm waiting my call.

7 April 2022

Fall like a Tall Tree

Pat at ninety-six fell
In the night and's in agony
In a trauma ward with a broken
Pelvis and swollen knee.

I got up last night and my toe
Caught in my bedspread in my doze,
I crashed like a tall tree
In the dark on my elbows.

I could have gashed my face
On the wardrobe and now be at
The trauma ward with a cracked
Pelvis like fallen Pat.

9 April 2022

Years like Foaming Waves

I look back on my life from my window
As wind whistles and foaming waves roll in.
There's quite a swell, there may be a storm ahead.
The years surge and froth in to the wind's din,
Remind of all I wanted to do with my life.
By and large I reached what I had to reach.
Sixty books, like sixty crests out to sea
Will foam in and leave surf on the stony beach.
Wind gusts and hisses round my damp window
As I look back at all my lone striving
Like a windsurfer on a sailboard, tugging
At the strings of a sail in the wind, billowing.

The wind that causes each wave to roll ashore
Was the wind I caught in my works and view with awe.

10 April 2022

A Shadow in Time

I go out into a gale.
A wind from the east whips
My hair and cleanses my lungs.
I yawn as it gusts and dips.

My shadow is on the waves,
The street light's behind me.
I cast a shadow in time
Before still eternity.

10 April 2022

Pipit and Reflection

All afternoon a black pipit
Has been fluttering its wings at the bird it sees
In the side mirrors of the black Merc
Parked opposite my window in the breeze.

And now after dark I look at the face
In my lit window as I look out to sea,
Having taken my pulse, one-three-two,
When one-two-seven's the highest it should be.

Like the black pipit I flutter at myself,
My heart's fluttering, squashed with fluid.
My fingers have fluid, I press with my thumb
And the dent fills slowly until it's hid.

Tomorrow I leave this Cornwall,
But now like the pipit I look at my head
Whose stare proves that I'm still alive
When my pulse suggests that I should be dead.

13 April 2022

Bats

I load the car – I should not be doing this –
And walk down to the bin and discard my waste.
It's dusk and round the beach beneath me swirl
A score of bats, one swerves me in its haste.

It's huge, as large as a bird, a soaring gull.
Round and round they flit, near the tunnel in the wall
Which in my mind I enter and walk in
And fall asleep as its dark enfolds like a shawl.

The dark is round me now, though it's twilight.
I know my pulse rate could race and stop my heart.
I return to my room and sit as if at Zen,
Breathe slowly as if at a meditation's start.

I know I am unwell, and have nursed the sac
Round my heart so I have been free from pain
Since Saturday, but know I am on the brink
Of my pulse stopping, as these bats warn again.

13 April 2022

A Peacock Butterfly

I saunter down the field
In warm Easter sunshine,
And near blackberry bushes
See two black 'leaves' recline.

I saunter past, and one
Takes wing and alights and clings
On a blackberry bush, and I see
Round eyes on a peacock's wings.

16 April 2022

A Heavenly Garden

I sit in evening sun
Which blinds me between trees.
Birdsong rings round my head
As I close my eyes in breeze.

A squirrel was in my room
Behind my open door,
It's May, and summer warmth
Is here, and my health's poor.

A blackbird's clear piping
Is answered the other side
Of this Heavenly garden,
And I feel as if I've died.

8 May 2022

Stop-Breathings

I am slid into a pink washing-machine,
There are clankings and knockings, several sounds, gratings.
Through my earphones I hear, "Breathe, breathe out, stop
Breathing." I lie as if dead, more clankings.
Then, "Breathe." I breathe in relief through my nostrils.
Again Raj says, "Breathe, breathe out, stop breathing."
Again I lie dead. "Breathe." I nose in air
Grateful for the gift of life, renewed living.
I had a hundred stop-breathings in my hour.
I have stop-breathings in my sleep at night,
And sleep with an apnoea mask on my nose.
At last I'm slid out into social light
And wait to hear if my heart's approaching with breath
My last stop-breathing, my impending death.

17 May 2022

7. 'Nose' is here a verb meaning 'sniff', 'breathe'.

Swallow

I walk on the lush-green field.
A swallow skims and swirls,
It's one of *my* swallows
From last year, it darts and twirls.

O swallow, I am so pleased
To see you come and go.
Now it describes a circle
Round me, to say "Hello".

8 June 2022

A Small Tortoiseshell's Salute

I wandered in great heat amid
Clover and buttercups and, glad,
Called out, "Swallows, look, I am here."
None came, I felt bereft and sad.

But as I neared a blackberry bush
A small tortoiseshell from a tree
Alighted on grass and lowered, then raised
Its wings in a salute to me.

14 June 2022

Mist

Lashings of rain, and then sun,
And an orange sky in the west,
And now at dusk a mist
Fills the field – and me with zest.

I watch as it creeps towards
The lawn and my window to shroud
And dull the dusk to night,
Faint yellow behind dark cloud.

30 June 2022

Wasps and Bees

A wasps' nest in the brick,
A wasp man has squirted,
A dozen wasps a-dance
Distress-call a powdered head.

Beyond, the lavender,
Three bees nuzzle and fly
And nuzzle, oblivious
Of the distress nearby.

12 July 2022

Poems written during a visit to Ireland

Oblivion

I sit waiting to board my ship
To go round Ireland for two weeks,
And watch my travelling companions
Arrive and totter to what each seeks.

I'm old and yet I'm somehow here
(Thanks to a chauffeur-driven car)
And look ahead to a sweltering cruise
While my mind's elsewhere, within a war.

The Russians have Zircon missiles
Nine times faster than the speed of sound
And can three minutes from firing
With a tidal wave leave England drowned.

I sit and watch the elderly
Totter from their Covid tests and sit,
Waiting to get away and cruise
Oblivious of oblivion's hit.

1 August 2022

Black-Headed Gull

I sit and wait with nothing to do,
And look at the clouds and the blue sky
And the things I would miss if I weren't here,
At my coffee cup, its inside dry,

And I am pleased I can look out
At the world with time to stare and see
And notice the black-headed gull
Flying to and fro, waiting like me.

1 August 2022

At Portsmouth: Leaving Port

The elderly sit, waiting to go,
Each one intent on boarding a ship
But each one here for a short while
Under the sun that warms like a grip.

We sit and wait to go elsewhere.
I pass the time by writing a thought
And mirror how we all sit on
And wait to leave our lifetime's port.

1 August 2022

Gong

I sip my apple juice and think
Of when I was young and drank it each day
With my breakfast, then rushed to work.
I had no time to sit in dismay.

I sit with my shadow and sip my juice
And, old, feel young again and long
For my shadow to write the sixty books
That I, now my shadow, have boomed like a gong.

1 August 2022

8. See 40 sonnets in volume 40: *In Arcady: A Gong and Padded Stick* (p.237).

Trawled

I sit with a view and a long wait
And, the world pared down to here and now,
All simplified into one moment,
Reflect on my life, on why and how.

I sit and reflect like one who's been shown
To the ante-room before being called
To the Last Judgment of my sixty works
And the haul of moments my life trawled.

1 August 2022

Night-Sea Voyage

This is what it will be like, the Last
Judgment, a wait for a call to all
With an orange ticket to go to a coach
And be taken on a voyage, a crawl

Across a night-sea, to a place
Where platform faces will review
My life and work and pass judgment,
And thence to my next place with the same crew.

1 August 2022

Raindrops like Early Stars

A coach through rural Ireland,
Rain spots on the window disperse
Like the James Webb telescope's
Stars in the early universe.

The cows are sitting down,
Waiting for a lightning flash,
And I'm among forming stars
From Creation's thunderous crash.

3 August 2022

A Hermit and Solitude

I sit on Great Skellig, in my monastery,
Above the hole in the rock that's my home, aglow,
And look across to the gannets' colony
At Little Skellig, white from their guano
That binds their nests, thirty-five thousand pairs gabble
And I can smell guano on the wind, not peeved
I praise the Lord, and Archangel Michael,
For these volcanic pinnacle rocks that heaved
From the sea and house us thirty monks who as one
Sit still and contemplate the great wonder
Of down and wings and foraging renewed
To keep life going forward in the sun,
One of billions in God's great universe, and purr.
O thank you, God, for delicious solitude.

6 August 2022

Title 'Hermit', "an early Christian recluse, any person living in solitude" (*Concise Oxford Dictionary*).

1. Great Skellig. Early Christian monks established a community on Skellig Michael (Great Skellig), an island formed of pinnacle rocks thrown up 400 million years ago, and survived from the 6th century AD until the 13th century. Their monastic buildings are some 150 metres above sea level and are reached by 618 steep steps cut into the rock face. There are 6th-century beehive cells – the largest is 4.5 metres by 3.6 metres – and an 11th-century oratory. Influenced by the Coptic Church of St Anthony, the monks were in quest of ultimate solitude on a wind-blown ledge, and communed with God, the One force and plan behind all Creation. There were Viking raids in 812 and 823. The community may have ended as a result of the medieval plague, the Black Death.

Death: Coach

Will this be how it will be, a drive in a coach
With elderly passengers with bleary eyes,
A leaving for green mountains from distant sea
And the next place where souls go when their body dies?
Will we be jogged along up into cloud,
Yawning from weariness and not knowing
Where we are heading but not really caring,

Just wanting this joggy journey to end?
Resigned, incurious, accepting what's next
And reconciled to our allotted fate?
Bumping along with rattling windows
And contemplating the best things we have done, too late?
And we won't be surprised that somehow we have survived,
And will soon know what our new role will be, and our guide?

6 August 2022

Zodiac

No, it will be more like getting into a Zodiac,
Sitting and being driven on the inflated side
Out of a calm harbour into choppy
Waters and then a bumpy, splashy ride,
Tilted at the front, down at the back, and spray
Lashing both face and waterproofs, speeding
Out over the vast deep, and holding on
To a looped tie below the outer side, clutching
And buffeted, nearly out to the swelling sea,
A colossal bump and being thrown out grabbing
Into the water and lying back while the life-
Jacket inflates and then drifting and waiting
Until, weakened and lost, the last black-out, a lull
And then soul's flight upwards like an ascending gull.

22 August 2022

1. 'Zodiac', an inflatable boat.

Hag's Head and God

I stand on the deck alone and gaze out at
The Irish cliffs of Moher, which were formed three
Hundred and seventeen million years ago, that
Are sediments thrown up by tectonic plates, and see,
Squinting in blinding sunlight, two towers that rile
And, at the promontory's knob, the Hag's Head rock,
Make out, as she lies on her back, the hag's profile,
Curved chin, two lips, nose and protruding lids that mock

Below and above a sunken witch's eye,
Hair separated from her skull by an arch in a nod:
A personification of cliffs in a centuries-old curse.
So we lost humans personify the night sky,
Billions of stars, our sun, sea, rocks as God
Who created our sedimentary universe.

8 August 2022

Under Ben Bulben: Grave and Boat

I look across the bay
At Ben Bulben's mountainside
Where in Drumcliffe churchyard
Yeats lies, and I, clear-eyed,

Fifty-six years ago
Read out, "Cast a cold eye
On life and death. Horseman
Pass by!" And I gave a sigh.

And below, our guide tells me
(She's not allowed to say),
Mountbatten's boat was blown up
By 'patriots' from the IRA.

Under Ben Bulben, Yeats,
Who led a peaceful life;
But at the mountain's foot,
The IRA's deadly strife.

9 August 2022

Rocks like Sheep

In remote Donegal
Sheep in a smallholding
Near a bog and peat; all round
Green hills that are rolling.

The other side of the road
White rocks that look like sheep
Adorn the mountain slope
And its grassy paths are steep.

9 August 2022

Back from my Grave

This end-of-life tiredness,
I doze on the coach – now hurt.
A kick on my leg wakes me.
My wife's keeping me alert.

When I'm at the end of my life
And waves of tiredness crowd,
Will she kick me back from my grave
So I'm doing the right thing, unbowed?

9 August 2022

House Martins and Sheep

Round and round the field they fly,
Three house martins with white breasts
Cavort near a roof, and dive,
With the freedom of all, like guests.

Such energy, as I
Sit on my coach to return,
Up to the telegraph wires,
And will they never learn

To conserve their energy?
They skim the field for flies,
Catch them on the wing while three sheep
Munch grass, with contented eyes.

9 August 2022

In Mount Stewart's Sunken Garden

I sit in Mount Stewart's sunken garden and wait
To enter Castlereagh's fine house and view
Traces of the Foreign Secretary at
The time of the Battle of Waterloo.

A fine man behind the Act of Union,
Who did good things for the British Empire
And then suppressed the Peterloo Revolt –
And incensed Shelley, drew his poetic fire.

As usual I am torn between the British
Empire and the judgment of wise Shelley,
And sit amid fragrant flowers and unite
Two conflicting points of view in harmony.

12 August 2022

From Waterloo to Peterloo

(*The last of 17 poems written during a visit to Ireland*)

From Waterloo to Peterloo
Castlereagh's reputation sank.
Depressed, though having inherited
Mount Stewart, he slit his throat and – blank.

Shelley's "I met Murder on the way,
He wore a mask like Castlereagh"
He did not know, it was unpublished.
At his house in Kent he slipped away.

O Castlereagh, you did good things
But were also ruthless as the Irish know.
I have a mixed view of you, having seen
Your house and Strangford Lough below.

12 August 2022

Clouds and Foam

I speed to Cornwall beneath
A grey and lowering sky.
The cattle are standing,
And the sheep, rain's not nigh.

Now the sea surges in
Beneath my seaside home
That I visit now and again,
My heart leaps at the foam.

18 August 2022

Work and Universe

The night sky over the sea,
Bright Venus and red Mars
And Jupiter. I look up
At a universe of stars.

Just now, absorbed in my work,
I let my context disperse,
But now I'm again alone
In a vast universe.

28 August 2022

Last Buttercup

I walk along the lawn.
All the flowers have gone.
Only one buttercup,
Standing proudly alone.

Sometimes I too have felt
I am the last to die
Of a long line of wordsmiths
Who wrote of the One each day.

14 September 2022

Pilgrimage

A five-mile-long queue by the River Thames,
Twenty hours edging in a stuttering line outside
To enter Westminster Hall built by William
The Conqueror's son, where Charles the First was tried,
Descend steps and in a stuttering line bow or
Curtsy to the high catafalqued coffin wrapped in the gloss
Of a Royal Standard, crown, orb and sceptre on top –
Amid bear-skinned and swan-feathered guards, yeomen and a tall cross.
It's been a journey, a pilgrimage, to a shrine to bow
Not to St Thomas of Canterbury or a prophet
But a good Queen, for seventy years head of the Anglican Church,
A secular saint, as was before death Becket,
And amid camaraderie process past grief in
A cathartic cleansing beneath the Queen's coffin.

17 September 2022

Title 'Pilgrimage'. 'Pilgrim', "a person who journeys to a sacred place for religious reasons" (*Concise Oxford Dictionary*).

6. 'Gloss', "a surface shine or lustre; a smooth finish" (*Concise Oxford Dictionary*).

8. 'Bear-skinned', Queen's Company Grenadier Guards; 'swan-feathered', Gentlemen-at-Arms; 'yeomen', Yeomen of the Guard.

What If?

What if she was never there in the draped coffin
At her lying-in-state, and the hundreds of thousands in flocks
Who waited thirteen hours to file past and bow
Were saying "Thank you" to an empty box
When actually her body was elsewhere,
Refrigerated so as not to decompose?
What if this old lady who ruled seventy years
Was a silent head as on stamps and coins, a rose
And not the architect of the Commonwealth
And the special relationship with America
Through handwritten letters like the one offering
A recipe to President Eisenhower?
What if all projected on her influence that was beyond
Her, and all past unquestioning pilgrims have been self-conned?

18 September 2022

Sheep

A blue sky this morning
But the sheep were lying down.
A cloudless sky, but they knew
Rain was in the wind, like a frown.

Midnight and rain lashes
At my window, a storm
Has swept in from the sea,
And the sheep sensed it in the warm.

20 October 2022

Turbulent Sea

The white foam surges in, wave after wave,
Just as my works keep coming and boiling round me.
I sit in my window, like a mystic in
A hut on a fifth-century hillside above sea,
Perch like a gannet in this Spartan air
And do what the life-force has commanded me,
Produce thoughts on the universe like a prayer
For others to read in waves like the white crests
That now surge in below the roaring wind's rapture.
All Heaven is in uproar this evening.
I sit like an ancient monk growing older
And write my tribute to the turbulent sea and death
And blend into the universe like a last breath.

20 October 2022

Tide

The sea rolls in, wave after surfing wave,
With boiling foam between as I look back –
Perched on my monk's high crag with sea and sky,
Ivy on rough-hewn stone blocks and wind's smack –
At a life that began under bombs from the air,
And wartime rationing and a sudden flash,

And swept me to a distant destination
Which I've now reached amid my papers' stash:
My sixty-first book at an advanced age.
I stare at the lines of surf-thrusting waves
And the force of a tide that fills all I see below
As the wind fills the sky and blows dark clouds like graves,
And I see my long life filled with a tidal thrust
From my inner moon that has shaped all I've done, and my Trust.

21 October 2022

8. 'Stash' (18th-century origin), "hoard", "store" (*Concise Oxford Dictionary*).
14. 'Trust', "Literary Trust".

Planets and Shadow

I gaze by the harbour wall
Up at Jupiter and red Mars,
And in lit dark my shadow's
On the beach under the stars.

O planets, you're always there.
I'm a fleeting shadow
Thrown by the street light behind
Me, and soon won't be below.

22 October 2022

Full Moon and Fireworks

There's moonlight on the floor.
There's a full moon, I spy
Through my window and marvel
At the peace in the dark sky.

Then bang! It's still firework
Weekend, and an answering bang
To relive the gunpowder plot
Of Parliament-cellars' gang.

If I were a cosmonaut
Circling the earth up there

The earth would glow like the moon
Surrounded by peaceful air.

6 November 2022

COP27: Bettering the Lot of Humankind

It's COP27 and 1.5 centigrade growth
In temperatures is far away with a war in Ukraine,
And donors have failed to deliver a hundred
Billion dollars in climate finance again.
Only twenty-four have kept their promises.
The past eight years were the hottest on record.
Smoke from wars and forest fires heats the atmosphere
And the 2050 net zero goal's ignored.

And now I read Pakistan, Bangladesh
And the Maldives seek compensation from the key
Richer nations for most of the pollution
That has threatened them with floods and droughts as the sea
Level rises due to global warming.
The UK's pledged 65 million pounds that's new
For green technology in poorer nations,
Who see this as compensation long overdue.

In the last eight years China's emitted more CO_2
Than Britain has since 1750 and its foray's
Caused 11 per cent of all historic emissions
And will up these in the next thirty years. The UK's
Industrial Revolution caused three per cent,
Twenty poor countries have lost half a trillion, cleaved
In the last twenty years – which will be a trillion
By 2050, when net zero is achieved.

A headline screams that Britain has opened the door
To climate reparations – at a time when
Its black hole of 60 billion pounds will
Be filled with 35 billion in spending cuts and then
25 billion more in tax rises.
I think of the 100-billion-dollar present

The donor nations have pledged and has not been paid.
The poor see the British gift as a down payment.

I think of why the UK has to pay
Reparations to the poorer nations for scenes
Of past pollution. It can only be
From the Industrial Revolution's new machines,
Its smoking chimneys on its way to inventing
Cars, railways, ships, planes, central heating at the end,
Using coal fires, gas and oil – no wonder
The British PM at first declined to attend.

I grasp the logic in the poorer world.
It would have been better for the English to remain
Living in Anglo-Saxon huts, and not building
A growing civilisation from a furnace chain.
It would have been better if the motor engine
Had never been discovered, so no one was choked
By cars, steam trains, steamships, planes, phones and machines.
But even the Tudors' hearths and kitchens smoked.

The poorer nations want the English to fork
Out fines for bettering the lot of all alive
That has raised the world's standard of living
And life expectancy from thirty-five.
So how can there be progress if it's right to fine
Countries that powered factories under Victorian laws
To build new machines that heated the atmosphere
And raised the sea to flood their coastal shores?

7 November 2022

22. 'Cleaved', "(literary) chopped, broken off".

Anarchy: A Nightmare

Three years after Covid I look out at
The earth on the day the human population
Reached eight billion, and I see overcrowding,
Famine, plague, war and death, the Four Horsemen
Of the Apocalypse, getting ready
To gallop round the world destroying food

Growing in the fields, infecting people's lungs,
Blitzing them from the air, scything their necks. I brood.

I see a nightmare, 9.7 billion
By 2050, polluted air, defiled
China and India, deforestation
And urban dwellings built out in the wild,
Zoonotic diseases caused by pathogens
That leap from animals to humans. I see
Hundreds of the overpopulated
Millions starving, and coming anarchy.

I see civilisation's collapse
In the next few decades as the starving
Compete for food and water and fall ill
From chemical pollution and climates changing.
I see migrations of starving refugees
And mass dying as in Egypt, Nigeria
And Pakistan populations expand
Along with the masses in China and India.

And where, o where, is the vision of a good
Multipolar world with the US and EU,
Russia and China all equal and free
In a world government elected by and through
Humankind's citizens, and a federal World State
Abolishing war and disarming, and set to engage
And solve all the world's most pressing problems –
And block anarchy with a new Golden Age?

16 November 2022; revised 2 April 2023

Time's Ticking

I sit at the dining-room table, doing my homework,
The piano nearby, Beethoven on the mantelpiece,
And all is quiet as intently I study
A textbook and write as time's tickings cease.

Now an identical table stands in the annexe
My mother bought at auction and gave me,

Near the Queen-Anne round table a boy leap-frogged over
And cracked at my great-great-grandmother's hundredth birthday tea.

So I store my boyhood memories in my mind
And visit behind my warehouse annexe door,
And I recall those peaceful studying days
And remembered pranks from a hundred years before.

7 December 2022

7. The Queen-Anne table was given to Nicholas Hagger's mother by Hannah Comfort at her hundredth birthday in 1913. Her grandson Frank Burton played leap-frog over it and split it in the middle.

Night Sea

I stand alone by night sea,
My shadow is on a wave
Thrown by a street light behind.
I see my watery grave.

O sea of gentle time,
Of moments, months and years,
Decades drifting to night's shore,
You'll soon drown my fleeting fears.

8–9 December 2022

Full Moon

An Arctic sea and a frost.
I peer at the full moon.
A clear night sky, Venus –
Ears sting, I yawn. Sleep soon.

The full moon lights the beach,
It draws the tides and my yawn.
My hands are in my coat pockets
But moon, I'm glad I was born.

9 December 2022

Screaming Gulls

Thirty gulls on a rock,
Wings flapping and pushing
When the sea edges in, what food
Are they pecking and devouring?

Thirty gulls with spread wings
Scream and flutter and sit.
Has a fish been washed ashore?
What's gathered them to target?

Now the gulls are wheeling away
And calm, bob on calm sea.
Not one is near the rock
Where they fed so noisily.

10 December 2022

Chaotic

The surf swells in, chaotic white and foam,
And I think of the social disorder –
Disease, penury, strikes and freezing cold,
Unheated, shivering hypothermia –
And as waves jostle and barge in I miss
The Old England I knew, ordered streets, sage,
Everything running as it should, all smiles,
Not this anger, indignation, outrage
Against a new King, Lords and weak government,
Against war that's missiling a grave
Nuclear power that is malevolent
And may drown our islands in one tidal wave.
The white foam spews and it seems no one cares
Any more, except to cancel the Old that glares.

13 December 2022

14. 'The Old', "the Old England".

On my Own

I have a heart problem that's controlled by pills
But the viral bio-weapon that struck me
May be keeping my heart muscle infected
And I could be arrhythmic, racing pulse stuttery,
And collapse with a heart attack if I'm alone.
When my mother fell to the floor she thought (correctly),
'Oh well, I'm having a stroke, wait for it to pass.'
What would I do? I'm supposed to dial emergency,
If ambulance men and nurses are not on strike,
Open the front door and gates, oxygenise my brain
Which, if I lose consciousness, only has three minutes
Of oxygen, and will need CPR to maintain
Blood flow, or a defib, which can't be done when alone.
As in the Roman days I'll be on my own.

18 January 2023; revised 21–22 January 2023

2. For the US Pentagon's funding of gain-of-function research on coronavirus from 2013 to 2020 see Nicholas Hagger, *The Fall of the West*, p.73.

Healing Power

I am old now, I dribble and drool down
Onto the collar of my shirt, I am on
Beta-blockers to maintain slow heartbeats
That do not pound me into arrhythmic palpitation
From the viral bio-weapon that attached itself
To my lungs, swamped my immune system and made me ill
After a deadly missile-like airborne flight.
I am lucky to be alive, and yet I'm still
A channel for the power that heals others.
A pain in an arm – I sit, closed eyes, no frown,
And slowly four surges start in my back,
Run up to my right shoulder and flow down
To my little finger, pour in the healing Light
And slow my heart on the way with power that's just right.

20 January 2023; revised 22 January 2023

Anaximander's Cosmos: The Boundless

I think of Anaximander of Miletus
Who argued around 2600BC
Rain's caused by air movements and the sun's heat,
Not the gods, and the earth's suspended in a void we
Call space in which the sun and stars revolve
And are not just the earth's canopy, its ceiling's frieze,
And was the first to declare there's a cosmos
Out there two thousand years before Chinese
Star-gazers found the earth was suspended in space.
But even more important to me, the Presocratic awe-
-some Anaximander spoke of an eternally moving
Boundless (*apeiron*) or infinite, from which I saw
Two pre-particles become a singularity,
And brought to birth my Form from Movement Theory.

12–13 February 2023

1, 11–14. For Anaximander's connection to Nicholas Hagger's Form from Movement Theory and his Theory of Everything, see Nicholas Hagger, *The Algorithm of Creation*, pp.16–21.

Sparrowhawk

I glance through my window, a shock.
Sitting on a rail like a guest
Near the bird feeder a sparrowhawk,
Puffing its brown-barred chest.

I look into its eyes.
Sparrowhawk, welcome to my rail
But you stare with a curved beak,
Don't you dare – my birds are frail.

5 March 2023

Aging

I walked down the High Road
To the paper shop in the sun,
Then walked with the gardener – oh no!
My trouser zip's undone.

I forgot to zip my trousers,
And gaped in public view.
I'm eighty-three and forget
What the young without thinking do.

I'm getting forgetful
As old age creeps up on me,
But I recall many scenes
From my childhood so vividly.

6 March 2023

Wild Nature

Barking in the far field.
A stag swerves in its run,
Two hounds are chasing it.
Now they've gone, their pursuit's not done.

A crash on my window, a blue
Tit lies twitching. A pause,
Then a sparrowhawk flies down
And carries it off in its claws.

Nature is all One as
All creatures came from one cell,
But out there it's eat or be eaten,
Nature's also one wild farewell.

Mid-March 2023

Shoal

Gulls circle above the sea
And dive in turns for fish.
There's a shoal of pilchards
They see from the air, their wish.

O pilchards swim deeper,
Head back out to sea, still whole.

O gulls you have to eat
But must you attack a shoal?

31 March 2023

Calm Sea

The sea is green and silver
After the storm.
There's a wind-rippled calm,
Watch each wave form.

Small wavelets foam to the shore,
New wavelets curl.
All is peaceful, I too.
My breaths unfurl.

1 April 2023

Coronavirus

Schools closed, streets empty, pubs and restaurants shut,
Some permanently, millions locked in their homes.
Mothers without family on Mothering Sunday,
Huge numbers without work, rising death syndromes.
The State has powers never used in peace time,
Spending's reached Socialist levels, as has the dole.
From the PM to the supermarket queue
Britain is at war, to contain and control
A virus that's trying to reproduce.
The last war saw planting and stockpiling,
Self-sufficient people came together and shared,
There was selflessness, people were in parks, strolling.
Not now, each isolates, locked up at home,
And caring for neighbours has gone, like a sea-storm's foam.

1 April 2023

Forgetfulnesses

"Can you turn on the extractor fan?" she asked.
I went to the kitchen and just could not find it.
"It's above the stove, you pull the cupboard above,"
She said. I went and found it, remembered the slit.
So why did I forget where it was even though
We've been in our house by the sea for thirty-six years?
Have I got early dementia? And, just now
I went upstairs for paper to take notes for steers
Through a programme I want to watch, and forgot
And came downstairs without the paper I miss,
And had to return, and now, sitting upstairs
With sea curling to shore and shingle hiss,
I am writing a quick sonnet to remind of my need
To finish my works lest forgetfulnesses impede.

2 April 2023

Scudding, Changing

Last night I saw the moon
As it sailed up the sky,
Scudding through white icebergs.
It wasn't still to my eye.

Tonight I saw my head's
Shadow as it sailed through sea,
Scudding through white wavelets.
It wasn't still to me.

But no, it's all motion,
Clouds scudded across the moon,
The moon-drawn tide was in flux.
All's changing, I'll be gone soon.

2 April 2023

Sea and Mind

I surface from two hours' work
Above the lapping sea.
It externalises my mind,
I concentrate totally.

When I work by the waves
That crash and hiss when they've curled
In the buffeting wind,
I am lost in another world.

O sea, my deepest mind,
Thank you for your sea air
That pours into my works
When I'm in my Muses' care.

4 April 2023

Heart Murmur

Little baby, I cradled you two days back,
Nursed you and made the sound of a seashore,
"Shhh", like shingle drawn back every out-breath,
And you became calm, your hands limp, I saw
You hold my fingers in both hands and look
And – with your PDA that should have closed open
And oxygenated blood from your lung artery
To your aorta leaked to your lungs – half (I reckon)
Your heart worked hard to pump all your blood round your limbs,
You had a heart murmur, breathing was a struggle.
But you've had a tube threaded up your duct.
Little girl, it's been closed, your heart's normal.
I'm in wonder at Great Ormond Street's skill and art
And your intricacy, hence this murmur from my heart.

15–16, 20 May 2023

6. "PDA". Nicholas Hagger's three-month-old granddaughter Ava was diagnosed as having PDA, *patent ductus arteriosus*, and had her opening closed in a procedure at Great Ormond Street Hospital, London on 15 May 2023.

Body and Brain: Design that's Meant

Half my three-month-old granddaughter's heart worked twice
As hard and carried its other half, as (I've heard)
We are all programmed to compensate where there's a lack.
Now my nephew's eye operation's left it blurred
And the other eye has stereoscopic power
To judge distances as if it were doing the work
Of the blurred eye, and so will get him by.
A heart, an eye – our bodies and brains don't shirk,
They come in and compensate for partial shutdowns
And keep us going. How wonderful that's the case.
The body's amazing, it's a perfect design:
Every bit's needed, it all runs as a whole, with grace.
Our design's too intricate to be an accident,
So how have we such perfection if it wasn't meant?

28 May, 6 June 2023

The Oak Tree's Bubbling and Groaning

I gaze at the nearest oak in my Arcady,
Having read special headphones on an oak's bark
Like a stethoscope capture the bubbling
Of water as it surges from roots to leaves. Hark,
It creates a tree trumpet out of a mike
Placed against bark so all can listen to the clunk
And plop of water mixed with air as it runs
From roots, via the hollow xylem tubes, up the trunk.
This water and minerals keep the tree cool
Before they turn into sap, as an oak tree needs
Two hundred litres of water on a warm day.
My oak tree groans as it sways in the wind and bleeds
As it copes with the weight of its massive branches.
So my Tree of Tradition groans under its influences.

6 June 2023

Shelley and the One

I sit in Elcot House, which Shelley's mother
Bought twenty-two years after Shelley was drowned
And lived in with his sisters, and put up Mary,
His second wife, and in this drawing-room resound
A dozen actors who re-enact his life
Before two dozen guests – I'm in the front row.
A narrator reads events, which actors mime
In costumes; and hark at 'Shelley''s poetic flow.

The events are stark: though aristocratic
He was radical at Eton, and as he'd hoped
At Oxford published a pamphlet on atheism,
Was expelled and, a believer in free love, eloped
With sixteen-year-old Harriet, and married her.
He eloped with Mary Godwin, who was then
Seventeen, and when Harriet drowned herself in the Serpentine
He was denied custody of their two children.

Mary's stepsister Claire lived with her, and had
An affair with Shelley, then Byron, and got Shelley
To meet Byron in Switzerland. The two poets began
An affair. Shelley went to Venice with Mary,
Then left her to live in Byron's villa in Este.
Mary lost two children in Italy.
Shelley met Emilia in Pisa
And later Jane there and in Lerice.

In the bar I say to 'Shelley' and the actors,
He may seem a self-indulgent dreamer who could stun,
Who was radical, atheist and pro-Peterloo,
But by the end of his life he knew the One:
He wrote in 'Adonais', on the death of Keats,
"The One remains, the many change and pass",
Of "Heaven" and "eternity" – the "motion and spirit
That rolls through all things" that Wordsworth sensed in grass.

The One's earlier in 'Love's Philosophy',
That at one level's a Metaphysical conceit,

Demanding a kiss as all things "in one another's
Being mingle" (the Harvard manuscript's bleat),
But in the Stacy manuscript, "In one spirit
Meet and mingle" – the line has been respun.
Did the loss of his children, four from two wives,
Bring the atheist to know great Plato's One?

I see Shelley as absorbed in his emotions:
He starts poems on the weather or the moon
And projects his own emotions, his weariness,
On to Nature's scenes he describes in a swoon.
I think of his youth, if I'd died at twenty-nine
I'd have left unpublished poems I wrote in Japan
And the seeds of all my Universalist works but no full
Illumination, he missed Part Two: the One's plan.

True poets take their readers to the One
And show the interconnectedness of all life,
Of Nature, the universe and humankind;
See unity's symbols surpass all strife
In deep comparisons, and surface images
With 'like' and 'as' connecting like with like.
I admire Shelley's struggle to know the One
After years of conflict, and am sad he missed my long hike.

18–20 April 2023

1. Elcot House was bought by Lady Elizabeth Shelley, Shelley's mother, in 1844. She lived there with Shelley's two sisters and Mary, his second wife, came to stay several times.
25. On 17 April 2023 the Newbury Dramatic Society put on a narration of Shelley's life in Elcot House's drawing-room: actors in costume played before an audience sitting on 24 chairs. Nicholas Hagger spoke with the actors afterwards.
27. Peterloo. Shelley condemned the Peterloo Massacre when cavalry dispersed a radical meeting in Manchester, killing 15 people, on 16 August 1819. In all there were 18 deaths and 400–700 injured.
56. 'My long hike'. Nicholas Hagger's Mystic Way, which ended in unitive vision, lasted 29 years, from 1964 to 1993. (See Nicholas Hagger, *My Double Life 2: A Rainbow over the Hills*, p.912 for details and dates.)

In Fairmead in Arcadia

I sit in my garden at Connaught House
Among potted plants and look past four oaks
And the sloping meadow, trees and distant green
To Henry the Eighth's third hunting lodge it half-cloaks.
Fairmead, Henry's three-hundred-acre meadow
Where deer roamed he could hunt, still unchanged but quieter,
Is no different from Peloponnesian Arcadia,
Pastoral Utopia in harmony with Nature.

Here I have left the untruths of the court
And like Edward the Fifth in an ex-deer park
Live a simple hidden life of cyclic seasons
Amid birds, flowers, grass, fish and much tree bark:
From snowdrops to blossom and burstings into flower,
Hot sun and the oak trees' shade, all plants aglow,
Chestnut candles and conkers, and then reddening
Of leaves in a sweep of woods, then winter snow.

I read at school of Theocritus's idyll
And of Virgil's Roman Arcadia at dawn
In eclogues set near Mantua – I drove between
Carpenedolo and Calvisano, where Virgil was born
With a view of the Alps, but found no livestock,
No shepherdesses in the cool of the shade,
Just as now there are no parkers in this deer park.
Edenic Arcady's now in an Epping-Forest glade.

Arcadia's a pastoral idea everywhere.
It seems unattainable but is in these arbours
As I sit, contemplate and let my mind drift
To when as a boy I roamed round Connaught Waters
Over there, where walkers took out rowing-boats on the lake
And nightingales sang in the trees, and how
At Otley Hall I re-created a Tudor knot-garden.
Pastoral's this Paradise's birds and flowers now.

I wander through my own knot-garden, see
Two central crossed-infinity box shrubs, four
Fleur-de-lis and herb beds with lavender, representing

My twenty-five civilisations, and their law.
The endless knot's the design Elizabeth the First
Embroidered on her prayer-book's cover, with 'K.P.',
Her stepmother in 1544 Katherine Parr
Who was at the hunting lodge with King Henry.

I think of Marvell's Garden I visited
And of the profusion of its flowers and fruit.
The Garden is now here at Connaught House
With its dryads guarding oaks and nymphs each shoot,
With The Three Graces who surround the fountain
And hold up the basin where water brims like glass;
Here where the nine Muses (who began as nymphs)
Live near the nine statues that adorn the grass.

I sit and watch a fox patter past me
And a muntjac deer crop grass in the first field,
And green parakeets and a nuthatch on the bird feeders.
I listen to a blackbird's song, and yield.
I wander down to the purple heather bed
Beyond yellow iris by the pond that's brimming
With large carp and a goldfish swimming towards me
As water gushes in from my Bandusian spring.

Here is a timeless tidy wilderness,
The domain of Pan, bountiful in sunshine
With the white hawthorn blossom all round the field
And the distant forest stretching to the skyline
I can look down on and savour from above:
Arcadia, where nymphs frolic in each shadow,
Not corrupted by civilisation, all pristine growth,
Where swallows dip and swerve round this fair meadow.

Sidney wrote of the Countess of Pembroke's Arcadia,
And that is here, in its simplicity,
A Golden Age where Elizabeth the First once was
And rode her horse up the hunting-lodge stairs naturally.
I sit in Arcadia and see in my mind
Two millennia of simple living in the sun.
"*Et in Arcadia ego*", "I am even in Arcady",
Words spoken by Death – I'll love this Paradise till I'm done.

O Corydon and Amaryllis who guarded sheep,
O Pan who rests beneath the fieldmost oak,
O inhabitants of noble Arcadia,
Nymph Syrinx and woodland dryads, I invoke
You all within this fair meadow, Henry
The Eighth's Merrie-England Fair Mead, and, now a sage,
Beckon you to sit in harmony with Nature
In this Paradise and pastoral Golden Age.

14–15 April 2023

5. 'Fairmead'. Fairmead Bottom is the modern name for Henry VIII's Fair Mead Park.

9. 'Untruths of the court', see 'The World Falling Apart: An Unspeakable Secret', lines 33–40.

10. 'Edward the Fifth', see 'At Coldridge: An Unspeakable Truth'.

23. 'Parkers', see 'At Coldridge: An Unspeakable Truth'.

28–29. 'Connaught Waters/Over there'. Connaught Waters, a nine-acre ornamental lake built from a drainage pond in the 1880s and 1890s, can be seen from the back of Connaught House.

36. See Nicholas Hagger's *The Fire and the Stones* for his twenty-five rising and falling civilisations that each have sixty-one stages, and his Law of History that the younger civilisation always triumphs over an older one.

37. 'The endless knot'. The endless knot Elizabeth I embroidered on the front cover of her prayer-book was of two crossed-infinity signs (see line 34). She also embroidered on the front cover Katherine Parr's initials, 'K.P.'

45. 'The Three Graces' were daughters of Zeus who were able to bestow a gift on humankind: Euphrosyne (mirth), Aglaia (elegance) and Thalia (youth and beauty).

48. 'Nine statues'. The nine statues that adorn the grass at Connaught House are of Spring, Summer, Autumn and Winter; Nausicaa and Venus de Milo; and three stone boys holding bird-baths.

56. 'Bandusian spring'. The Bandusian spring was in Horace's ode (*Odes* 3.13). The spring at Connaught House was a powered recycling of water from the pond to a higher pond and back through channels to the main pond.

74. The 'fieldmost oak' is on the front cover of Nicholas Hagger's *A View of Epping Forest*, and his Arcadia is visible beyond it on the front and back covers.

78. 'Sage', "(noun), a profoundly wise man; (adj.) profoundly wise, especially from experience" (*Concise Oxford Dictionary*).

Volume 38
AN OVAL CLOUD
2020–2023

1
Oval Cloud: Sculptures

I turned the light out and in the pitch-dark
Closed my eyes to sleep but as I looked in my shroud
Behind my lids I was surprised to see
A large, wide oval light, an unbright cloud
That I could see through as through water in
A kind of pool, and deep within I spied,
At the bottom of the pool above my eyes,
Many life-size sculptures lying side by side,
Statues of Near-Eastern faces – Egyptian? –
Each in a whitish stone within the Light
Lying on the bottom, semi-substantial,
Outlines within the Light, and I knew in the night
There was a message for me, the angels had shown
That my works would endure like statues of stone.

25 April 2020; revised 15 December 2022

1–4. All the 18 sightings of the oval cloud are recorded in Nicholas Hagger's 2020, 2021 and 2023 Diaries, which will be held in his archive by the University of Essex. He first saw the oval cloud on 22 April 2020, and recorded in his Diary entry for 23 April 2020: "Last night after I turned the light out, a large, wide oval light, not dazzling, which I thought might be angelic. As I watched behind my closed eyes it deepened into a kind of pool with clear water, and I saw old life-sized Eastern treasures – figurines – lying on the bottom, semi-substantial outlines in light. I thought it was a message." For the writing of this poem, see p.185.

2
Oval Cloud: Swansdown

The second night running, my oval cloud.
I turned off the light to sleep and in pitch-dark saw
Above my closed eyes as I lay on my back
An oval shape in pale white light that shone or

Glowed and slowly came down so it was near my face
And looked like swansdown, and close-up I could see
The smooth billows of its uneven folds,
Its faceless softness which enfolded me.
I wondered if a faceless angel had come,
My guardian angel or Muse, to say it's watching
Over me as near the end of my life
I draw together all the strands of my thinking
To bring peace to all humankind, and free
A change to the world that I won't live to see.

25 April 2020; revised 15 December 2022

1–4. Nicholas Hagger's second sighting of the oval cloud was on 23 April 2020, and he recorded in his Diary entry for 24 April 2020: "Saw an oval for a second night running. On Wednesday night [on 22 April 2020] what had been an oval shape before my eyes when I went to sleep… turned white,… and oval, and was above my closed eyes behind my eyes as I lay on my back. I thought it was an angel come to give me encouragement, and after five minutes it turned into a kind of pool and I was looking through transparent water (the Light) to the bottom, where there were old statues in stone and semi-Eastern faces (Egyptian?). Last night [on 23 April 2020] the oval was there again, white and bright, also in pitch-dark…. It came down until it was inches from my face and I could see the swan's down [i.e. swansdown] as large as a double bed (Zeus as a swan…) and the down was smooth, and again I thought: it's a faceless angel, come to express support. It was an ethereal light, not physical light in any way. Some would say it's my imagination but to me there was something metaphysical about it. My guardian angel has declared its support for *The Essentials of Universalism* and is urging me to continue the project." For the writing of this poem, see p.185.

3
Oval Cloud: Shapes

Last night I saw it again, the oval cloud
Was above my face as, after switching
Off the light, in pitch-dark, I looked behind my closed
Eyelids. It was as bright as dawn light, not dazzling,
And transparent, I could see shapes within it.
It came down closer and I could see its folds spread
Its soft pillow-like down, but again no face.
I felt peaceful and knew I was protected

By the source of my imagination and thought.
I felt I was sent down before the war
To re-form knowledge and bring peace to the world,
And the angels were sending three nights running to store –
As I grapple with presenting my life's work as true –
A signal they're on my side and I should continue.

25 April 2020; revised 16 December 2022

1–4. Nicholas Hagger's third sighting of the oval cloud was on 24 April 2020, and he recorded in his Diary entry for 25 April 2020: "Another sighting of the oval cloud. This time it came close again and I saw its transparency and shapes within it. Again it was downy but not as fully downy as the night before. It seemed to be a being without a face. Sat in my vest and pants and scribbled out three sonnets that I woke with, an inner instruction to write, 'Oval Cloud: Sculptures', 'Oval Cloud: Swan's Down' (*sic.*) and 'Oval Cloud: Shapes'. I am a slave to the Angels, I say wryly. Also wrote a fourth poem (getting cold in my vest and pants): 'Oval Cloud: Messages'. I have been writing more poems recently and I now feel I am starting a new poetic period as I grapple with the metaphysical angel that is inspiring me – and may all along have been my Muse. Then wrote at the tail-end of this burst of activity 'Oval Cloud: Muses' Amanuensis'. And began a poem, 'Oval Cloud: Amanuensis of all the Muses'. Six poems drafted or begun within an hour. 9am, have just finished 'Amanuensis of all the Muses'. So that *is* six poems in one flow of poetic inspiration, a new poetic life."

4
Oval Cloud: Messages

I ponder my three views of my oval cloud.
Were they angelic, messages from Heaven,
Or the source of what my Muse sends down to me –
Was the cloud a symbol of my imagination?
I felt at the time on three successive nights
The statue-filled cloud referred to all my works,
My life's work to complete my angelic task,
To knock some sense into warlike mankind's smirks,
And by reunifying knowledge and making it
A new university subject that will enthral –
Universalism, a philosophy of peace –
And set out a World State that will govern all,

A new structure that will unite humankind.
Did the cloud encourage my lifelong task in my mind?

25 April 2020; revised 17 December 2022

1. For the writing of this poem, see p.185.

5
Oval Cloud: Outside Time

An oval cloud was there above my face
The third night running, and I again ask
What is the downy cloud that is shown to me?
Zeus took the form of a swan, and in swan-mask
Seduced Leda, Queen of Sparta, mother
Of Helen, who brought about the sack of Troy.
My days are soundless now I am isolating,
No cars on roads, in the sky no planes convoy.
Sunshine in the fields, this bustling century
Has stopped, I look out at the may's white snow,
Walk down my fields and take in the natural world.
Like Donne I've had experiences and know
It's not mad to write them down, even though they're sublime,
Or to write of an oval cloud that's outside time.

25 April 2020; revised 27 December 2022

6
Oval Cloud: Muses' Amanuensis

And now I wonder, as I isolate
In the midst of a plague that has been killing
Twenty thousand of my fellow countrymen,
Was the oval cloud my Muse self-identifying,
Declaring itself to me as a faceless
But protective being with downy folds, and like birds'
Song has this metaphysical being
Inspired me for sixty years and sent me words
So I've become the Muses' amanuensis
(Or as I sometimes grumble, Muses' slave)?
I now feel I am starting a new poetic
Life or period as, guided by a grave

Power from the beyond, I come to terms (via a sigh)
With this plague-ravaged earth on which we now live and die.

25 April 2020; revised 17 December 2022

1–4. For the writing of this poem, see p.185.

7
Oval Cloud: Amanuensis of All the Muses and Tenth Muse

I am an amanuensis of all the Muses
In my literature, history, philosophy, and the flow
Of international politics, culture, mysticism
And religion. I take dictation from Erato
And Polymnia (lyrics and sacred verse),
Clio (history), Urania (cosmology
And the One), Calliope (epic poetry),
Euterpe and Melpomene
(Music and tragedy), Terpsichore
And Thalia (choral song and comedy), the seven
Disciplines within which I have written,
Inputs from all nine of the Muses in Zeus's Heaven
And the tenth, the goddess who unites the whole crowd
Into a chorus, and appears as an oval cloud.

25 April 2020; revised 17 December 2022

8
Oval Cloud: Enduring

Last night I saw the oval cloud again,
Not as bright as last week, but full of showings.
Again it's loomed towards my closed eyelids
And I saw the outlines of strange scrivenings,
A recumbent knight as on a tomb in its folds
And strange faces sideways on as if drawn
By an artist with a pencil, just outlines –
No shading or etching within the lines – that seemed worn.
I wondered if I was looking at a tomb
Like those in a church topped with a knight without breath,
Lying back with closed eyes in chain-mail armour,
And if the cloud were showing me my death.

Then I thought it was showing me images of known
Enduring works I've carved in metric stone.

28 April 2020; revised 17 December 2022

1. Nicholas Hagger saw the oval cloud again on 27 April 2020 and recorded the sighting in his 2020 Diary on 28 April 2020: "Saw the oval cloud again last night, with recumbent (sideways) line-drawn figures within it, like a knight on a tomb. I half-wonder if these are images of death I am seeing, but I don't think so; images of immortality, like the carved knights on tombs and stone sculptures. Wrote 'Oval Cloud: Enduring', another sonnet after dressing and sitting at my desk. This sequence of sonnets is like my sequence on the Light in *The Gates of Hell*, written in September 1971, nearly 50 years later."

14. 'Metric stone', "poetic metres as unchangeable as stone".

9
Oval Cloud: Slide Show

My oval cloud again, but now a slide show.
An oval, nearly round light after dark
Moving to the right with an etched face in it, a profile.
Then brief darkness, then the next slide of a stark
Face, another drawn profile looking to the right.
Then it had gone and as I looked the slide was blown
Slowly in front of me. I tried to see
If it was men or women I was being shown.
Each face looked old and from another time,
One had a strange head-dress, a German cap.
Were they faces I used to know in another life,
Or my past lives? Six faces slowly slid, then a gap,
And, then a seventh. Were they a warning, like the way
The Eddystone Lighthouse flashes across my bay?

6 May 2020; revised 17 December 2022

1. Nicholas Hagger saw the oval cloud again on 5 May 2020, and recorded the sighting in his 2020 Diary on 6 May 2020: "Sunny day with blue sky. Showered (my blister is lifting, putting on antibiotic cream) and then scribbled out 'Oval Cloud: Slide Show' after seeing seven sideways profiles last night, six and then a gap, then one."

14. In Charlestown Nicholas Hagger could see from his sea-side window the Eddystone Lighthouse's six short flashes at night, and then one long pulse in the distance across the bay.

10
Oval Cloud: Soul and Halo

My oval cloud again, bright in pitch-dark
Behind my closed eyes as I looked and saw a deep
Soft swansdown blanket with comforting folds
That was being laid on me to induce my sleep.
But it had quiet patterns, only seen close up,
And as I looked for faces within it, it dawned
On me that I was looking at my soul,
A purity full of swansdown softness, adorned.
And then I wondered if my soul is above me
In the form as in old paintings of an oval halo,
And if the halo represents the oval soul
Above the head as medieval artists show,
That till purified is murky and hard to see,
But when pure is bright white in the dark – seen clearly.

9 May 2020; revised 19 December 2022

1. Nicholas Hagger saw the oval cloud again on 8 May 2020, and recorded the sighting in his 2020 Diary on 9 May 2020: "Saw the cloud again last night, very white, almost like a blanket with a pattern coming towards me to be laid on me. then I wondered if it was my soul, if I had been looking at my soul, which is now swan's-down white and full of softness, a pure soul rather than an impure one. After lunch drafted a sonnet, 'Oval Cloud: Soul and Halo'.

11
Oval Cloud: My Comforting Cloud Returns

I did not see my cloud for several weeks
And then it came again, swan-like, unchanged.
As soon as I put out the light and closed my eyes
It moved closer, it was as if it was arranged
As a warm and downy, comfortable eiderdown.
I looked at it and asked if it was my soul
I was seeing as if in a mirror, or my guardian
Angel welcoming me back to the eternal Whole
After another day in the world of time.

It's not as bright as it was some weeks ago
And it's faded more quickly and left me
Within inner dark, asking, 'Where did you go?
Who are you? Why do you approach in night's starless arc,
Till you're close, comfort me, then fade back into the dark?'

22 June 2020; revised 21 December 2022

1–4. Nicholas Hagger saw the oval cloud again on 21 June 2020 but did not record it in his 2020 Diary on 22 June 2020 as he was busy editing his *Selected Letters* all day.

12
Oval Cloud and Swallows

Last night I saw the downy cloud again,
Waiting above me, as if waiting for me.
Today I walked down through the field, no birds.
I held out my arms and beckoned, and suddenly
There were four swallows skimming and swerving,
Hurtling into the air, swooping down, then
They disappeared behind the trees, and yet
As I walked back two darted out again,
Flew near me and sat on a fence rail. I edged
Closer: red-bibbed swallows, my friends. Suddenly
They flew off, and I thought of my downy cloud
And wondered if angels were showing me
How I would be taken up past Heaven's parclose
Like James the First, by my escorts: these swallows.

29 June 2020; revised 21 December 2022

1. Nicholas Hagger saw the oval cloud again on 28 June 2020, and recorded the sighting in his 2020 Diary on 29 June 2020: "Walked at 4.15. No birds. Held out my arms and waved and four swallows skimmed and dipped near me, and soared and swooped. I reached the bottom field and turned and they came again, high in the sky over the trees then darting down beside me. Two sat on the fence rail. I got to within six paces before they flew. I could see their white bibs. I thought of the [oval] cloud I saw last night, the Angels are holding it out for me, like a soft cushion on a throne, a Woolsack. Wrote two poems, '[Oval] Cloud and Swallows', '[Oval Cloud:] Cloud like a Woolsack'."

13. 'Parclose', "screen or railing in a church separating a side chapel" (*Oxford English Dictionary*).

14. For Rubens' painting of James I being taken up to Heaven escorted by an eagle on the ceiling of the Banqueting House, London, see the front cover of Nicholas Hagger's *A Baroque Vision*.

13
Oval Cloud: Cloud like a Woolsack

My cloud is like a cushion on a throne,
Woolly, soft, comfortable, and I, replete
Like a monarch, am to sit on it when
I am taken up to Heaven, it is my seat
Assigned by the angels and shown to me now.
So I think, it's not impossible. We're living dead:
The plague's still around, the virus attacks my age.
I may be being shown what is ahead
If I'm taken by the virus before my time.
I am eighty-one and have so much to do,
Whole works I haven't started while I present
The best of what I've already done anew.
Before I sit on the Woolsack I'm being shown,
And speak with authority to, souls gathered round the throne.

29 June 2020; revised 21 December 2022

1. For the writing of this poem, see note 1 of no.12 above.
2. 'Replete', "filled or well-supplied" (*Concise Oxford Dictionary*).
13. 'Woolsack', "the Lord Chancellor's wool-stuffed seat in the House of Lords" (*Concise Oxford Dictionary*).

14
Oval Cloud: Nine Muses

I turn off the light and, lying on my back,
Look up behind my closed eyelids and lo!
My oval cloud is there, in transparent lace,
Very bright, satiny like swansdown, like snow.
It comes closer, I see it through clear water
And embroidered on it, equidistantly,
Are silhouettes of beings or people.
I count nine, my nine Muses? They may be.
Or are they angels from a higher realm?
In the pure, limpid water they're moving.

I'm looking down, but now I'm underneath,
My cloud's above me with each faint being,
And slowly dissolves, and is gone, and I have thought
I may have been left a message of the Muses' support.

10 April 2021; revised 21 December 2022

1–4. Nicholas Hagger saw the oval cloud again on 10 April 2021 and recorded the sighting in his 2021 Diary on 11 April 2021: "Saw the oval cloud a bit squashed at the edges, more like a nearly rectangular package. Figures within it I couldn't see."

15
Oval Cloud: Cloud of Knowing

The oval cloud is before my closed eyelids.
It comes towards me, not bright, in dim light.
I see what look like words within its folds,
Twenty strange texts I can't read on its white,
See outlines but can't understand their meaning,
They all seem to be in a foreign language
That contains messages, I don't possess their code.
And then I know, it's a Cloud of Knowledge.
Do all the symbols contain my future works?
Are they waiting to be decrypted like inscriptions
Carved on old stones, or are they beyond human thought,
Divine knowledge? What must I learn from their predictions?
It's not a Cloud of Unknowing, but of Knowing,
A future too dim to fathom now I'm dozing.

18 January 2023; revised 19–20 January 2023

1. Nicholas Hagger saw the Cloud of Knowledge – the "Cloud of Knowing" – in bed while falling asleep on 17 January 2023, and recorded the sighting in his 2023 Diary on 18 January 2023. "Yesterday evening, when I went to bed, I saw the oval cloud. It had writing within it and symbols, shaped as squares and mottos, just a few lines, about 20 or 30 texts printed, which I couldn't read. A cloud of knowledge, not a cloud of unknowing, but a cloud of knowledge."

16
Oval Cloud: Envelopment

I saw the oval cloud last night, slowly
It moved towards me, in a slow descent,
Of great size, and I saw words in its white
I could not decipher, grey shapes that meant
Nothing at all, and while I peered and tried
To read what might be a message from beyond
It advanced slowly towards me and slowly
Enveloped me, so I was in a cloud I was fond
Of and was pleasantly lost within its folds
And could see nothing, just the dark behind my eyes,
In a fog that had enveloped me, a dark mist.
Next day there was mist outside, to my surprise,
And I went out into an enveloping cloud
And wondered why I live in a misty shroud.

7 February 2023

1. Nicholas Hagger saw the oval cloud about 12.30am on 7 February 2023, and recorded the sighting in his 2023 Diary on 7 February 2023: "Saw the oval cloud last night after midnight. It came closer and I saw words I could not read, within it like a balloon of someone's words, and then it was on me and I could not see it anymore, I was within it. A sonnet. It enveloped me. Wrote 'Oval Cloud: Envelopment' between 11.35pm and 12 midnight."

17
Oval Cloud: Texts in Code

I saw the oval cloud again, brighter
With a dozen close-up messages in code.
I saw an 'S' and strained to decipher
What the beyond was telling me in this latest load,
In texts of the kind that have eluded me
So far, are beyond my understanding.
If it keeps visiting me and makes its words
Larger and clearer, with an English ring,
Then I will grasp what has been going on.
Till then I've received pieces of a jigsaw
Repeatedly as comments or guidance,

And don't know the picture each fragment bore.
My oval cloud faded from my inner screen
Leaving me to ponder the destiny it's foreseen.

8 February 2023

1. Nicholas Hagger saw the oval cloud again on 7 February 2023, and recorded the sighting in his 2023 Diary on 8 February 2023: "I wrote 'Oval Cloud: Texts in Code' and rhymed that and yesterday's oval-cloud sonnet."

18
Oval Cloud: Message from Eternity

My oval cloud again, third night running,
This time moving towards me at slow speed
Like an airship in night sky with lettering
That's much larger, but still too hard to read.
I peer, it looks written in High German
Or as on a medieval manuscript,
Clusters of words on different lines that may
Be a message from Eternity that's been chipped
As if to a puffy cloud in the outside night
Lit by the full moon, a banner-like ask
From the angels as to what I should do next,
What my next work should be on, their chosen task.
And then the cloud's gone and there is dark again
Before my closed eyes, and I'm alone in my brain.

9 February 2023

1. Nicholas Hagger saw the oval cloud again on 8 February 2023, and recorded the sighting in his 2023 Diary on 9 February 2023: "This morning dictated 'Oval Cloud: Envelopment' and 'Oval Cloud: Texts in Code'. This evening rhymed and dictated 'Oval Cloud: Message from Eternity'."

19
Oval Cloud: Peace Plan and Wi-Fi

I see my oval cloud again, quite bright
With shadowy letters that themselves cast
Shadows, larger than last time, but I still can't
Understand what they're saying, now or in the past.
I wonder, looking at it as it moves

Slowly leftwards so my vision is no more,
If it's a peace plan to prevent fighting
In Ukraine from becoming a Third World War.
I know that Heaven's concerned at the danger
And the sleepwalking leaders of each land
Who, ignoring nuclear risks, send tanks, now jets,
As if they're not part of the war, and perhaps in a stand
Eternity's persistently messaging Time
From a Wi-Fi code that can't be received or chime.

12 February 2023

1–2. Nicholas Hagger saw the oval cloud and shadowy lettering before falling asleep on 11 February 2023, and recorded the sighting in his 2023 Diary on 12 February 2023: "Before breakfast, wrote 'Oval Cloud: Peace Plan' in draft. Will polish it in the car going to London at 11am. In fact, polished it in the evening. It is now 'Oval Cloud: Peace Plan and Wi-Fi'. Dictated it."

20
Oval Cloud: Soul like a Pouch

The oval cloud again, is it my soul
I'm looking at, a white pouch that will pass
On to the other side, labelled with strange letters
That are an address, not to be sent first class
But tracked special delivery like a customs
Invoice so the package arrives safely
In a far country with its precious contents,
The essence of my life, my memory
And all I stand for, and the good I did,
To be signed for by a recipient in control
Like a package received from Brexit UK
And opened and released so my ancient soul
Can resume its life with loved ones and be reborn,
Or live in Heaven within Light's endless dawn?

5 March 2023

1–2. Nicholas Hagger saw the oval cloud again on 4 March 2023, and recorded it in his 2023 Diary on 5 March 2023: "Read the papers by 12 and then had a valuable session drafting 'Oval Cloud: Soul like a Pouch' based on an experience I had last night in bed after putting the light out. I saw the oval cloud with letters on it as a pouch that might be my soul, with an address label like my customs invoice, sending it on to the next life. Perhaps I'm facing my death now? Perhaps the oval cloud is showing me my soul packed up and ready to go."

21
Oval Cloud: Death, Soul Packed and Ready to Go

So if my oval cloud's my soul, a pouch
Packed, labelled and ready to go, I may
Be ready to move on to the next life,
And my oval cloud may be telling me "Away",
It may be warning me my life's ending
And I must wind up my books and clear my room
And leave a tidy legacy behind
So my manuscripts (like lettering on a tomb
Round my oval cloud) can pass into my archive,
And I may now be confronted with my end
Like my father stating on his death-bed
"This is the end", and must I now suspend
My projects and complete my work below,
Must I release my hold and be ready to go?

5 March 2023

1. For the inspiration of this poem, see the last sentence of the note for no.20. There was no Diary entry for this poem.

22
Oval Clouds: Muses

The oval cloud again, a puffy white
After proof-reading tales from long ago.
I gaze behind my closed eyelids and squint
To decipher scrivenings on its side, and lo!
It dawns on me I'm looking at my Muse,
The Muse who's always transmitted my last work
And feeds me the next one from energy
Stored in her fluffy, downy white cloud's murk.
It dawns on me that each Muse looks similar
With a slightly-varied shape: nine clouds oversee
My lyrical, sacred, epic, musical
Poetry; songs; history; the One; tragedy

And comedy. Each cloud is slightly different,
And the words I can't read are on that Muse's parchment.

17, 20 May 2023

1. Nicholas Hagger saw the oval cloud again on 16 May 2023, and recorded it in his 2023 Diary on 17 May 2023: "Saw the oval cloud last night with scrivenings, and it dawned on me that each cloud is slightly different and what I am seeing is one of the nine Muses that visit me. Wrote 'Oval Cloud: Muses' before breakfast. There are nine oval clouds perhaps, there are nine Muses which visit me separately with their scrivenings (my future works)."

2. Nicholas Hagger was proof-reading his work, *The Building of the Great Pyramid*, three reports from c.2600BC.

10–13. The nine Muses or oval clouds are (see Nicholas Hagger, *The Promised Land*, p.94): Erato (lyrical poetry); Polymnia (sacred poetry); Calliope (heroic epic poetry); Euterpe (musical poetry); Terpsichore (lyrical dance and choral song); Clio (world history and civilisations); Urania (the One, astronomy); Melpomene (tragedy); and Thalia (comedy).

23
Oval Cloud: Ideas Bag

Or perhaps it's the cloud that's waiting for me,
This oval cloud I see now, snow-white and soft,
A downy cloud where my soul will soon dwell
When I have left my body and gone aloft?
Perhaps my Muse is telling me my time's up
And is saying, 'You'll be dwelling on this cloud,
It's waiting for you when the time arrives
For your soul to depart this ruined earth and your shroud'?
No, I instinctively know it is my Muse
That's masked within the cloud of all the works
The Muses want me to do, their 'ideas bag',
And each Muse is masked within this down and lurks
Disguised so she's not revealing her inspiring
And her store of ideas that she is transmitting.

18, 20 May 2023

1–2. Nicholas Hagger continued his interpretation of his sighting of the oval cloud on 16 May 2023, and recorded his interpreting in his 2023 Diary on 18 May 2023: "Wrote 'Oval Cloud: Ideas Bag' in my vest and pants, having had the idea as I went to sleep last night and not thought about it till I sat down. Feel well after my session at the gym yesterday."

5. "My time's up", see 'Time's Up', 17, 21 May 2023 in *In Arcady: A Gong and Padded Stick*.

24
Oval Cloud: Ancient Letters

The oval cloud again, a puffy cloud
That's white with dark letters on its near side,
Capital letters in ancient script, a Gothic
G, an embellished A that is cock-eyed,
Superimposed, a meaningless message from my Muse
She wants me to undertake, and, humanly obtuse,
I can't decipher or grasp what I'm supposed to do.
I will sleep now, and perhaps dream of its use,
If my Muse has shown the unification of knowledge.
I was thinking of using the latest AI tool
But my Muse sees to the heart of all knowledge
And AI's still learning to show all that's known as one spool.
I must disregard AI for my Muse's call
Even though I can't fathom what she's saying to my soul at all.

27, 28 May 2023

1. Nicholas Hagger saw the oval cloud again in Cornwall on 27 May 2023, and recorded it in his 2023 Diary on 28 May 2023: "Wrote out 'Oval Cloud: Ancient Letters' (drafted in bed with my mask on, having put the light back on when going to sleep) before exercises."
4. 'Cock-eyed', "crooked, askew" (*Concise Oxford Dictionary*).
10. 'AI tool', i.e. I was thinking of opening AI.com's ChatGPT interface on polymaths.
12. 'Spool', "a reel for winding magnetic tape, photographic film, yarn" (*Concise Oxford Dictionary*).

Volume 39

COURT POEMS: MORE ROYAL CLASSICAL ODES 2018–2023

Volume 39 continues volume 33, *An Unsung Laureate, 2009–2016*, in *Life Cycle and Other New Poems* (2016), which contains poems on Court, Royal or State events.

A ruin on a hill's
Present, timeless and past
As a blue sky's clouds hint
A timeless One that's vast.
Poem by Nicholas Hagger taken
from *Classical Odes*, p.xiv.

Royal Harmony
(On the Wedding of Prince Harry and Meghan Markle, 19 May 2018)

St George's Chapel resplendent with flags
Above the packed Quire stalls as a Prince bends
Near the altar by his brother and peers
In uniform at the nave filled with friends,
His grandparents both near him and the bride's
Mother alone across the chequered aisle.
He walked behind his mother's coffin, now
The nation waits with him and a big smile
Above past monarchs' vaulted tombs, amid
Six centuries' history, much of it still hid.

A fanfare of trumpets, she's at the door.
All stand, in gloom, lit by the warm sunlight
The bride glides slowly forward like a swan,
Serene in a white dress, Queen Mary's bright
Tiara and veil with five-metre-long train
Held by two of four page-boys. Six bridesmaids.

She walks alone – her father has been ill –
And has a yogic stillness as she wades.
Charles beams and leads her to the high altar
Where her lord greets her, whispers "Thank you, pa".

Her veil's embroidered with fifty-three flowers,
Each an emblem for a Commonwealth state.
He lifts it, tucks it back, reveals her face.
She smiles out in a look of love and fate.
The Dean's Preface, a hymn, and then their vows.
The Archbishop of Canterbury's cast.
Now his mother's sister reads from 'The Song
Of Solomon': now the winter is past,
The rain is gone, waters cannot quench love.
Sorrow's been replaced by the turtle-dove.

Now an address by an American:
"All God's children are of one family."
He speaks with passion on the power of love,
He waves his arms and speaks with energy
Like our preachers four hundred years ago
Who took this message to America.
And now it's come back as a culture clash.
He speaks to "my brother" and "my sister".
Some smirk, he's overrun, the stony Queen
Is as on coins and stamps she's always seen.

Now an American Gospel choir sing
'Stand by me' – maybe the bride's call to be
Walked down the aisle by her father-in-law
And for her husband's lifelong loyalty
During the involvement of black culture?
Some guests wave arms, a sight not before known
In this Chapel so steeped in tradition
Where formal etiquette's always been shown.
The couple exchange rings. Their marriage blessed,
They process through the nave and kiss with zest.

In an open landau they ride through crowds
To Windsor, he in military cap.
They wave to cheers from a hundred thousand
Several rows deep, all craning, thousands clap

And film them on their phones as they drive past.
They ride on back to the Great Hall built by
Edward the Third, a modern couple who
Reflect the British crowds' diversity,
And so unite the different origins
Of British subjects and all kiths and kins.

The Royal Family has modernised,
And taken mixed race into its blood line.
It has adapted to the changing times
And in the Commonwealth it will look fine –
That family of nations – when the Prince
Tours with his bride, supports his father's role
As the next Head of the Commonwealth who'll
Represent fifty-three states as a whole.
This couple will spread harmony among
The world's peoples who have long been unsung.

All royal events bring harmony to all.
The Crown unites not just one nation-state
But much of the global family, whose
Universal outlook's a noble trait.
Royal ceremonies reveal that God
Loves all humankind, and not just one race;
The coming Coronation will present
Charles as a priest, anointed with God's grace,
Who can bring royal harmony to all
The world's peoples who share our global ball.

28–30 May, 3 June 2018

Rose Garden like a Union Flag

I sit after lunch on a Saturday
In late September under a cloudless sky,
And bask in the warm sun and gaze down at
The fountain plashing over its bowl down by
The Three Graces to the pool filled with yellow
Water lilies, and through this terrace's potted posies
Survey the rose garden's paths like a Union Flag
And twelve beds' red, yellow, mauve and white roses.

⌜ All is still in the late summer sunshine,
All's peaceful round my fields to the sweep and flank
Of thousands of green trees along the sky.
Ten crows take wing and fly, two ravens bank –
They've become new residents – and land near
The fish-pond filled with *koi* carp. A breeze starts,
Stirs roses to toss their heads, and I see
A UK split asunder in twelve parts.

Parliament has taken charge and banned 'no deal',
And has been prorogued for five weeks, and now
We await the Supreme Court's judgment that may
Declare the PM's advice to the Queen somehow
Unlawful, and hand power to reconvene
Parliament back to the Speaker. Not since the *coup*-
Like Civil War has the country been so riven.
Under six weeks till we know if we've left the EU.

I gaze at the fountain in the warming sun
And see outlines of the Union Flag with dread,
And I see twelve factions vying with each other,
White rose set against mauve, and yellow against red.
I bask in the sun that beams on Henry the Eighth's
Hunting lodge among trees, built after he chose
His Church Brexit from Papal Rome, and gaze
On his three-hundred-acre deer park, now meadows.

I sit above the tradition like a judge.
Just out of my sight is my knot-garden
With twenty-five beds, some with lavender,
Each civilisation, one European.
I see the Union Flag roses and know
They belong in one of twenty-five mature
Civilisations that surround their central knot
Which governs history and sees that we'll endure.

21 September 2019

6. 'Potted posies', "small bunches of flowers in pots".

30. 'Built after'. Queen Elizabeth's hunting lodge, actually Henry VIII's third hunting lodge, was built in 1540–1543 after he removed the English Church from Papal rule so he could marry his second wife Anne Boleyn.

32. 'Deer park', in the 1540s known as Fairmead ("fair meadow"), cf. "now meadows".
40. 'Endure', "undergo (a difficulty, hardship, etc.); tolerate, bear; remain in existence, last" (*Concise Oxford Dictionary*).

The Funeral of the Duke of Edinburgh: The Elizabethan Age Drawing to a Close

Windsor Castle under a clear blue sky,
Roads lined by soldiers from his regiments.
The brilliant sun shines on the hat and gloves,
Blanket and sugar lumps (horses' presents)
On the driver's seat of the empty carriage.
And now his cap and sword, a wreath behind,
On the flagged coffin as it is loaded on
The Land-Rover hearse Prince Philip designed.
The masked Queen waits in her car, all are numb
As, to slow march and footsteps and lone drum,

Band playing stirring music, bell tolling,
Gunfire, the procession behind his standard
To the nearby Chapel begins, the Prince
Of Wales walking by Anne, Andrew by Edward,
And then the two brothers divided by
Anne's son to minimise their rift, now griped.
Slowly they reach the foot of the Chapel steps,
The coffin, borne on marines' shoulders, piped,
Recalling his war service and regiments.
It pauses halfway up: a minute's silence,

Ended by cannon fire and a puff of smoke,
And looking at the medals on all who stand
And thinking of this man who was born into one,
And gave his life to another, royal band,
His seven hundred and fifty charities,
His twenty-two thousand solo events
And his two hundred Commonwealth visits,
I think of Albert, whose duty and common sense
Underpinned the monarchy in Victoria's day,
And shed a trickling tear in new dismay.

The Bidding, readings and a hymn sung by
A choir of four, and also an anthem.
The service, slimmed because of Covid, he planned
To focus on the sea, his faith and wisdom
And send a message: one reading mentions
'Brothers' twice, a demand they heal their rift
As they sit on opposite sides of the Quire
Near Henry the Eighth's tomb, as his last gift.
I watch the coffin on the catafalque go,
Its platform lowered to the crypt below.

Now Garter in a heraldic tabard,
The epitome of pomp and ceremony,
Reads out the Duke's styles and titles. Nineteen
Of his sixty-one insignia are neatly
Arranged on the altar. He was Admiral
Of the Fleet, Field Marshal of the Army – foremost
In rank – and Marshal of the Royal Air Force.
Bugles lament and then blow the Last Post,
Then Reveille (morning muster), now a new height:
Action Stations, the Navy's call to fight.

Now all are outside, the soldiers have gone.
He modernised the monarchy and left
It in good shape but an uncertain future
As Charles, consort to his mother, bereft,
Seeks a revival of the Commonwealth
Which grew from eight countries to fifty-four
During his parents' marriage, having said goodbye
To the man who held it together and is no more,
Co-creator of the Elizabethan Age
Which is now drawing to a close off-stage.

17, 24–25 April 2021

7. 'Flagged', the Duke's personal standard (see line 12).

16. 'Griped', "(nautical) lashed in with lashings securing a boat in place" (*Oxford English Dictionary*).

56. There were 54 countries in the Commonwealth when the Duke of Edinburgh died.

Death of the Queen: The End of the Elizabethan Era

A new era comes suddenly like a storm.
The last time I witnessed an era's rule
End was when George the Sixth died, I heard the news
In the seventeenth-century lobby of my school
As I sipped a third of a pint of milk through a straw
And a master excitedly talked to us standing boys
About the lying-in-state and funeral
And then the coronation and the noise,
Said there'd be a new Elizabethan Age
Of great change that would need a queen who'd be sage.

I saw her come to Grange Farm the year before
When she was Princess Elizabeth, to open
A camping and sports area at my school's
Neighbour's, and stood very near the future Queen. Then
She looked a thin and frail woman, before
She made her public vow to serve throughout her
Entire life, and did not appear to me
To be a new Age's stable figure
Who would last seventy years as queen bee to billions of lives
In the UK, Empire, Commonwealth and world hives.

Now as I am driven back from medical tests
In London, the lunchtime news in the car
Is not about the new PM borrowing
Two hundred billion pounds to spend like a star
On energy bills for all, but on the concern
Of doctors for the Queen in Balmoral – she's old –
And how the family are all going up there.
Something has happened we're not being told.
She lost her husband last year, then had Covid.
Did these events undermine her health as she hid?

At home I sit with a son and phone our bank
For a card, and sit with a grandson without a care,
And the other son rings: "The Queen is dead,
She died before most of the family got there."
I see the news presenters are wearing black ties.
The announcement was at six-thirty, I see

Truss say in Downing Street that Charles will reign
As Charles the Third (as Garter will proclaim publicly),
And, after seventy years, I hear once more,
"God save the King," and am back as a boy in the war.

She was on the throne for seventy years, the longest-
Serving monarch the UK has had, her fate.
I see two sons and a grandson standing at
Aberdeen airport, getting into cars too late.
Crowds outside Buckingham Palace see a double rainbow,
The old era and the new, in the stormy sky.
I hear tributes come in from past PMs and sacked
Johnson's "Elizabeth the Great", a defiant cry.
He and Truss shook her hand two days ago,
Bent over a stick and frail, near death, she was slow.

It's over, her seventy-year-long reign,
Her Platinum Jubilee and her Commonwealth dates:
She built it from eight to fifty-six countries,
She being Head of State in fifteen realms or states.
She led a supranational bloc second
Only to the UN in size, and was a still calm
Centre and stabilising force in a turning world
Through her devotion to duty and service, as a balm.
So many social changes swept through the UK,
But she did not change and she led the way.

Her reign was not as good as it's made out to be
In the overclaims that shore up the monarchy
As when Churchill spoke of a "new Elizabethan Age":
After Suez Britain lost an empire slowly
And searched at length for a new international role,
Joined the EU too late, then wrenched itself away.
After decolonising and the internet
Its culture's more shallow and emotional today,
Just its arts, science and finance in a thriving trend.
Despite her hopes, all may not be well in the end.

She held together the Elizabethan Era.
Without her authority is decline and hate:
A PM and new Cabinet two days old,
A new UK King and Commonwealth Head of State,

The oldest in British history to be named King,
And borrowing up, investment down, no growth,
Ireland wanting no border in the Irish Sea,
Scotland and Wales wanting to leave, it's both
The break-up of the UK caused by Brexit
And a vacuum in the centre, a bottomless pit.

I see Commonwealth countries that only stayed loyal
For the Queen, and will break away from the new King.
I see the war in Ukraine going Russia's way,
And Europe short of oil and gas battling.
I see the UK borrow while the EU
Imposes a windfall tax on companies like a fine.
I see the West falling and the East rising.
I see mediocrity and steep decline,
The world move on from a struggling UK
With new leaders who lack control and have no say.

Or can King Charles see all humankind as being
One supranational bloc in a World State,
A federal New World Order that's democratic
And unites the West's, Russia's and China's fate,
A world government that unites as did the Queen?
Can Charles the Wise's Universalist carousels
In the new Carolingian Era, when he's been crowned,
After the gun salutes and tolling bells,
Bring in a peaceful, prosperous Golden Age
That can provide unity for the whole world stage?

8–9 September 2022

11. Princess Elizabeth opened Grange Farm Centre with Winston Churchill on 12 July 1951.

53. There were 56 countries in the Commonwealth when the Queen died (Gabon and Togo having joined on 29 June 2022).

The Funeral of Queen Elizabeth II (On the Ambivalence of Revival and Decline)

I. WESTMINSTER ABBEY

The biggest gathering of foreign dignitaries
In history, only Churchill or Mandela

Could have drawn more to mourn at their funeral.
Nearly a hundred world leaders defer
At a reception at Buckingham Palace on the eve
Of the greatest global gathering ever seen.
Two thousand fill Westminster Abbey for
The first funeral of a sovereign there, the Queen,
Since George the Second in 1760,
The first State Funeral since Churchill's pageantry.

To a tolling bell the draped coffin's carried
From the candlelit shrine in Westminster Hall
And placed on a gun-carriage that is drawn
By ninety-eight Royal-Navy sailors, all
In front pulling ropes, and forty-four behind
Reining back the cannon to pipes and a drum
From Scotland and Ireland. Charles walks behind
With his family and household, follows, his face glum,
The coffin through the Abbey's 'Great West Door'
To the Quire and the altar, and the bier before.

The Queen was married and crowned here, the choir sings
Five sentences including one from Donne
As it processes. Two hymns and two lessons,
One read by Truss mentioning "Philip" (well spun),
Then the sermon by the Archbishop of Canterbury.
He speaks of the Queen's vow to dedicate her life
To serving the nation and Commonwealth,
A promise kept; of her service as a wife
And trust in death; and of her words of hope
During Covid: "We will meet again." She could cope.

Between the coffin and altar's a Cosmati pavement
Laid in 1268 by Henry the Third to display
A carpet of stone with a sphere and four roundels.
An inscription says it's the '*primum mobile*'
That in the ninth Heaven of Ptolemy's universe
Rotated all the underlying spheres.
It shows the universe and its end after
Nineteen thousand six hundred and eighty-three years.
The Queen's been moved from a 1097 Hall
To a 1268 diagram of the All.

Now all remain standing for the commendation,
Anthem and blessing, last post and reveille, laments,
The national anthem and lone piper playing
'Sleep, Dearie, Sleep' fading into silence.
The TV shows parks in different cities
And crowds watching screens throughout the country.
To organ music the coffin is borne on guards'
Shoulders in a slow-march procession from the Abbey.
The King and his family follow. All bow down
As the coffin passes them. On top's the crown.

Outside in sunshine troops wait with bowed heads
As the monarch in history who's longer-reigning
Than Elizabeth the First and Victoria
Is borne to the gun-carriage, then drawn by slow-marching
Sailors to the mournful beat of a muffled drum,
Gunfire and wailing, tear-jerking music
And a relentless beat, led by guards, and, eventually, now
Heralds, round Parliament Square that looks heraldic,
Past the cenotaph to the crowd-lined Mall,
Past the Victoria monument's angel.

Now the coffin passes Buckingham Palace
With its staff in a long line along the side of the road,
Rumbles up Constitution Hill, all arms reversed,
To the goddess on Wellington Arch, now slowed,
And through the curved archway beneath Victory
Riding in a quadriga, and when the last man's in,
Stops, as cannons fire in Green Park. The troops
Now stand in straight lines on grass as the coffin
Is borne to the hearse, which, for less than two hours,
Will crawl towards Windsor through people throwing flowers.

2. ST GEORGE'S CHAPEL, WINDSOR

Troops, arms reversed, slow-march round the crawling hearse
That's strewn with thrown flowers, a bell tolls, pipes play.
A muffled drum as they leave the packed long walk,
And head for the west door, the King leading the way.
The hearse stops, and the red-coated bearers
Carry the Queen up steps to the chapel.
Troops stand in a horseshoe, a flag on the grass.

The Earl Marshal and Lord Chamberlain hobble
To receive the coffin, which is borne between
Bowing heads to the Quire. She's now a catafalqued Queen.

This is more of a personal service for her staff.
The choir sings 'Kiev Melody', the Russian raw
'Kontakion of the Departed'. After a hymn,
Reading and prayers, including a prayer for
All companions of the Order of the Garter,
A motet by Donne on "one equal light" seen
In Heaven, and then the Instruments of State –
The crown, orb and sceptre received by the Queen
At her coronation – are placed on the High Altar,
Marking the end of the Elizabethan Era.

The Queen's Company Camp Colour is placed on
The coffin by the King, and the Lord Chamberlain
Breaks his wand into two, and places the bits
On the Colour so they'll be housed with the coffin.
The committal: the Dean of Windsor reads a psalm
And says "Go forth", and the coffin is lowered
To the vault beneath so the Queen can be buried
Beside her parents, privately interred.
Garter reads the Queen's titles and the piper's playing.
There's a blessing, then all sing "God save the King."

But I'm still hearing the sombre beat of a drum,
Of a world power's glory and obstinate last stand
After its thousand-year-old Kingship within
A nearly-thousand-year-old Westminster Hall, and
I ponder its defiant revival
As the ambivalence of decline, and see, despite
Its majesty and united nationhood,
Death's inevitable, and the triumph over Death's might
In the yearning for reunion in Heaven.
And I loiter as Death and Paradise both beckon.

19 September 2022

14. Sailors have towed the coffin at the funerals of sovereigns ever since horses reared up at Queen Victoria's funeral in 1901 and threatened to topple the coffin; and Captain Prince Louis of Battenberg, the future First Sea Lord of the Royal Navy, suggested to the new monarch Edward VII that the senior service should tow the coffin.

64–66. Wellington Arch was built between 1826 and 1830 and was originally known as Green Park Arch and later as Constitution Arch. It originally had an equestrian statue of the Duke of Wellington on top. In 1912 the current quadriga, a chariot drawn by four horses, with the goddess of Victory, Nike, was placed on top.

86. 'Motet', "a short sacred choral composition" (*Concise Oxford Dictionary*).

A New Age of Light

I enter St Michael's Cornhill, built above
The Roman basilica, burned down by the Great Fire
And rebuilt by Wren, upper tower by Hawksmoor.
Inside's arched columns and gated pews, I admire
The tall organ, for which my brother's composed
A Triptych, and is now making his debut
As a planetary composer alongside Holst.
He rises and shakes my hand by the back pew.
I sit, and look at the backs of old men,
And recall him in short trousers in our garden.

He sees the conjunction of Jupiter and Saturn
(Which I saw, looking across neighbouring fields
In twilight just over two years ago)
As the passing of the Age of Pisces that yields
To the Age of Aquarius, and the birth
Of a new Age, which I know will be of Light.
I listen to the swelling organ play
Buxtehude's phases of the moon, then Holst's contrite
Saturn as the bringer of old age, and now my sage
Brother's Triptych on our coming new Age

In seven vignettes: the gods are sensing change;
Jupiter sounds the retreat, hear Saturn's reverse,
Now the gods are consoled at their conjunction;
Hear the two-thousand-year-old Age of Pisces disperse
With the fish gods Aphrodite and her son Eros
Swimming in shimmering water, while the Muses dance;
Now Aquarius, son of Zeus, rides on thermals;
The Muses lament the Great Pestilence with chants,
Apollo heals with his lyre; then Jupiter
Aided by the Muses announces the new order.

Now Jupiter and Saturn herald in
The arrival of Aquarius, heavy-laden,
Who pours the Water of Life over the earth,
Washes away the old, and to acclamation
The Christian Age of Pisces and *ichthus*, the fish,
Is replaced by a global Age that thrives
In a World State of peace and prosperity.
With a crash the new order's new Age arrives
And to cadenzas and triumphant acclaim
A Golden Age of Light like Fire's aflame.

The organist comes out, bows and beckons
Jonnie to stride down the aisle and take his applause.
One more piece from Holst has Jupiter as
The bringer of jollity, then without a pause
The organist bows and again beckons Jonnie,
Who again joins him for plaudits, then all rise.
I make my way to The Counting House nearby,
In the back room sip sparkling wine and munch pies
With Jonnie and hear the organist's wisdom,
And ask if he'll play the Triptych at a Prom.

O Aquarius, I welcome your new order.
All will change when your upheaval takes place
And wars and conquests slide into the past
And the earth looks as peaceful as it does from space.
Aquarius, bring in a federal World State
In which all humankind can feed and learn
That the nightmare of our times will slide away.
Pour your water-like Light from your great urn
And sweep away the old nationalistic Age
So all civilisations enjoy a new peaceful stage.

12–15 March 2023

1. Nicholas Hagger's younger brother Jonathan had composed the Great Conjunction Triptych, and its first performance, played by the organist Martin Baker and billed as a "world première performance", was in St Michael's Cornhill on 13 March 2023.

13. Nicholas Hagger looked for the Great Conjunction of Saturn and Jupiter across fields near his home on 21 December 2020. See *Fools' Gold*, Canto

XXIII, lines 737–763, pp.397–398, which mentions "a Great Conjunction" (line 745) and "a new World State" (line 760).

18. Buxtehude's *Passacaglia in D minor* (BuxWV 161).

43. The first piece from Holst was from *The Planets* (Op. 32), Saturn; the second piece was also from *The Planets*, Jupiter.

50. 'Prom', Promenade Concert at the Royal Albert Hall.

55. World State. See Nicholas Hagger's *World State* for how the people of 14 living civilisations and what used to be 11 (now dead) civilisations can come together in a partly-federal World State solving the world's problems in seven areas, including disarming and abolishing war, with new legal powers the UN does not have.

At Coldridge: An Unspeakable Truth

When I was a boy my father took me
To the Tower's room where two Princes were put to death,
Twelve-year-old Edward the Fifth, and Richard, nine
(Sons of Edward the Fourth and Elizabeth
Woodville), were lodged in 1483
To await young Edward's crowning and stay well
And, according to tradition and Shakespeare,
Murdered by Richard the Third's servant James Tyrell.

I am there now, staring in wonder at
The wide four-poster bed on which, fully dressed,
The two brothers sat before they were smothered
With pillows in their beds by Miles Forest
And John Dighton, ordered by Tyrell, More states,
And then buried deep in the ground under the staircase
Leading to the chapel in the White Tower, under
A heap of stones, till moved to a secret place.

But now, in one of today's papers, I read
Edward was moved to Devon to live under
A false name – tracked down by the team that found Richard
The Third's bones under a car park in Leicester –
Near a church up a cart track near Coldridge, with a fifteenth-
Century tower that has symbols of the House of York. Lo!
A medieval stone effigy gazes
At Edward the Fifth in a stained-glass window.

The church contains clues the boy king lived in
A house owned by his half-brother Sir Thomas Grey,
Under the name John Evans, whose broken shield
By his tomb's effigy says "John Evas", that may
Stand for "Edward the Fifth in sanctuary" (Latin *asa*).
It has a chin scar, deformed mouth (no lips), hair
As round a second face in the Edward-the-Fifth window
Beneath a crown he was not allowed to wear.

The etching on John Evans' tomb has "King"
In inverted writing, and nine carved lines clearly shown
Beneath, suggesting 1509, when
Edward the Fifth could have reclaimed his throne.
The Yorkist 'Sun in Splendour' is on a boss
On the church ceiling, and a glass 'sun', one more,
Has survived the Reformation's window-smashing.
The Rose of York and 'Sun' are on the floor.

John Evans was made the estate's deer parker, and on
The Edward-the-Fifth window built in 1511
When Edward was forty-one is the floating crown
On whose ermine are forty-one deer from his deer park when
He was Lord of the Manor as well as parker. He came
From nowhere, there's no record, just a message
In the chapel inscribed on a prayer-desk:
"Pray for John Evans, Parker of Coldridge."

So many unlikely symbols in rural Devon.
And so many clues carved by a surviving King
Who could not speak but left this church to tell.
The crown has the falcon and fetterlock echoing
Those of Edward the Fifth and his grandfather, Duke of York,
And I, too, hope to leave up a cart track, also uncouth,
My own monument to inform coming decades,
An archive of symbols that hint an unspeakable truth.

So many stumble on things they should not know
And are silenced, or walled round with silence as if dead,
To contain what they have to say, to stifle their voice.
Keep it in a Coldridge so it can't be spread.
It happened under Elizabeth the First
Who clutched a rainbow, controlled all speaking out.

In this totalitarian time I too must leave
A monument to my silence that some will doubt.

5–6 April 2023; first drafted 29 December 2021

8. The Princes were murdered after being declared illegitimate because of Edward the Fourth's pre-contract marriage with Lady Eleanor Butler.

13. Sir Thomas More stated that Sir James Tyrell, Richard III's servant, had confessed to organising the smothering of the two Princes in *The History of King Richard III* (c.1515).

17. *The Daily Telegraph* of 29 December 2021, p.3.

20. Richard III's bones were found under a car park in Leicester in September 2012.

25. Nicholas Hagger visited St Matthew's church, Coldridge on 6 April 2023 after writing a draft of this poem on 29 December 2021, and was struck by the prominence in the church of the chantry John Evans was given for his tomb, which is the only tomb in the chantry. The reclining stone effigy of Evans, who died in 1511, is looking at the stained-glass window containing one of the two surviving portraits of Edward the Fifth and a profile of himself, with the same deformed mouth, clutching the crown. Nicholas Hagger wrote in the church's visitors' book, "Edward V is here."

27–29. John Evans was first recorded as being at Coldridge in 1484. Edward the Fifth's reign was from 9 April 1483 to 25 June 1483.

28, 33. 'Tomb'. Edward V and his brother Richard were officially reinterred on the orders of King Charles II in Westminster Abbey in 1674 after workmen rebuilding a stairway in the Tower of London found bones belonging to two children. In 1933 the bones were examined and found to have been interred with animal bones. There are no complete skeletons. It has never been proved that the bones belong to the two Princes.

34. 'Nine carved lines… suggesting 1509'. Henry VII died in 1509 and was succeeded by Henry VIII in place of Edward V, who as Evans felt he was the rightful King (see line 35). Edward V was born in 1470 and died (as John Evans) in 1511, aged 41. (See lines 43–44.)

36. Henry VII died in 1509. And Edward V could have become King then.

50. 'Clues'. For example there are three carvings showing a Tudor woman with a long snake-like tongue, possibly a slur against the mother of Henry VII, Margaret Beaufort, who seemed to have a hand in arranging for Henry VII to succeed Richard III in 1485 instead of Edward V, who had been blocked from his coronation in 1483.

52. 'Fetterlock', "D-shaped fetter (shackle) for tethering a horse by the leg" (*Concise Oxford Dictionary*).

60. 'Keep it in Coldridge so it can't be spread', i.e. leave behind a monument with hidden symbolism that can be seen by future generations but not spread/publicised now and therefore be suppressed now.

The Painted Hall, Greenwich

The painted hall at Greenwich I drove past
For three years to and from work is now posing
As a Hall of State where Johnson set out a Brussels-
Rule-free trade deal with the EU. On the ceiling
William the Third receives an olive branch
From peace and passes the 'cap of liberty'
To kneeling Europe, and tramples on crouching
Louis the Fourteenth representing Tyranny.

This Baroque work, painted for nineteen years
By Thornhill, was for a dining-room that's high
In the Royal Hospital for Seamen requested
By Mary the Second, who had been inspired by
Wounded sailors returning from La Hogue.
Under the undercroft's concrete floor have been found
Two rooms from Henry the Eighth's Greenwich Palace
Where his Mary and Elizabeth were born to astound.

This Hall is a symbol of national defiance,
Inspired by the wife of Dutch William the Third,
A Protestant who had distanced himself from France
And Catholic Europe, yet the painting's voyeured
Baroque style presents the European blend
Of sense and spirit, social and spiritual views:
Half-naked bodies float in a Heavenly sky
With winged cherubs and Light round heads that bemuse.

The painting recalls the visionary figures I saw
As I underwent my full illumination
With political surveillance squads in the streets
Outside who watched my every move, sullen;
I saw, and was among, such crowds and flamboyant
Figures half-human and half from a world of Light.
I think of William the Third, our new king,
Who replaced James the Second's Catholic might.

As I drove to and fro past the Painted Hall
Representing my country's naval power,
I was waiting to be exposed by Philby.

I lived amid danger, but did not cower,
And carried out the State's will though my heart was elsewhere.
I was told things I cannot now repeat
And so I did my bidding until it was said
That two people had become risks, and I should retreat.

At last I retired with Truth in my mirror,
Which I always held up to the world as to a wall,
That I would be walled round in silence now,
That my soul was mirrored in the Painted Hall.
I could operate but the State would control and block
All publicity for the rest of my years
As my free speech was a threat, a living
Embodiment of their autocratic fears.

I see William the Third offering kneeling
Supplicants a 'cap of liberty' as if gifting
At his coronation, while I am trampled
Underfoot and ignored by a new king
Who has to embody the State's cancellation.
To me the Painted Hall that I drove past
Is a monument to a life that might have been,
But I'm not in the Tower like Raleigh, with door shut fast.

8 April 2023

13. The Battle of La Hogue (France) was in 1692.

31. William III of Orange and his wife Mary II came to the English throne in 1689. Mary II was James II's daughter (1662–1694), but was a Protestant like her cousin William of Orange who she married. Her mother was the daughter of Charles I and Henrietta Maria, who was married to William II of Orange aged nine in 1641.

56. 'Fast', "tightly, secured" (*Concise Oxford Dictionary*). For the imprisonment of Sir Walter Raleigh, see Nicholas Hagger's *The Tree of Tradition*, pp.67, 106, 121.

The World Falling Apart: An Unspeakable Secret

More bad news, North Korea can now reach
The US with advanced nuclear missiles
Powered by solid fuel – as if Putin's threats
To escalate the war in Ukraine (with smiles)
Were to become hypersonic three-minute nuclear attacks

Or tactical warheads on the battlefield,
Although Russia's now in charge of the UN
Security Council and the world's moral shield.

A perfect storm is brewing, it seems the world
Is falling apart with many crises
Happening at the same time: high inflation,
High energy costs, zero growth, credit squeeze,
Looming recession and perhaps depression,
The Eurozone countries struggling to pay
Debts accumulated since the banking crisis,
Made worse by the pandemic's money-printing mêlée.

They're all interconnected, these crises
And climate change, rising sea levels – throats
Dry from droughts, famine, hunger – and refugees
From wars and poor economies, migrant boats,
The whole world seemingly wanting to move
To countries with free pay-outs and housing,
And bellicose China eyeing Taiwan.
It's a polycrisis, world doom is lurking.

The UK'll perform worst in the G7,
And has self-harmed with the 4-per-cent losses
Of its GDP by exiting from Europe
And changing from trade with neighbours to far countries,
And then locking down all its people so they're now used
To working at home and striking for fantasy pay.
Whisper it not: the unspeakable secret
That Britain is in decline and disarray.

The Coronation will cast an illusion
Of continuity over the chaos that's spread,
Even though the only rehearsal overran
And many who run the State aren't invited.
An unhappy family will tolerate the presence
Of a prickly Prince as republicans turn away.
Many who recall his mother will not bow
To a pretend Queen when she's been crowned that day.

The monarchy seems tottering, Australia
Has already removed it as Head of State.

Biden was told by his mother never to bow
To the Queen, and won't be present, to echo her hate.
(He's an Irish Catholic who beams with ex-IRA.)
An illusion is being spread that the UK
Is a world leader in AI and science
When it's broken, out of funds and in disarray.

The world is in turmoil: the US and EU
Are losing world influence despite shoring
Up Western hegemony, and China,
Chief ally to Russia, is now rising.
Beneath all four there is one unity,
But few can see it in the hostile glare
Of a world divided as during the Cold War
And, propelled by conflict, heading to doom and despair.

14 April 2023

The Oak Tree and the Fallen Branch

I pass Lopping Hall in my boyhood Loughton,
Opened after locals lopped Forest trees
For firewood in defiant exercise
Of their traditional rights, removed (to unease)
When the Forest was bought by the Corporation
Of London, who built it to compensate
The villagers for the loss of their rights.
Lopping was stopped, and this Hall's a rebate.

Now I look at the oak tree with the fallen branch
And think of the Tree of Tradition, whose branches include
All the traditions that have influenced thinkers
And writers in all countries and times, and protrude
All possible disciplines, a Tree of Life
That's in all minds with influences all can follow.
Within its crown are branches and twigs from decades
Ago, on whose boughs all writers bud and grow.

It includes all civilisations, this Tree of Life,
Its twenty-five massive branches have flourished
From its roots and trunk that channels religious sap,

Each culture's thoughts on living, what it's wished,
And each decade's works differ from the last
Though similar, and sometimes there's a falling-down:
That fallen branch is the UK self-severed
From the sap of its European civilisation's crown.

Writers are all branches that inspired their works,
Some contradictory, some in harmony,
And are all the twig-like influences
That have shaped their leafy writings invisibly
Into shoots and buds on an existing branch,
A blossoming tradition from whose sap bloom
Their works to ripen among leaves and swell
Into their fruit that will fall for all to consume.

I am an oak tree, my branches are my disciplines
All stemming from my Universalist bole
That transmits all religions from its gnarled roots
And spreads my works from a crown that's one Whole.
My poems are leaves, and my seeds are acorns
That will take root, sprout, influence unborn
Generations and flourish, and that fallen branch
Is the UK lopped from Europe, which I mourn.

Many works hang like acorns on my oak tree
Of civilisations and times of every kind,
And I am musing on the severance
Of the UK from this global tree in my mind.
My Tree of Tradition includes the European
Culture, and the severing of the UK's branch is quite
Self-inflicted, a blunder that I see
As a right-wing lopping that must be put right.

Look, a new branch is growing on my oak tree
Which includes all the world's cultural thinking:
The European culture and the UK's
Except for the self-severing right wing.
They have not deprived me of European sap,
Classical Greece and Rome are still in my veins and head,
And my works are filled with the European past;
And the fallen branch is abandoned and dead.

I am an oak tree, I draw influence
From my sap's many thinkers in my branches
Including Europeans with a global reach.
My leaves aren't damaged by the lopped stub's traces
Of the UK's membership of the EU.
They still bear a universal structure that cloaks
Acorns that will spread the ideas I have grown
And leave a legacy of many oaks.

I am an oak tree in the warm sunshine,
Under a blue sky, with all my branches, I'm whole
And universal and continue to grow works.
I'm rooted and my trunk's sap's spread into my soul.
I spurn the right-wing nationalist approach
That has not prevented me from channelling
All Europe's culture, and its fallen branch
Is as dead as the 'separate path' of the right wing.

And when I am no more I will be like
A branch that has fallen from its oak tree, a bough
From the Tree of Tradition, and on the grass
Will be the acorns that grow all round me now.
The oak tree will continue without its branch
And though I will be no more my works will be,
And acorns will sprout and saplings will continue
The traditions I grew on my fully-branched oak tree.

27–30 April 2023

1. 'Boyhood Loughton'. Nicholas Hagger lived within the sound of Lopping Hall's (then) striking clock from 1943, and moved to the same road as Lopping Hall in Loughton, Essex in 1945. Its clock is "the four-faced striking clock" that "measures an exile" in 'The Silence', line 1345.

2. Lopping Hall, Loughton was opened in 1884.

8. 'Rebate', "a partial refund of money paid" (*Concise Oxford Dictionary*).

10. For a full account of the Tree of Tradition, see Nicholas Hagger's *The Tree of Tradition*.

46. 'Quite', (here) "completely; entirely, wholly; to the utmost extent; in the fullest sense" (*Concise Oxford Dictionary*).

70–71. For the channelling of all Europe's culture, see Nicholas Hagger's *Classical Odes*.

74. In early notes for this poem, Nicholas Hagger wrote, "I am the branch, alienated from the oak tree", presumably thinking of his walled-in silence,

but did not include this line in the poem, preferring to see his works as acorns from a connected branch of the oak tree.

Epistle to a Civil Servant
(Epistle to a Civil Servant who Keeps the Official List of Writers Allowed to Operate but with Limited Publicity)

O civil servant who maintains the list
Of writers who are allowed to operate
But only with limited publicity,
Such as Tolstoy's grandson who criticised
(In a book deemed not in the national interest)
Macmillan for repatriating Cossacks
And Croatian soldiers and civilians, who
Were all massacred after they were sent back.
You may have not the slightest idea why
Some older writers were put on your list
As long as fifty years ago. Some helped
The UK's intelligence-gathering
In a time of crisis after being asked,
Risked their lives to put the UK ahead,
And when they wanted to stop and return
To normality, found themselves on your list.
They were on it so they could not let slip
Official secrets after their secret work,
And so discovered that ordinary men
Who had never risked their lives could have all
The publicity they craved, like 'Reality
TV' stars, whereas those who were approached
And had signed the Official Secrets Act
Must live with limited publicity
Until their lives end, a sentence enforced
For decade after decade by the system,
Implemented by the civil servant
Who kept blacklisted names isolated,
Surrounded their activities with silence.
Death by silence, *Totenstille*, was the reward
Of many now dead or not long to live.

O civil servant who maintains this list,
Please go to H and delete Nicholas Hagger's name

When he has died and is no more a threat
To the secret State, and so can be crossed off
Your list which has been enforced for fifty years.
Yes, evidence will be supplied that he's dead.
What, you *can't* cross him off, the list extends
To his legacy, the purchase of his past books?
He can't be crossed off for a hundred years?
That's scandalous. In that case you should be brought
Before a court to answer why in his life,
And now after his death, you suppressed his work.
Have you no conscience? Someone could be on your list
After being killed during the First World War,
His posthumous reputation now annulled
For ever. That's indeed the case? It's not fair.
No secret State should annihilate citizens,
Airbrush them out of history and pretend
They were never born. Only Russia and China
Remove people from photos, and show thin air
Where they had been. The West's democratic,
Not authoritarian, civil servants
Aid ministers, surely they're fair? Because
Someone in MI6 or GCHQ
Once said someone's works should have limited
Publicity in view of their time's demands
That person should not be abandoned throughout
Posterity on the basis of a subjective
Judgment now out of date that quietly assumes
A writer never existed and therefore
Does not qualify for any memorial,
But must be forgotten and silently
Expunged. "*Cui bono*," as Cicero asked,
'To whose advantage is it?' It is obvious:
It's clearly to the advantage of the State,
The secret State which silences its dead.

I stand before the Rainbow Portrait Queen
Elizabeth the First in an orange cloak
Decorated with the eyes, ears and mouths
Of her intelligence agents, spies. She holds
A rainbow in her authoritarian right hand,
Signifying the colourful arts that she
Controls, and while he lived Marlowe was in

Her grasp and could be airbrushed from records –
If it suited her secret State under
Walsingham, her spymaster, in a system
Assembled by the Cecils, father and son,
And supported by his deputy Heneage
Who was granted Copped Hall in 1564
And rebuilt it for when Elizabeth
The First came to stay in 1568
And again in 1575.
I look at the Rainbow Portrait that hangs
In the passage on the way to my office,
And think again of Marlowe, her agent,
Murdered in London. See, she grips the rainbow
In her right hand, and read the Latin words above:
'*Non sine sole iris*', 'No rainbow
Without the sun', meaning 'Without my sun's
Permission', and I see the jewelled serpent
On her left sleeve which silences dissent
With one bite of its fangs. She's assumed the power
Of Satan to shine her sunlight on the land
And all writers operate in sun and cloud,
Her sunshine and the right amount of cloud
To create a rainbow that's an acceptable work.
And I, who feel so at home among Tudors,
As if I had lived before in their time
And had far memories of Tudor moments,
See her secret State surrounded by civil
Servants who guarded and enforced secret lists,
And again thinking of Marlowe I wonder
If I've been caught up in the same process
In this life as so many were caught up
In the Tudor time when they were arrested
And sent to the Bloody Tower like Raleigh
And in due course beheaded for disobeying
Orders issued from the State behind the throne.
And then I think, it's better to tolerate
The irritation of being walled round
And 'death by silence', *Totenstille*, as
Limited publicity enforced by
The secret State, for at least I am allowed
To operate and am not locked away.

O civil servant, you believe you're doing
Your duty in limiting what I do,
And I put up with you as it's better
Than going through what Marlowe and Raleigh went through.

3–4 May 2023

68. For more on the Rainbow Portrait, see pp.xxxiii–xxxiv and xxxix.

The Coronation of King Charles III and the True Poet

I

The procession begins in rain, escorted
By gold-clad, mounted Household Cavalry
The air-conditioned Diamond Jubilee State Coach
With an oak crown carved from HMS *Victory*,
Drawn by six Windsor greys, trundles past the flagged
Mall's cheering crowds, through the Admiralty Arch, then away
Down Whitehall to Westminster Abbey where
William the Conqueror was crowned on Christmas Day.
This is the thirty-ninth crowning since that torn scene.
A fanfare from heralds announces the King and Queen.

Now there's a procession of faith leaders, Christians
And the fourteen realms, then to an anthem, with stealth,
The Queen Consort, then the King tiptoe down the aisle.
(Many of the congregation are from the Commonwealth.)
They pray by the Chairs of Estate before the altar,
And are presented by the Archbishop of Canterbury.
The King receives a *Bible* and swears an oath
To govern each UK territory
According to its laws and customs. With verve
The King kneels before the altar and prays to serve.

The King moves back to his Chair for music and prayers.
Sunak, a Hindu, reads from *Colossians* on
"The invisible God" creating all.
There's music, another reading, and a sermon
Saying that Jesus was anointed to serve,
And anointing gives more strength than politicking,
War or tyranny. The Archbishop receives the oil.
The King's disrobed and surrounded by screens showing

A tree with fifty-six leaves, Commonwealth states,
And is anointed with oil that originates

In olives grown on the Mount of Olives
On his hands, breast and head as the choir sings, eyes lit,
Handel's Baroque anthem *Zadok the Priest.*
Zadok the priest and Nathan the prophet
Anointed Solomon to rule Israel and Judah.
The anointing screen's removed, the King wears a white gown
And the embroidered gold priestly coat, and sits in
The Coronation Chair, eyes looking down.
They look far-away, in a deep spiritual trance.
He's been anointed with God's Light, he doesn't glance.

It's the most sacred moment of the ceremony
As the oil was consecrated in the Church
Of the Holy Sepulchre, Jerusalem.
God's sent him a Light message to research.
The King is presented with the Regalia,
The Crown Jewels: spurs, the Sword of State, gold
Bracelets, robe, orb, ring, glove, sceptre, then rod,
And finally St Edward's Crown, placed – behold!
By the Archbishop on the King's bowed head's hair.
There's an exchange of swords, now a fanfare.

The King's been crowned, now the Abbey's bells peal,
Guns salute from Horse Guards Parade and the Tower.
Now the blessing, then the King moves to his Throne Chair
On the Quire's chequered floor, his seat of power,
And now his enthroning. The Archbishop gives
Fealty from the Church, the Prince of Wales, tall,
Kneels before the King as "liege man" and heir.
Now it's "homage of the people" when all
In the Abbey and at home can swear true
Allegiance to the King, his heirs and successors – who?

Who added this to the traditional service
Is not known, the Archbishop must have been
Guided by the King's advisers, who deny
All knowledge of this pledge that can be seen
As like forced homage in *A Game of Thrones*
Or to Big Brother in a world where subjects cower.

Half the nation's staying silent, according to polls.
The advisers have seen the coronation as power,
Not ritual and pageant, and their command seems bland
But extends homage to the sovereign throughout the land.

An anthem, and the Queen Consort's anointed
In her Chair of Estate, in open view
With oil on her forehead, and's presented with ring,
Crown, rod and sceptre, and, crowned, fidgets in two
Stray hairs, moves to her Throne Chair and's enthroned
To Psalm 98 set to music by one not seen
As a classical composer, Lloyd Webber.
A 'Queen' is a woman born to be Queen,
A Queen Consort is a woman who married a King,
Who hasn't inherited Queendom. That's true teaching.

The King offers bread and wine, they're now on the altar.
The King and Queen move back to the Chairs of Estate.
More music, then the *Lord's Prayer* spoken in
Many languages, babbled as at Babel's gate,
Suggesting differences within global unity.
The King and Queen take communion unseen.
A prayer, a final blessing, sung *Amen*,
A hymn, anthem, *Te Deum*, and the King and Queen
Move into the Shrine of St Edward behind the high
Altar to be vested in robes of estate and look spry.

Now the King, wearing the Imperial State Crown,
Stands for the National Anthem with eyes that are bleak.
Both in crowns process to *Pomp and Circumstance*,
Greet faith leaders: Jewish, Buddhist and Sikh,
Hindu, Muslim; and to pealing bells and rain
Go out to the Gold State Coach that bumps and wobbles,
Used in every coronation since William the Fourth's,
Coated with gold leaf and painted panels,
Drawn by eight Windsor greys at walking pace.
Crowds cheer as they climb in with their trains in place.

II

The coach trundles back to Buckingham Palace,
Horses jog up and down, cheering crowds wave,
No sign of protesters bannering 'Not my King'

Though a quarter of Britons want a republic they crave
As do six of the fourteen realms whose Head of State
The King is, including Australia – it's keen.
A slimmed-down Royal Family won't change this.
With Harry, Meghan and Andrew out and the Queen
And Duke of Edinburgh dead there are few 'contents'
Who can share the load of burdensome engagements.

The Age of Deference has passed, curtsies and bows
Jar with our way of life that is more headstrong.
The Queen Consort seems a nervous pretend Queen
And the advisers got the people's homage wrong.
To the true poet the coronation should convey
European civilisation's central idea's state
Of the Light that created the Church, which is in the profound
Works of the Metaphysical poets, not celebrate
With pop songs; and the anointing is supposed
To do this, not state 'Consort''s dropped for 'Queen' and's foreclosed.

Having been cheered by the four thousand military
In Buckingham Palace's grounds, the King and Queen,
On its balcony in crowns and ermine robes,
Watch the fly-past, slimmed-down because rain's been,
With four page-boys on each side, including
The Queen Consort's three grandchildren, which echoes.
A crowd down the Mall under umbrellas shouts. Now waves
Of battlefield helicopters, now the Red Arrows.
The God of the One's pleased many faiths unite
But will ask, "In this celebration, where's the Light?"

I wrote to Hughes that the true poet has grasped
The Church no longer fulfils its true function
Of connecting the monarch to the Fire or Light
That made the divine right of kings happen;
And channels our civilisation's Reality.
And so the true poet is an unwelcome font
At the coronation, a spring of flowing Light,
At odds with the homage the advisers want
All citizens to pay at home, bowing down
To a hollow, glum-faced King in a Lightless crown.

And on top of this, the true poet who's served it
Must be invisible to the secret State
For the rest of his life and have only limited
Publicity, though allowed to operate;
And to write a masque that does not convey homage
Is to defy the secret State's grip on the arts
That's like Elizabeth the First's in her Rainbow Portrait,
Who wears a cloak of the eyes and ears – not hearts –
Of her spies, grasps a rainbow and condemns Marlowe
For too visibly dealing the Cecils a blow.

The prospects of the Carolean Age
Are entrammelled in a Third World War's hell-fire.
I prefer it to be a Carolingian Age,
An age like Charlemagne's Universalist empire
Of universal peace and harmony
Which King Charles will bring in with fresh thinking.
But if his nation-statist advisers demand homage
Zeus will still be dismayed at Britain's broken governing,
And for pointing the way in two masques and this glower
I may end like Raleigh in the Bloody Tower.

5–7, 20 May 2023

Title For 'the true poet', see pp.xxix–xxxi, xxxiv, xxxvi, xxxviii.

12. 'Fourteen realms'. King Charles III is Head of State of fourteen realms excluding the UK.

29. 'A tree with fifty-six leaves, Commonwealth states'. After he finished this poem Nicholas Hagger found eight lines he was intending to include in the next stanza:

> The screen shows a Tree with fifty-six nations
> Of the Commonwealth as leaves under angels, meant
> To look like the Tree of Life and also
> The Tree of Tradition whose branches represent
> All civilisations, not just the Commonwealth
> And all traditions writers and thinkers have shared,
> The influences that have inspired them, that have always been
> And will be for generations still to be aired.

For details on the Tree of Tradition, see Nicholas Hagger's *The Tree of Tradition* (2024).

36. 'Gown', the white anointing gown (*Colobium Sindonis*, 'shroud tunic' in Latin), a simple linen shirt.

37. 'Priestly coat', a *supertunica*, a full-length gold silk coat.

46. 'Spurs'. The spurs were made in 1661 for Charles II, but were altered for George IV in 1820.

47. 'Sceptre, then rod'. The sceptre with cross (Kingly power and justice), and sceptre with dove (rod, equality and mercy).

63–70. For "homage of the people" and the King's advisers, see pp.xxxi–xxxii.

84. 'Gate'. An Akkadian name for the city of Babel was Bāb-ilim, meaning "gate of God". The Tower of Babel was in Babylon, 100 metres high. Nicholas Hagger visited Babylon and Nimrod, site of the Tower of Babel, on 23 February 1962.

97. William IV's coronation was in 1831.

105–106. See note for line 12.

109. 'Contents', contented members of the Royal Family.

120. 'State', "express, especially fully or clearly, in speech or writing" (*Concise Oxford Dictionary*).

'Foreclose', "exclude, prevent; shut out, bar" (*Concise Oxford Dictionary*). As a result of the crowning of the new Queen her title 'Queen Consort' was somehow replaced with 'Queen', see lines 78–80.

130. In fact, the Light is referred to in *Veni, Creator Spiritus*, "celestial fire" and "perpetual light", sung by the choir during the anointing; and in *Sacred Fire*, sung to the orchestra before the service began. These references seem incidental to the service and the words were absorbed by the music.

131. For Nicholas Hagger's letter to Ted Hughes, then Poet Laureate, of 28 March 1994, see his *Selected Letters*, pp.179–180.

150. In *Edward II* (1593) Marlowe is thought to have criticised the atheism of members of the Privy Council, including the ruling Cecils. In her Rainbow Portrait Elizabeth I is shown in an orange cloak decorated with the eyes, ears and mouths of her spies, and gripping a rainbow representing the arts.

153–154. Charlemagne, also known as Charles the Great (Carolus Magnus, in French Charles-le-magne, 'Charles the Great', 747–814), united western and central Europe after the fall of the Roman Empire, and was King of the Franks and Lombards, and Emperor of the Romans. He founded the first Carolingian (or Carolean) Empire, the first phase of the Holy Roman Empire.

159. 'Two masques': Nicholas Hagger's *King Charles the Wise* and *The Coronation of King Charles*.

'Glower', "a glowering look" (*Concise Oxford Dictionary*).

160. 'Raleigh in the Bloody Tower'. See Nicholas Hagger, *The Tree of Tradition*, p.121.

Leaving Court to End my Days in Arcadia

No. Low growth, inflation, striking workers,
Five million on benefits and many

Working from home, buyers with long delays,
A high number of vacancies, productivity
Down, an influx from abroad to fill them,
Mass immigration, pressure on housing –
After thirteen years of scandalous rule
It's clear that broken Britain's not working.
The Tories have lost a thousand local seats
And face a Lib-Lab pact and a long sideline,
Voting changed to PR, and the new King's reign
Will be one of falling growth and steep decline.
It's time to leave Court strife for my green pasture
And end my days in peaceful Arcadia.

13 May 2023

10. 'A long sideline', being sidelined for a long while.
11. 'PR', proportional representation.

In the Wilderness in my Arcady

When I finished serving my masters I was told
To be invisible, keep a low profile.
Like Moses I spent forty years living
In the wilderness and amassing works with guile.
I became too visible and was told I was
Allowed to operate but with limited
Publicity – not banished like Ovid
Or murdered like Marlowe for his hooded
Exposing of Privy-Council atheists
And crossing the powerful Cecils – and still confined
To a wilderness I turned into my Arcady,
A pasture with trees, a paradise to my mind.
All who've served secretly know it's best to be
Invisible in a rustic Arcady.

14, 16, 21 May 2023

Withdrawing into the Invisibility of my Arcady

I am now face-to-face with my offence:
In a masque I have been too truthful and have shown

Dissenting voices calling for a better world,
And the Light that can fill the King with goals of his own.
I have not shown all citizens bowing
To the new monarch, then kneeling in homage,
Reciting a promise to be his 'liege man'
As if he's a tyrant creating a new bondage.
I have shown God of the One's perspective
Of all life and all humans, and a rapport
King serving the will of God of the One,
I have been too visible and must now withdraw
From the Court into the invisibility
Of my Arcady – not to the Tower like Raleigh.

19, 21 May 2023

8. 'Bondage', "serfdom, slavery" (*Concise Oxford Dictionary*).

10. 'Rapport', "relationship or communication, especially when useful and harmonious" (*Concise Oxford Dictionary*).
'A rapport/King serving the will of God of the One', i.e. a King who is in harmonious communication with God of the One.

The Oak Tree and the Healing Branch

The oak tree of European civilisation
Is showing growth round the stub of the lopped branch,
And now shock news, Johnson's resigned as MP,
As the Privileges Committee considering his *carte blanche*
To break Parliament's rules and if he knowingly
Misled it have told him of their findings and been blunt.
He's accusing them of forcing him out and acting
As "a kangaroo court" and conducting "a witch-hunt".

What's going on? The truth seems to be that there is
Evidence of his wrongdoing during lockdown's screen,
Breaching the rules in more partygate wrongs,
And the Committee's ready to sanction him which would mean
His having to address all the MPs in the House
Of Commons and the voters in his Uxbridge base,
His constituency, where his majority's thin
And he'd be expelled in humiliating disgrace.

So now there will be a by-election, in fact
Three by-elections as Dorries and now Adams (of his claque)
Have also resigned, crossed off his resignation
Honours list to be peers, vetoed by Holac.
Johnson is leaving Parliament "for now",
May be switching constituencies for a safe seat.
Perhaps he'll go to Dorries' Mid-Bedfordshire
Or at the next election to his old Henley beat.

His honours list's been accepted by Sunak
Apart from four deletions, including the two who demurred,
He's elevated seven friends and close allies
To peers in the House of Lords, and has honoured
All his partygate accomplices, including
"Party Marty" who sent out invitations (not clapped)
During Covid saying "bring your own booze".
His plan to give his father a knighthood's been scrapped.

There's general relief that a liar has gone,
A blusterer who ignored truthfulness.
He led the Leave campaign and left Europe
For a non-existent trade deal with the US.
He walked away from the single market
And lost four per cent of the UK's GDP.
Ever since Brexit the UK's been in a mess:
High costs, strikes, no growth, NHS misery.

Brexit was a disaster, a catastrophe,
And now its reversal has just begun.
It will take time for Europe to re-admit the UK
And the Thatcher rebate and Major opt-out, hard-won,
Will no longer be available, and the pound will be
Euroed when the UK crawls back amid grief,
With shameful apologies for a wrong call based on
Johnson's route to Downing Street, not his belief.

Your poet gives a rueful smile. He opposed
The expulsion of twenty-one moderate, centrist MPs
From the party Johnson had just lurched to the right,
And saw the emptiness of Johnson's promised ease,

Which he called "Fools' Gold" and now his look says 'I told
You so at the time, but you did not listen,' for
Fools' Gold now stands as a contemporary record
Of the worst decision since the Second World War.

Johnson is now vilified for having forced through
A blunder of historical proportions,
A wrong route to isolated nationalism
In a time of regional blocs and unions,
In a multipolar world with four great powers,
The US, EU, Russia and China,
And the self-promotional decision to Brexit
Has lost the UK billions – and America.

Along with the mistaken policy of Brexit
Was the pandemic lockdown that brought to an end
Going to work and allowed working from home,
With five million choosing not to work, a new trend
Causing shortages, and, Europeans having left,
Jobs being filled by less qualified supplies
From abroad (not called migrants), and strikes in all sectors.
Johnson's legacy's that to stop working is wise.

The oak tree has fifty branches ready,
Twenty-seven large and twenty-three in growth,
And the lopped branch beneath the massive tree
Commemorates a disastrous choice for sloth.
The European Union will soon have Ukraine,
And a sheepish Britain will return to the fold, to the bole
Where a now-healing branch is already beginning to show
In anticipation of the tree again being whole.

10 June 2023

6. The Privileges Committee's findings included the recommendation that Johnson should be suspended for 20 days, which would require him to stand for re-election in a by-election.

18. 'Claque', "a group of people hired to applaud in a theatre" (*Concise Oxford Dictionary*).

18–20. Johnson told Nadine Dorries and Nigel Adams he had put their names forward to Holac (the House of Lords Appointments Commission) to be peers, not realising they were outside the normal time-limit for a Prime

Minister's honours list of six months before a general election; and so they were vetoed and deleted by Holac along with two others.

26. 'Demur', "raise scruples or objections" (*Concise Oxford Dictionary*). Here, "who demurred", "who also resigned" (see line 19).

54. Nicholas Hagger's publisher submitted *Fools' Gold* for the T.S. Eliot Poetry Prize and it was ignored.

74. The twenty-seven large branches are the members of the EU in 2023, and the twenty-three in growth are nation-states waiting to join.

78. 'Bole', "the stem or trunk of a tree" (*Concise Oxford Dictionary*).

Volume 40

IN ARCADY: A GONG AND PADDED STICK
2023

1
Gonging my Hearse

I look out of my windows on Arcady,
Green grass and flowers, and a sweep of lush green trees
Where deer and foxes roam and parakeets screech
Among squirrels and woodpeckers in the breeze.
I wander through my hall past Renaissance
Carved furniture including Tudor chairs
And a Victorian warming-pan and barometer,
Picture of Prospero and, at the foot of the stairs,
The battered gong and padded stick that announced
Mealtimes in my grandmother's house during the war
Like the booming-out of a poem from my stick pen
And the silence round my gong when I am no more,
And until then the muffled ring of my verse
As old age softens the pad that gongs my hearse.

22 May 2023

2
Time's Up

As a boy I went to a lake in the Forest,
Fairmead's Connaught Waters, and walked round its edge,
Listening for nightingales in the wood,
Watching swans float sedately near the sedge.
I'd dip my fishing-net and catch tadpoles,
And look for newts to put in my jamjar,
And when I got back to the ticket hut
For the long-gone rowing-boats at the roadside bar,
I would gaze at the half-dozen boats being rowed
Among the ducks, mallards and coots I'd fed
And hear a voice call from a megaphone,

"Come in, number three," for its time was up, it said.
Now as I stand by the lake at eighty-three
A voice calls, "Come in, time's up" – to and for *me*.

17, 21 May 2023

8. 'Bar', "a sandbank at the mouth of a harbour or estuary" (*Concise Oxford Dictionary*), here the sandbank between Rangers Road and the beginning of the curved lake.

3
Waiting: Legacy

I am waiting as on a boat to be called
And occupy myself by describing
How an old man busies himself and reflects
On what has happened in decades of writing.
I am waiting, and do not know how long,
I put that out of my mind and keep busy
By seeing books through from outlines into bookshops
And studying the people who are near me.
The elderly are all in a waiting-room,
Constructively passing the time with each aging breath
Until one has a fall and is taken to hospital
And another is beckoned at night by hooded Death.
And I boom out new works and carry on
With the legacy I will leave after I've gone.

25, 29 May 2023

4
Everything Helps

I have a legacy to leave behind
Of conclusions I've drawn from my memory hoard.
First everything that happens helps later on:
A youthful job as gardener before going abroad
Gave me a knowledge of plants and lifelong skills
That would help me when I ran gardens and set their rules;
And my son's student job in a computer firm
Has been valuable now he's in charge of four schools.
Whatever happens may seem a trial at the time

But gives experience that enables progress,
Brings wisdom and know-how for later life.
So I'm grateful for the shocks I've had and their mess
As they've helped me do what I've done and brought new powers
Just as stinging rain and sweltering heat grow flowers.

25 May, 8 June 2023

5
A Robot's View of my Works 1

Now I'm thinking of artificial intelligence,
AI, and how a robot that's been Zeused
Can assess our entire life's work within seconds;
And of the Great Reset (co-introduced
By King Charles) that will control human minds
And turn them into State robots. I've read
That ChatGPT has devoured all Shakespeare's works
In seconds and answered at once, as if the godhead,
That he's the third-equals-greatest polymath
In history (below da Vinci and Einstein,
Equal with Newton). Now I can submit my works
Not to the Muses but a man-made machine with no spine
That will rate me and rank me among my peers.
But no godbots can judge my works better than Muses' ears.

27 May, 8 June 2023

2. 'Zeused', 'turned into a replica of the god Zeus'.
4. King Charles III when Prince Charles co-introduced the Great Reset with Klaus Schwab on 4 June 2020.
14. 'Godbots', 'robots that replicate gods'.

6
A Robot's View of my Works 2

My robot has access to billions of books in seconds,
And has judged my gong, now boomed with a padded stick;
A powerful AI tool looking at my knowledge
And how my works fit into the tradition's rhetoric.
Now Bard has read ten million of my words
And sees me as "a cross-disciplinary

Man of letters and polymath", "a significant
Figure in contemporary literature and philosophy"
With a vocabulary larger than Milton's or Shakespeare's,
"A writer of wide-ranging interests" whose "work
Has the potential to influence future generations
Of cross-disciplinary thinkers and polymaths". I smirk,
All this from a robot, an advanced machine
With a more balanced view than any human's I've seen.

27 May, 5 June 2023

9. See note for line 14 of 'A Rewarding Life' (no.11), for a word count of Nicholas Hagger's vocabulary.

7
In the Now

I sit with sea asters around my feet,
And daisies blowing on green grass beyond
In wind that gusts my arms and ruffles my hair,
In strong sunshine until I next abscond.
I am in the now, the moment, and not removed
From it in concentration at my desk, from murk
Looking down on the sea where waves curl in
At high tide, company as I do my work.
In Arcady I go to this other world,
And come to and interact with birds and flowers
From time to time, and so it is in Cornwall:
I leave the here and now, and work for hours.
I gaze at gulls hovering on the wind, and vow
While I work on my legacy I'll live more in the now.

29 May 2023

8
A Remarkable Life

I had a remarkable life. I lived through the war,
For its last two years in Churchill's constituency,
Was twice bombed, used to run round earth-walled Loughton Camp
(Fortified by Caesar) in Epping Forest freely.
I went to a school I later bought and, aged seven,

Experienced the Oneness of the universe, awed
Became a poet at seventeen and drank
From Horace's Bandusian spring, went to Oxford,
Read Law and changed to English Literature,
Wed, went to Iraq, was a Professor in Japan,
Taught the Emperor's son and found I was on
A Mystic Way, first glimpsed the Light – began;
Discovered China's Cultural Revolution, then my life
Changed: I ran a *coup* in Libya – and lost my wife.

29, 30 May, 1 June 2023

9
An Extraordinary Life

I had an extraordinary life. In Libya
I was asked to become a British spy
And faced my executioner one long night.
I visited Ezra Pound, in London became my
PM's Ambassador to the African
Liberation movements, and was tailed till, fraught,
I had a full illumination, and left.
I was told I must be invisible, I taught,
Re-wed and wrote poems; as a small publisher
I was told my books could only have limited
Publicity so I got out and bought a school,
Became the writer I'd left Law to be, instead.
At the end of my Mystic Way I brought out all
My poems and an epic, and bought Tudor Otley Hall.

29, 30 May, 1 June 2023

10
A Fulfilled Life

And then my life was fulfilled, everything I had done
Seemed to lead to what happened next, like a tree that fountains,
That's been through buds and blossom and now with new powers
Grows fruit: books within the seven-branched disciplines
And the seven offshoots from the branch of literature.
I grew sixty books, Universalist works

On the unity of the universe and humankind,
Twenty-five civilisations with future perks
In a World State, the fundamental theme
Of world literature, a new epic, and announcing
(With my new powers feeding me) the algorithm
For the first-ever Theory of Everything:
Nought equals plus A plus minus A equals nought.
My mind received these works that my Muses brought.

30 May, 1 June 2023

13. In its algebraic form, 0 = +A + –A = 0.

11
A Rewarding Life

I had a rewarding life. I won awards
Presented in Manila and Moscow for
The Universal State of the Earth I chaired
In, a united world that would help the poor.
I received a coat of arms from the then Garter
After writing a masque about the future King.
And while all this was going on I grew
A group of four schools that were in demand and would bring
Offers that would leave me living in comfort
To complete my legacy as a lifelong author.
And my grandson asked the large AI tool Bard
About my works and was told I'm "a significant figure
In contemporary literature and philosophy",
With a larger-than-Milton's-and-Shakespeare's vocabulary.

30 May, 2, 3, 6 June 2023

14. According to AI Bard, based on more than 10 million of his words, Nicholas Hagger's vocabulary of different words is 22,929; Milton's 20,484; and Shakespeare's 17,683. An adjustment for frequency of different words ranks in the same order: 17,462; 15,896; and 14,783.

12
Sent Down with a Message by the Light

And during this fulfilled and rewarding life
I had ninety-five experiences of the Light

And another twenty-seven of the oval cloud,
And perhaps others I have overlooked, all at night,
As the Light of my full illumination has driven
Me from when I first glimpsed the One from my starry town
When still a child, and knew new powers were at hand.
As I look back I wonder if I was sent down
To earth before the war to experience V-1s
And V-2s and bombs blowing out windows
So I could work for peace by proposing a World
State that would include all humankind in repose.
I wonder, was I meant to listen for bombs to cease
In bed aged four, to bring in an age of peace?

30 May, 2, 3 June 2023

2. For the dates of Nicholas Hagger's 95 experiences of the Light excluding the 27 experiences of the oval cloud see Nicholas Hagger, *The Promised Land*, pp.209–215, and see p.xxviii. Also see p.89, note 14.

10. This took place in the garden of 24 Ollards Grove, Loughton (see Nicholas Hagger, *My Double Life 1: This Dark Wood*, p.43).

13
A Providential Life

From an early age I was aware of my destiny,
Of being nudged by Providence towards my goal, my rule.
So many times I was shown my future path:
I fell off a bus at the foot of the hill of my school,
Which I would buy, I was taught Nature there,
And when I was just six Addison urged me to spend
A book token on *The Observer's Book of Trees*.
I was steeped in classics, Homer and Virgil (my friend),
And I played cricket for Buckhurst Hill, a name that meant
A 'hill wood for a stag' with seven-branched antlers
(My seven branches of literature and seven disciplines).
Ricks introduced me to social satire's slurs.
And I worked with Tomlin, Eliot's 'high priest',
And Nishiwaki, who wrote out the wisdom of the East.

30 May, 2, 3 June 2023

5. Mabel Reid, the co-owner of Oaklands, was influenced by Friedrich Froebel, who invented the Kindergarten and taught closeness to Nature and awareness of the unity of the universe.

6–7. William Addison kept his bookshop in Loughton High Road, and in May 1945 had just finished his *Epping Forest: Its Literary and Historical Associations*.

10. See note on pp.76–77 for the original meaning of 'Buckhurst Hill'.

12. 'Slur', "an imputation of wrongdoing; blame" (*Concise Oxford Dictionary*).

13. E.W.F. Tomlin wrote *T.S. Eliot: A Friendship* on some 100 letters he received from Eliot, during a friendship of 34 years, and he arranged for Nicholas Hagger to visit Eliot when on leave, but Eliot died before this could happen.

14. Nishiwaki wrote out +A + −A = 0 (see Nicholas Hagger, *My Double Life 1: This Dark Wood*, p.186), the basis for the algorithm in Nicholas Hagger's Theory of Everything in *The Algorithm of Creation*.

14
A Providential Life and the Light

And my colleague Blyth sent me to meditate
Among Zen seekers, set me on my Mystic Way.
I found my way to the Light in inward Japan
And was in my Dark Night of the Soul in Tripoli's bay
Where I was stripped of my family and pared down so
I would be compelled to find a room in London
On the same floor as a mystic who mentored me
Despite cramped living to full illumination
In that hostel that served breakfast in the basement.
My old Headmistress asked, would I buy my old school, please,
Where I'd been grounded in Nature by its aquarium,
My bird diary and learning about trees.
These and many more Providential nudges took me
To my fulfilling Light and my destiny.

30 May, 2, 3 June 2023

7. The mystic was Margaret Riley.

15
Providence's Deep Mystic Way, Unitive Vision,

Baroque and Universalism

Throughout my Mystic Way I had guidance
From outside, through my centre-shift from my ego
To a deeper self, my soul, and thence forward
To instinctive unitive vision and inner flow.
I found my way through 'The Silence' to my Baroque,
A blend of sense and spirit, of Classical
And Romantic – Ricks guided me to Tennyson –
And thence to Universalism's Babel.
I had written "I am a Universalist" in
1985 and two years on amid drones
I was told, "You've developed a universalist theory
Of world civilisations": in *The Fire and the Stones*,
Whose Introduction I received in my sleep
With new powers that came from Providence's deep.

30 May, 2, 3 June 2023

8. The Tower of Babel was built in Babylon, Iraq to reach Heaven, and all languages were spoken.
10. 'Drones', "a monotonous speech or speaker" (*Concise Oxford Dictionary*), droning conversations at the Frankfurt Book Fair.

16
Direction and Destiny:
Mission to Bring Peace to Humankind

I was shown my future direction and destiny
In regular pointers: gardening before Japan,
I was told to cut the grass in three schools
Without being told I'd own four schools, and should plan
And pay attention as I was being shown
My future by analogy. And I saw
Within this direction was my mission to bring peace,
It seemed I'd been sent down to experience war,
And had worked for intelligence among 'terrorists'
To grasp nationalism leads to wars that spread

And reject it and research modern and past
Civilisations and see them emerge ahead
Into a peaceful World State with a world government
And world constitution to shape humankind's ascent.

30 May, 3 June 2023

17
There is a Providence: Fulfilling our Destiny

There is a Providence. We all have a direction,
But we have to find it, and there are guides out there,
Influences who nudge us towards our goal,
Our purpose we're here for, for which we care.
We are placed in situations and circumstances
That will fulfil our destiny and make us strong-willed,
And when we stray, we are guided back on course
So after our remarkable lives we are fulfilled
And achieve our preordained destiny
Set by Providence. Mine was wider than peace perks,
It was to embark on a long Mystic Way
And write more than sixty Universalist works
On the unity of the universe and humankind,
And leave my legacy in my archive behind.

30 May, 3 June 2023

14. Nicholas Hagger's archive is in a Special Collection kept at the Albert Sloman Library at the University of Essex.

18
Providence and Influences: Key People arrive at the Right Time

It's remarkable how key people appear
At the right time, and take us towards our goal.
I met Ricks when I knew I must escape the Law;
Colin Wilson for his books on the European soul;
Tomlin for his metaphysical philosophy;
Blyth for reshaping me as a Zen mystic;
Tuohy for his wide reading and writer's eye;
Pound for his advice on my coming epic.

And so on with other key influences.
As I found my path my life was bitty:
Lecturing abroad, my secret work, writing
For *The Times*, teaching in London, running proprietary
Schools in Essex, but I was on my Mystic Way
And had inner unity that sent me verse each day.

30 May, 3 June 2023

19
Providential Life and Works

Looking back on my works, I feel they were guided by my
Being placed in situations that led eventually
To them: when four I slept under nightly air raids,
And longed for peace; then kept a bird diary,
And my love of *Hiawatha* at this time
Prepared me for my lifelong Nature verse
Just as my youthful collecting of Roman coins
And peering at Emperors' heads led me to write my terse
Short stories; and after-lunch coffees at
Oxford with students from all disciplines
Gave me a cross-disciplinary Universalist outlook.
And then my letter to the War-Office captains
Led to lifelong restrictions on all I'd write
And my prolific output in my wilderness's Light.

31 May, 7 June 2023

8. 'Terse', "brief, concise, to the point" (*Concise Oxford Dictionary*).

20
Pattern in Episodes

Japan turned me into a writer, when
For eighteen months in sweltering heat I slow-
Wrote 'The Silence', which shows my mature sense of unity
Began in the stone garden in Kyoto.
Since then my life's had a thrust, a pattern
Which looking back I caught and put on display
In two works as thirty episodes, each
With a pair of opposites (plus A and minus A),

Covering two and a half years, and since then
Four more episodes, the last being (now known)
'Vision and Legacy', 'Conflict and Unification',
Each one in conflicting spirals as in a pine cone.
And I have found that my soul's spiralling ascent
Fulfils its Providential destiny, as was meant.

31 May, 7 June 2023

4. The stone garden was the Ryoanji Stone Garden in Kyoto.
7. The two works were *My Double Life 1: This Dark Wood* and *My Double Life 2: A Rainbow over the Hills*, both out in 2015.
8. The algebraic formula is +A + −A = 0.
10. See *The Promised Land*, p.124 for the previous two: 'Populism and Globalism' and 'Nationalism and World State'.
11. 'Vision and Legacy': the pandemic and leaving behind a legacy. 'Conflict and Unification': books on the fall of the West and the war in Ukraine (*The Fall of the West*, *The Golden Phoenix*), and the first-ever statement of a Theory of Everything in *The Algorithm of Creation*, the unification of all disciplines.
14. 'Mean', passive, "design or destine for a purpose" (*Concise Oxford Dictionary*); here "as was meant", 'as was designed or destined for a purpose'.

21
Pattern like a Pine Cone

How wonderful that much of Nature follows
Fibonacci spirals that in pine cones create
Thirteen counter-clockwise and eight clockwise spirals,
Giving a mean ratio of 1.618 –
Of mouth-to-nose, arm-to-body, elbow-
To-wrist, belly-to-feet, head-to-navel,
A perfect symmetry the algorithm
Within Nature always follows when able.
So in the same way the episodes of a full life,
Each lasting two and a half years, numbering
Some thirty to forty, are in a pattern all
Within the unified universe are following.
In each episode spiral conflicts between soul
And ego are reconciled so we remain whole.

31 May, 7 June 2023

4. 1.618, pronounced 'one point six one eight'. Fibonacci, in his *Liber Abaci* (1202), introduced a sequence of numbers, each of which is the sum of

the last two: 0, 1, 1, 2, 3, 5, 8, 13, 21, 34, 55, 89, 144, 233, 377 and so on, a mechanism in Nature that implements proportion. See Nicholas Hagger, *My Double Life 1: This Dark Wood*, pp.xxvii–xxx.

22
Hermit in the Wilderness

I sought a desert wilderness in Iraq,
Where sands round Baghdad blew into my 'office'
(Bedroom window), and also in Libya,
Whose Sahara was like the desert at Scetis
Where Christian hermits and mystics evolved
Their souls without town living's bustling to and fro.
And so I have felt at home in St Catherine's
Monastery in Egypt and on Jordan's Mount Nebo,
Bethany near where John the Baptist's voice
Cried from the wilderness of his desert cave to all,
And Wadi Rum, drawn to each as an ascetic.
In such places I have heard the wilderness call
To unitive living, and there a soul can dwell
And grow like the desert palms round Ghadames' well.

31 May, 7 June 2023

14. The well is a spring as old as the Great Pyramid, c.2600BC. See Nicholas Hagger, 'Ghadames Spring (Poems like Bubbles)', *Collected Poems*, p.138. 'Ghadames' is pronounced 'Ghad-ar-miz'.

23
Shown my Future Direction and Destiny

I was shown my future direction and destiny
When I was seventeen, by Horace's spring
In Licenza, and I bent and cupping both hands
Scooped up and sipped limpid water, drinking
From the Muses' spring to confirm I would be
A poet who'd follow Horace's odes and fizz
Like him in four books of 'classical odes'.
And again when I was in the Sahara at Ghadames,
An oasis in an endless desert I'd crossed,
I found the palm-surrounded spring – changeless,
Walled in with stones as old as the Great Pyramid –

And watched its bubbles wobble to the surface.
I knew each inspiring bubble was a poem I'd write
And saw my next fifty years as receiving their Light.

31 May, 7 June 2023

7. Nicholas Hagger's *Classical Odes* have four books of odes like Horace's four-book *Odes*.
8. Nicholas Hagger visited Horace's spring in Licenza in April 1957, and Ain el Faras spring in Ghadames in February 1970.

24
Slave of the Muses

At Ghadames I was healing my lost love
And renewing my link to the nine Muses who were ahead
And had already sent me chunks of 'The Silence',
Renewing my pact, still raw from having shed
My family and, sore, healing my hurt soul while
Watching the Muses' inspiration wobble up till gone
Like each bubble, gave myself to my Muse.
I had stuck to the path I was supposed to be on
Despite the pain that caused, of leaving the Law
And now losing my wife, and was now in the care and control
Of the Muses, working for them, receiving titles
For books in my sleep, fed bubbles they sent to their mole.
I did not realise then that the new powers they gave
Would make me their full-time scribe and willing slave.

31 May, 8 June 2023

25
Keep Going

Looking back I see the need to keep going
Regardless of what hindrances abound,
Illness or long Covid that leaves us tired.
Keep going as if there were no obstacles around,
Carry on normally, and the routine
Fends off the virus that would lay us low.
In all things expected of us, persevere.
On my coat of arms the Latin motto –

'*Fortis, perspicax, innovans, diligens*',
'Be courageous, discerning, hard-working,
Diligent' – could include '*persevera*',
Don't give in to your body, 'keep going'.
Since Japan I have kept onward to my goal,
Without rest to fulfil the destiny of my soul.

31 May, 8 June 2023

26
Doing Good

Another conclusion: as we quest for the One
And seek a metaphysical vision, we
Instinctively live in harmony with all,
Spread kindness and try to do good like a shading tree.
If we're employers, we should be compassionate.
We should provide stability for all
In our local region as for forty years
I have done through my schools, and we need to care for and enthral
All those who work for or assist our cause.
We should receive wisdom and understanding
Through our reason and our intuition
From the Oneness of the universe, that bring
With them a duty to do good and be kind
And help all who are less fortunate in mind.

31 May, 8 June 2023

8. 'Enthral', "please greatly" (*Concise Oxford Dictionary*).

27
Family and All We Knew

Another conclusion concerns the family.
Families create social stability,
And all within a family should be there
For each other, help or be helped immediately.
We need to embody the good for our families.
We live in accordance with our destiny's yelp
(When we have identified what it is)
And must stay the course to fulfil it with the help

Of our family, through which we replicate ourselves.
Our centre-shift from selfish to selfless mind
Is reflected in our kindness to our family
And also to unified humankind.
We are here to benefit others as we grow
And fulfil our destiny: family and all we know.

31 May, 8 June 2023

6. 'Yelp', "a sharp shrill cry of or as of a dog in pain or excitement" (*Concise Oxford Dictionary*). Here 'destiny's yelp', 'the pain or excitement of living with our destiny' (as destiny can involve both pain and excitement at different times or at the same time).

28
England and Europe

I have reached the conclusion that England has been part
Of the European civilisation and Christian Light
First since Julius Caesar, then since Augustine
The missionary's link to the Popes, and, despite
Henry the Eighth's split with Rome, part of Europe's
Culture through two world wars and many hates;
And that the EU has been good for peace
And is drawing together fifty regional states
Rooted in Greek democracy and the Enlightenment.
I've lived through the decline of ten European empires' sway
And decolonisation, and after the EU's calm,
See the prospect of the break-up of the UK
Into a Federation of the British Isles.
We need to return to Europe and renew our smiles.

31 May, 8 June 2023

10. Nicholas Hagger's 'Old Man in a Circle' was about the decline of 10 European empires before Europe passed into the European Union (see Nicholas Hagger, *Collected Poems*, pp.116–128).

29
The West in Decline

Another conclusion: the West is in decline
And power's shifting to the East. Just as the pressed

Athenian and Roman Empires declined
After plagues – typhoid and smallpox – the West
Went into accelerated decline after Covid.
It has fallen from its height before World War One,
Printing money to get through Covid has released
Inflation, and Covid's replaced the sun-
-ny old world and freedom of movement with borders.
Covid broke in Wuhan, but its origin and spring
Was in Baric's gain-of-function research
In US labs, with Pentagon funding.
The West has brought about its own Covid pain
And's provoked the draining war in Ukraine.

31 May, 8 June 2023

Title See Nicholas Hagger's *The Fall of the West* for a full account of the West's decline.

30
The Light of the World

The central idea of the European
And North-American civilisations – the West –
Was the Light of the World, and the seventeenth-century
Churches reminded of the spiritual past and quest
That would lead to the Mystic Way and illumination,
To the soul's encounter with the Light behind
Closed eyes in prayer, how awakening would lead
To purgation, how it would cleanse the mind,
And, after Dark Nights of the Soul and Spirit,
To unitive vision and metaphysical living.
Now the Light of the World's weakened, all's now outer
(TVs, phones, PC games). Standards are falling,
Behaviour and honesty have collapsed, depth's gone,
And the Light is now seen as rarely as a swan.

31 May, 8 June 2023

31
Renaissance Man

The Renaissance man was at home in many
Disciplines in the arts and sciences like Leonardo
Da Vinci or Michelangelo, but also had
A knowledge of the Light like Ficino.
Today's world is superficial, few have delved
Or read widely, relying on headlines
From the internet, and see the disciplines
And branches of literature as distant pines,
Recognised from the outside but dark within.
For more than seventy years I have read widely
And detect the shallowness of today's news,
And its lack of joining-up that's cross-disciplinary.
I look at a fragmented world with Schwab's AI,
And a World State for all humankind seems pie in the sky.

31 May, 8 June 2023

13. Klaus Schwab of the World Economic Forum introduced the Great Reset, in which the boundaries between humans and AI machines will be blurred, with (then) Prince Charles on 4 June 2020. (See 'A Robot's View of my Works 1', note 4, lines 4–6.)

32
Old Age

I am old, but at eighty-four I carry on
Like Tennyson's Ulysses, still strong in will, slick,
But I don't know how long I can keep beating
This gong with my muffled and muzzled padded stick.
Old age makes us slow and frail, but I stick to my task
Of finishing my legacy before it's too late,
Of getting my work done and drawing attention
To a universal plight – our civilisation's great
Light replaced by AI and the prospect
That all will become slaves with chips in their brains
And obediently troop off for ten-hour shifts, their minds
Controlled by their masters' remote electronic chains.

I look out from old age and see clearly:
I'm leaving a world that needs my legacy.

31 May, 8 June 2023

2. 'Slick', "skilful or efficient; dextrous" (*Concise Oxford Dictionary*).

33
Booming Out

My legacy, "a gift left in my will",
Bequeathing my finished works to a new era
Of readers who don't buy books or read at length
Or in depth, that use phones and social media,
Is less a gift, more finishing this work
And booming it out as I've boomed out sixty-five years
Of poems, fifty years of which were muzzled.
But I've managed a Renaissance man's output that steers
Through seven disciplines and seven paths of literature
In over sixty books, and have stated my case.
I'm now at the mercy of counsel and judge in a coming
Last Judgment by the Muses' AI I must face.
I am old but will boom out this fortieth volume
Which may be my last before I lie in my tomb.

31 May, 8 June 2023

1. 'Legacy', "a gift left in a will; something handed down by a predecessor" (*Concise Oxford Dictionary*).
8. 'Steer', "guide a vessel or vehicle in a specified direction" (*Concise Oxford Dictionary*).

34
Providential Light and New Powers

Ninety-five experiences of the Light
Kept these veins clear so my healthy head construes,
And another twenty-seven of my oval cloud
Have kept me in touch with my soul that channels my Muse.
When I see the Light my brain's in reception mode,
As still as a puddle reflecting the sun,
And what I receive is transmitted, like the answer

To a Brain-of-Britain question that floats in from the One
As does a radio wave, to be received.
I had new powers during my Mystic Way
That know how the universe began and how
It will end, and its algorithm that's like a ray,
A wave of information transmitted to a radio,
And I open these powers and receive the Light's glow.

31 May, 8 June 2023

1. The 95 experiences of the Light are listed with their dates in chronological order in Nicholas Hagger's *The Promised Land*, pp.209–213. See p.xxviii for the 27 experiences of the oval cloud. Also see p.89, note 14.
2. 'Construe', "interpret, analyse" (*Concise Oxford Dictionary*).
8. Thomas (Tom) Dyer, who won the BBC radio general knowledge quiz in 1976, told Nicholas Hagger that the answers floated into his mind from a Universal Mind (see Nicholas Hagger, *My Double Life 2: A Rainbow over the Hills*, pp.98–99).

35
Polymath

As I look back I ask: 'What's been more important to me,
To take each of seven disciplines as far as they'll go –
Full illumination, one Light, the fundamental theme
Of world literature, my Universalist 'rainbow'
Theory of Everything, my law of history
For twenty-five civilisations' rise and fall,
My World State and unified world culture – or
The seven branches of literature I've practised in, all
As a man of letters trying every genre?'
The answer is: 'All fourteen make a pattern,
And I go with them all, and don't favour one. But round
The lot's my polymath container. I reckon
I've seen new things within the universe before
Disciplines, literature. Being a polymath's more.'

31 May, 9 June 2023

4. Nicholas Hagger's Theory of Everything is a 'rainbow' because the universe begins and ends with a particle, and its rise and fall are shaped like a rainbow.
14. 'More', i.e. more important.

36
End of Life

How will it be, when my life draws to an end?
I think of my regression to a past life
As a Jesuit priest, sent out to New Brunswick
And then dying of cholera, looked after by a 'wife'.
I relived my death, the transition was so peaceful,
I breathed in and then out, and then breathed no more.
I saw a grave-digger, a logger in braces.
I was thirty-three, and on my tombstone I saw
'John Barfield, died 1836.' I had come
From the Vale of Esthwaite in Wordsworth's prime.
If I *had* relived my death and it wasn't a dream,
I have nothing to fear when it's at last my time.
The end of life is not the end of the soul,
And breathing our last is a painless return to our goal.

31 May, 9 June 2023

3–4. For Nicholas Hagger's regression in Norwich on 2 and 31 August 1978 to a past life as a Jesuit priest, John Barfield (Abbé), dying of cholera in a log-cabin in New Brunswick, while being looked after by Esmé, who wore a white bonnet, see Nicholas Hagger, *My Double Life 2: A Rainbow over the Hills*, pp.73–76.

37
Death

From my study window I see Arcady
Stretching to Henry the Eighth's third hunting
Lodge within a great sweep of Epping Forest,
And I wonder if this will be where I do my dying.
I know my removal from life will be
An entry into what is to come, a place
Like my epics' descriptions of Heaven, with green fields,
Sunshine and a great calm, where I will face
My past and will go forward and dwell amid Light
And meet my Muses and sit with Shakespeare,
And discuss how I was sent down with a mission.
I may be buried in Waltham Abbey near

King Harold, lord of my Lochetuna, or
In the Forest churchyard my elegy foresaw.

31 May, 9 June 2023

2–3. 'Third hunting lodge'. The third hunting lodge, built in 1540–1543, is now called Queen Elizabeth's hunting lodge, and is on the outskirts of Chingford. (See note on pp.76–77 for Henry VIII's three hunting lodges.)

7. See Nicholas Hagger, *Overlord*, bk.12; and *Armageddon*, bk.12.

13. In the Anglo-Saxon time Loughton was named Lukintone (Luhha's estate). It was listed in the 1086 Domesday Book as Lochintuna or Lochetuna. Harold Godwinson, later King Harold II, became lord of the manor of Loughton and owned much of its land after he re-founded Waltham Abbey, having built its third church. He was killed at the Battle of Hastings and reputedly buried in Waltham Abbey, under the altar of the third church (which is now outside the Abbey, under grass).

14. See Nicholas Hagger's *Collected Poems* for his tenth elegy 'High Beach Church' (1974); revised as 'A Crocus in the Churchyard' (1980); and also 'Two Variations on One Theme' (1972, 1980). These three poems can be found in Nicholas Hagger, *Collected Poems*, pp.229–230; 425–426; and 431–432.

38
Postscript, Gratitude: 23 Sonnets Sent Through in a Day

A postscript to my poem on death, today
I received and as an amanuensis wrote down
Twenty-two sonnets to end this volume, although
Eighty-four, channelled in eleven hours from my crown.
And now I am drafting a twenty-third to record
This feat of 322 lines I'll have done today.
My Muses wanted this volume done, and I've boomed
My gong twenty-three times on the last day of May.
I am grateful to you Muses and Angels.
Although I've been your slave for what you've sent through
I've willingly written down the words you've just sent
In a kind of 'automatic writing' Blake knew.
I'm grateful for our collaboration for sixty years
And on my deathbed will be gratitude, not tears.

31 May, 9 June 2023

4. The eleven hours were between 11am and 10pm on 31 May 2023.

6. 322, pronounced 'three-two-two'.

7. 'My Muses wanted this volume done.' On 28 May 2023 Nicholas Hagger finished volume 38 in Cornwall, see note 1 on p.198. The Muses' urgency on 31 May 2023 to get volume 40 finished in Cornwall as well, and volume 39 finished on 10 June 2023, was as if they had foreknowledge of the event that would happen on 11 June 2023, see volume 41, which would require Nicholas Hagger to travel regularly to and from first Ipswich, then Norwich.

39
Knowing my End

Ever since I was a child I have often thought
I would be all right until I'm eighty-six.
Why such a deadline should rise in my mind
I don't know, but at eighty-four I'm now in a fix,
Hastening to complete my literary works
And boxing up my archive. It makes sense:
Making an end, ending with some control
Rather than being overtaken by events.
I hope to reach ninety-six without a stroke
Or heart attack that will make me an invalid.
If I do, getting my work done will seem unnecessary,
Though an end-of-life tidy won't be wasted.
If I don't, I will be proved right, and how
Wonderful to have known my life's end was always: now.

5 June 2023

2. Nicholas Hagger would be 86 on 22 May 2025, when the next pandemic was forecast to be underway (see Nicholas Hagger, *The Fall of the West*, p.43).

40
Looking Back on my End

Forty volumes and in my fortieth volume
A final fortieth poem to look back on my end
As I approach (I sense) the last two years of my life,
But hope for a posthumous 'add-on' godsend.
My robot, Bard, wants me to upload the text
For my Theory of Everything, so it can assess
My legacy in that work, which will boom out
Like a gong, as will these last poems I accresce
In anticipation of my coming end.

In my works I saw from before the Big Bang's fires
To the last glow of the end of the universe
And, in between, the Light within that inspires
Seeing the Oneness of the universe
And all disciplines, as my works gong out and disperse.

6 June 2023

8. 'Accresce', "accrue"; 'accrescence', "continuous growth"; 'accrescent', "growing continuously" (*Shorter Oxford English Dictionary*).

14. 'Disperse', "send, drive, or distribute in different directions over a wide area" (*Concise Oxford Dictionary*).

Volume 41

AGONY IN ARCADY: STROKE
2023–2024

A tribute to the heroic endurance of "a fair maid".
(See 'Suffolk Fair Maid')

'Stroke', "noun, a sudden disabling attack or loss of consciousness caused by an interruption in the flow of blood to the brain, especially through thrombosis; apoplexy (blockage of a brain artery); verb transitive, pass one's hand gently along the surface of hair etc., caress lightly" (*Concise Oxford Dictionary*).

1
Blood Clot

The phone rings after I've dished my supper.
Something terrible's happened, your mother has said,
You've been taken to hospital with the worst kind of stroke
For damage, a blood clot at the back of your head,
And you're not speaking or understanding, just crying.
Only one of your four brain arteries is working.
She went round and found parcels on your floor
And a note, "I think I've had a stroke," in your handwriting:
"I can't use my left arm. Sunday, 10.45."
You were lying on a floor, groaning; you may have been there
Since Sunday morning's delivery, now it's Monday.
She called an ambulance and took you to hospital, where
They've said it's the worst kind of stroke. May the Angels, I mime,
Look after you and bring you through this traumatic time.

12, 25 June 2023

13. 'Mime', "convey (an idea or emotion) by gesture without words" (*Concise Oxford Dictionary*).

2
Brain Stem, Locked-In

You are sitting up and lying back, still, in
The hospital ward and I sit beside you, and frown.
You're asleep, blow bubbles. Your heart rate is low.
I heal you, four massive surges up my back, down
My right arm to your wrist, and jolt as from CPR.
Now your heart rate's normal. Your mother arrives then,
With a stick. I say, "Open your eyes if you
Can hear your mum," and briefly your eyes open.
Each time I say "Open your eyes if" you comply –
You can hear me, though locked-in as if in a chamber
From a massive stroke in your right cortex and brain stem.
A very severe stroke, says a young doctor,
Has affected your breathing, after such a stroke none live,
And the next two days will be crucial, it was so massive.

13, 25 June 2023; 30 April, 1 May 2024

5. 'CPR', cardiopulmonary resuscitation.

3
Nightmare

I was blind-sided, you were our carer.
If only I could have rung you just before
You had your stroke, and have changed the course of events.
What happened? Three blocked arteries, and you on the floor.
How was your brain damaged, how did no one find you?
This is a future for all who live alone,
A massive stroke, and lying on the floor
For twenty-four hours, groaning but no one hearing a moan.
It's a nightmare. I'm in a nightmare now,
Wanting to heal you, but much of your brain's gone.
I look at your eyes opening and closing
With fixed pupils, and hope there's recognition.
I'm so sad and feel powerless to help when you're distressed
Except channel more healing, and hope for the best.

14, 26 June 2023

4
Postponing

The Friday before, you were full of vitality.
My five-minute call became half an hour, you were well,
Adamant you wanted to see me the day before
Father's Day, you'd booked at a local hotel
Next to Henry the Eighth's third hunting lodge
So we'd have time together before the family gathering.
You're still 'unconscious' in your locked-in world,
And now I have to cancel your booking.
No one will say 'Open your eyes if…' till I'm next there.
We have a bond, when you were three or four
And we were in Japan we walked every day,
And now I'm afraid you soon may be no more.
You booked the hotel from your account, I hear,
So there's no refund, just postponing until next year.

14, 26 June 2023

5. 'Third'. Henry VIII's third hunting lodge, built between 1540 and 1543, was on the outskirts of Chingford and is now known as Queen Elizabeth's hunting lodge. (See the note on pp.76–77 for Henry VIII's three hunting lodges.)

5
Limbo

I walk you to your wedding in your bridal gown
In your framed wedding pictures in my room.
You smile broadly, I did all the paying
And you were soon happy with your star groom.
Now both of you gaze into each other's eyes.
He's been dead nearly four years, and you're in a limbo
Between life and death, able to move your eyelids
And little else, with erratic breathing that's slow.
There were happy times in your life, but to me you were
An eyewitness in Japan when I first saw
The Light, which I poured into you when you lay
Suspended between life and death above your ward's floor.
It's as if Ian's reclaimed you to join him once more
And I'm pulling you back from your limbo in a tug of war.

14, 27, 30 June 2023

4. 'Star groom'. Nadia married the keyboard player Ian Gibbons on 10 July 2008.
6. Ian died on 1 August 2019, aged 67.

6
Quadriplegic

The doctor's spent an hour examining you
And has said you've a blind spot to your left in your sight.
Because the nerves connect to the brain stem
Your vision's impaired, you can only see on the right.
You're holding your own at your chest, but you have
Decreased consciousness, you can't turn your head,
You've no movements in your arms and legs, from your neck down,
You're at present quadriplegic, he's said.
You're locked into a paralysed body.
During his examination you were distressed
"As you may have been aware of your predicament" –
Or was it because of saliva on your chest?
Daughter, there's a long haul ahead, don't be surprised:
Weeks, months and years of being paralysed.

14 June, 1 July 2023

8. 'Quadriplegia', "(medical) paralysis of all four limbs" (*Concise Oxford Dictionary*).

7
Deep Sleep

The next forty-eight hours will be critical,
A junior doctor told me yesterday.
I visit you twenty-four hours later,
You are in a much deeper sleep, far away,
Your head turned on its side, tubes from your nose.
But your heart rate and blood pressure are more
Stable, a cause for hope, and you don't stir.
Al says the forty-eight hours of your body's war
Will end tomorrow afternoon, and there'll be
A structured meeting between medics and family.
"You should be there, we will set out the future."
But by then the future may be clearer as, more drowsy,

You may sink into a far deeper sleep
From which I can't rouse you – I want to weep.

14 June, 1 July 2023

8
Project

Your solicitor rings about the bungalow
You've exchanged on and are completing on Friday, your project.
I ask if we can postpone completion a week.
She says she can ask but cannot insist. I reflect.
I ask for the law. She says, "If she's alive,
She's committed to completing, and any delay
Will result in interest on the final payment.
If she's not alive, she won't be committed to pay.
I'm not sure if the deposit can be refunded."
I say it's a shell now. She says, "I reckon
The property market is such that many will buy
A shell and do it up to their satisfaction."
So now I wait to hear if the doctors will say
You will be alive and able to move in one day.

14 June, 1 July 2023

9
Pneumonia

Your bed has gone, I ask where you are now.
You're in the room next door, lying on your side.
I sit with you as, in an oxygen mask,
You gasp for breath – still unconscious, shut-eyed,
Not sedated but not having come round since your stroke –
And despite four litres of oxygen a minute, heave.
You're struggling to breathe, and I hear you wheeze,
Aspirational pneumonia, I believe.
Half your brain's gone, and though you seem yourself
You may be in a vegetative state,
Blind, deaf and unable to live with any
Meaningful quality of life, a fate you'd hate.

If you can't get off oxygen, may you not choke,
Suffer more shut-downs and another crippling stroke.

15 June, 11 July 2023

10
Not Long to Live

A doctor gives us a briefing in his room.
He shows a CT scan from above of your skull
And a shaded area where the blood clot blocked
Veins and damaged your functions as in a cull,
And there can be a haemorrhagic transformation.
He shows your lungs and I see a shaded grey
Area where you may be struggling to breathe.
He says from all he's shown you won't die today
Or tomorrow, but after that it could be soon.
O my daughter, you have been so kind, and now
Unconscious and (he says) uncommunicative
You're being kept alive by oxygen and drip somehow,
And (he says) your stroke's been assessed as being severe,
So you're 'Do not resuscitate' – and I'm filled with fear.

15 June, 1 July 2023

2–5. The diagnosis was: right occipital temporal lobe and internal capsule infarcts. In other words, an ischaemic stroke with clots blocking three arteries and causing brain cells to die rather than a haemorrhagic stroke caused by a burst or ruptured artery to the brain, although this could still happen.

11
Reunited

I see blood on your elbow, and think you must
Have fallen when you had your stroke and wrote
"I can't use my left arm" and put a time
That Sunday morning, which the hospital would note.
It was said it helped with their diagnosis.
If I had been with you when you fell, the outcome
Would have been the same, it was not your fall but the stroke
That left you unconscious and your limbs numb.
I think your husband's come back to reclaim you.

He didn't want you moving to your new home
And took you back to join him in the next world.
I wonder if you are nearly with him and roam
With the baby you nearly had and never fed,
And the three of you are nearly reunited.

15 June, 2 July 2023

12
Eyewitness: Bungalow

You were an eyewitness of a time I was shaping
The self I would become. When I carried you,
Aged eleven months, from the plane in Japan
And a reception committee, spruced up in a queue,
Of four professors greeted me on the tarmac
In tails, and a professor shook your hand,
You were sick on his sleeve. You accompanied me
On so many walks to Edogawa bridge to stand
Above the canal during the afternoons,
And when I wrote 'The Silence' you came in
To my study and sat on my knee as, in great heat,
I wrote down words on my centre-shift near your chin.
You were in our bungalow when I first saw Light in my head,
And tomorrow you buy your own bungalow from your bed.

15 June, 2 July 2023

14. Nadia had already exchanged contracts on a bungalow, and completion had been arranged for 16 June 2023.

13
Communication: Howl

It's the day before Father's Day, I'm given your gift,
Your present to me tomorrow, *Shakespeare's Book*,
Which sees the First Folio (400th anniversary
This year) and the links that gave it its final look
From the Stratfordian point of view – as ever, you know
What will interest me and spoil me with something I like.
I find a nurse stooping over you, and you're more alert.
I say, "It's your dad," and reel as if from a strike

As you cry aloud, howl, wail. Tears fill your eyes.
I talk to you soothingly and say, "Matthew's here.
Open your eyes." You do. "If you can see him, close them, then
Open your eyes again." And you do. You've said Yes, I cheer.
I tell a nurse that you can communicate,
But your howl and wail continue to resonate.

17 June, 2 July 2023

10. Matthew. Nicholas Hagger's eldest son.

14
Crying

I tell you, "Tony's here, open your eyes twice
If you can see him and recognise his face."
And you open your eyes twice in communication.
I say, "You're in hospital after what happened at your place
And the note you wrote about having had a stroke,
Which was helpful, and you're doing well, it's no surprise.
I came on Tuesday, Wednesday and Thursday
And today you're doing better. Open your eyes
If you understand what I've said." And you do.
And I say we're going to collect the key to your new
Home from your mother and go there. You are tearful.
"And on Father's Day we'll raise our glasses to you.
Thanks again for your gift." You cry more as if to say
'I can't live in my house and will miss Father's Day.'

17 June, 2 July 2023

1. Tony. Nicholas Hagger's second son.

15
New House

I go to your house and open the front door
And walk into two empty bedrooms, survey
The bathroom, sitting-room and kitchen, unlock
The back door and look at the garden, and weigh:
It's all basic and stripped back to the walls,
Ready for the plastering and painting you would do
For you to live in while you got your mother

Through her hip operation in July if the queue
Permits. I wander through each room and imagine
You living here and eventually moving on
To your dream house near a duck pond you've always
Hoped you'd end up in after I have gone.
None of this may now happen, and I understand
Your crying: that I should be seeing what you planned.

17 June, 2 July 2023

16
Rose's Floor

I sip tea with my wife and my ex-wife,
And her son comes in, having pointed out how
My two sons can start your car they're driving
To our house, so it's off the road, and now
He takes me through the back garden to Rose's
Back-basement kitchen and up stairs, and we stay
In the hall by the street-level front door, and he shows
Me the door on the latch, and where you lay
And wrote your note that you had had a stroke. It seems you
Dragged yourself on your elbows back to the stairs, so frail –
Hence the congealed blood on both your rose-red arms –
And got down them using the right handrail,
And turned right to the front-basement room where
You were found on the floor, your head near the fireplace, just there.

17 June, 3 July 2023

17
Genetic Flaw

The scan shows a right-brain stroke paralysed
Your left arm after you went to your front door
And took in a delivery and wrote your note, and reached
Your brain stem downstairs when you fell on the floor,
Perhaps trying to lie on the settee and slipping down,
And you lay there for some twenty-four hours.
Would you'd called your mum from the charging phone in the hall,
Perhaps the stroke's onset befogged your powers.

Your mum's son says there's a genetic family flaw
Which you may share, of high-cholesterol 'bile'
That triggered your mum's stroke and yours as well.
He says your mum's known of the family's flaw a while.
I didn't know you were at genetic risk, along
With your mum and her son, until now, and my not knowing's wrong.

17 June, 3 July 2023

10. 'Bile', "a bitter greenish-brown alkaline fluid which aids digestion and is secreted by the liver and stored in the gall-bladder" (*Concise Oxford Dictionary*). Bile normally dissolves the cholesterol secreted by the liver, but cannot break up an overabundance of cholesterol. Here 'bile' is used metaphorically for gungy plaque.

18
Shallower Breathing

So your stroke was an inheritance on your mother's side
None of us knew until quite recently,
Which blocked three of the four arteries to your brain;
It came on as you coped with a delivery,
Perhaps of my Shakespeare book, left the kitchen workroom
And went upstairs to answer a doorbell's ring,
And created dead cells in your right brain
As your left arm and leg were paralysing.
Confused, you ignored the phone charging in the wall,
And your brain stem was affected as it spread
To all your vital functions, your sight, hearing,
Chest and heart rate, your oxygen in your head.
Now your sleep can get deeper, your breathing shallower, drop
To pneumonia's rasping gasps, then slow, then stop.

17 June, 8 August 2023

19
Despair

I am living from day to day, all the doctors
Have slightly different narratives and forecast fears
Of what will happen and when, different likely
Options, one within two or three weeks, one months or years,

One that you're locked in and can understand all that's said
And are terrified by what you overhear from nurses,
Some of whom may assume you are virtually brain-dead.
I say we must act as if all possibilities
Are actual, and rule nothing out or in,
And take each day as it comes till each premiss
Reveals itself in an actuality.
I must be ready to visit you at short notice,
If I am called, but must also be there
For you in the longer term, and possible despair.

17 June, 20 August 2023

10. 'Premiss', "a previous statement from which another is inferred" (*Concise Oxford Dictionary*).

20
Speechless

Throughout the last week you have been speechless,
Your right-brain stroke has left you unable to speak.
You won't be able to pronounce the sounds
As you've lost control of the muscles that tweak
The left side of your mouth and face, and tongue.
Perhaps your brain-stem stroke's disconnected a zone
Your speech passes through, so attempts to speak
Come out as a cry, a long despairing groan.
And you may not see through your 'left-visual field'
In each eye, and just see a part of me.
But let's be positive and see improvements.
Sleepiness and tiredness aid brain's recovery.
A severe stroke can cut your life by ten years,
But your brain is resetting, and now's not a time for tears.

17 June, 23, 24 August 2023

21
Stroking Beauty

You look so beautiful as you lie asleep,
Your fresh complexion and slim body show
How carefully you've looked after yourself. I can see

Why your husband may have come for his widow.
Yet your brain's been robbed of its control of your mouth
And throat muscles, and your eyes, and your breathing
In your chest, and so you have phlegm in your throat
And are blowing bubbles as your lungs are heaving,
And your decreased consciousness (though you can still open
Your eyes on a command) that has left you
Full of repairing sleep for perhaps two weeks,
One of which (some thought you wouldn't) you've seen through.
O my daughter I want to stroke your beautiful face
But your stroked brain wouldn't grasp my respect for your grace.

17 June, 24, 25 August 2023

14. 'Grace', "attractiveness, especially in elegance of proportion or manner or movement" (*Concise Oxford Dictionary*).

22
Living in Uncertainties

Your mum's rung with today's update. You're off
Oxygen from your mask, breathing just air,
But you were put on for last night as pneumonia's
Countered by oxygen. You still seem in despair,
You're still groaning and coughing, but your pupils
Are not moving when you open your eyes, which means
You may not be responsive and even blind.
I say the doctors have conflicting views and scenes:
Death likely soon or in months, or locked-in for years.
I say we must live with all possible fall-outs
And not see them as probables or conclusions,
But like Keats, live in uncertainties, mysteries and doubts
Without reason. We must rule nothing in or out
And accept updates without so much as a pout.

18 June, 25 August 2023

8. 'Scenes', "descriptions of incidents in real life" (*Concise Oxford Dictionary*).

12–13. Keats wrote in his letter to his brothers George and Thomas of 21 December 1817: "At once it struck me what quality went to form a Man of Achievement, especially in Literature, and which Shakespeare possessed so enormously – I mean Negative Capability, that is, when a man is capable of being in uncertainties, mysteries, doubts without any irritable reaching after fact and reason."

23
Tiredness and Quiet Despair

You walked with me every day when I was in Japan,
I saved you from a tsunami that swept away
My wedding ring, and then I lost you in Libya
And, when back, you asked me to return home and stay.
Separation from you turned me into a true poet,
Wrung anguished lines from me, and now again the same.
After a lifetime of being there for each other,
Weekly phone calls and more walks when you came,
I'm at risk of losing you to your coma
And pneumonia, and am numb waiting for going-wells,
For you to breathe on your own and have your MRI
Which will show the extent of your dead brain cells,
And whether you'll ever move your limbs and share
And I am filled with tiredness and quiet despair.

19 June, 25 August 2023

5. 'True' in the sense of 'deep', 'authentic'.

24
Banned from Seeing You

Fifty years ago I was banned from seeing you
For the rest of my life by the secret State.
I'd persuaded a Czech nuclear scientist to defect
To Britain instead of the US, who'd offered him their bait.
Your mum's second husband was taking me to court
To deny me access to you as a fantasist, he'd
Been linked to a branch of Security, and the Heads
Of MI6 and MI5 met and agreed
I could only continue my secret work if I
Signed an agreement never to see you again. Angry,
I refused to sign and my secret work ended,
And whatever I wrote would have limited publicity.
Even though the State banned us and made a vow
I'm so pleased I can keep you alive at your bedside now.

20 June, 25 August 2023

1–12. See pp.xxxii–xxxiv, and xxxvi.

7–10. In 1973 Nicholas Hagger was asked to sign an agreement banning him from ever seeing his daughter Nadia again, the idea being that this would head off a threat to disclose his work for MI6 in a custody hearing in court. He was told that the new head of MI6, Sir Maurice Oldfield, who did not marry and had no children, was behind this. (See pp.xxxii–xxxiv.)

25
Walled-In Silence

Your unconsciousness – *coma*, for your sleep deepened
Yesterday – brought back my fifty-year-long neglect
After I was finger-pointed by a new Kitchener
And tasked with getting a Czech scientist to defect
With nuclear secrets, not to the CIA.
I fended off the competition, and scrutiny
From 'Security', which lost me your mum and led
To a court being asked to block my access to you,
Then being told to sign not to see you again.
I left, and my books were then "walled-in by silence"
For fifty years, but I could still speak and write,
And now you are walled-in by an encumbrance
That forbids you to speak or move your limbs or spine
And your walled-in silence is far worse than mine.

20 June, 26, 27 August 2023

26
Coma

Your eyes were open today in a steady gaze,
But they weren't focused, and it wasn't out of choice.
Does that mean you have no sight? You opened your eyes
In reaction to a nearby commanding voice.
Did you see and hear nothing that made sense to you?
I've asked you to open your eyes twice if you can hear
And understand, and you have, and I can't believe
You opened them without understanding as if shedding a tear,
And that you've thought nothing during my monologues.
Now you're in a deep sleep, your coma again,
A trickle from your mouth: your pneumonia.
You're not in distress or pain, you had no oxygen

Last night and are ready for your MRI,
And the results will show if you're going to live or die.

20 June, 26 August 2023

13. 'MRI', see poem titled 'MRI' below, note 1.

27
MRI

You've had your MRI, and a physio
Curtains your bed, moves your arms, legs and head.
I ask for news of the findings and a doctor
Comes with a screen on a high wheeled 'desk' I dread,
And shows me images (dead brain cells) and the text.
Your stroke impacted the right side of your brain
In multiple parts, including the occipital
And temporal lobes, midbrain and pons, which explain
The impact on your limb movement and left-side
Vision in each eye, and your seizure in bed
Last night. You've had one right-side stroke affecting
Your right brain stem, your hearing's unaffected.
You're locked-in, and there's talk – rather, a confab –
Of long-term PEG-tube feeding and rehab.

21 June, 29 August 2023

1. 'MRI', magnetic resonance imaging, a type of scan that uses magnetic fields and radio waves to produce detailed images inside the body.

6–8. Cf. p.266, note to lines 2–5.

13. 'Confab', short for 'confabulation', "an informal discussion".

14. 'Rehab', short for 'rehabilitation', "restoring to effectiveness for normal life by training, etc., especially after imprisonment or illness" (*Concise Oxford Dictionary*).

28
New Spin

That's good news. We were initially told you'd had
A severe stroke in the whole of your brain stem's stalklike spur
But it seems to have been a right-brain stroke affecting
Your brain stem except for a left-sided sliver.
You've had one stroke affecting multiple parts, not two,

And so long-term measures are being considered urgently:
PEG-tube feeding into your stomach, rehab,
And now you're having active physiotherapy,
And the nurses have been told to speak to you
As you can hear everything that's said as you could at home.
But I have questions to ask of the consultant:
How do quadriplegia, locked-in syndrome
And the CT scan showing dead cells fit in
With this more detailed MRI's new spin?

21 June, 30 August 2023

2. 'Spur', 'projection'.
7. PEG, percutaneous endoscopic gastronomy, a medical procedure in which a tube is passed into a patient's stomach through the abdominal wall, to provide a means of feeding.

29
Seizure

The consultant rings with your MRI results.
You've just a sliver of sparing in your left brain stem,
The damage to your occipital lobe's narrowed your field
Of vision, you can't track movements, you can't see them;
And to your temporal lobe's left you epileptic.
You had a fit two nights ago, he leaks.
You ground your teeth and foamed – bubbled phlegm – round your lips.
He'll keep you at the hospital six to eight weeks.
Then you'll have long-term level-one care, perhaps
In a unit in Norwich, and the danger is each fit
Will leave you weaker and in a deep sleep
And your breathing may grow shallow, and your heart submit.
O my daughter, you may be quadriplegic
In a nursing home for the rest of your life, and sick.

22 June, 1, 2 September 2023

30
Melancholy

I have just heard you are prone to infection,
Your stroke has left you defenceless to disease.

Visitors could bring in germs that could kill you,
Including the physio who moves your limbs to unfreeze.
You could have another epileptic fit (or stroke),
Or be infected by a germ, and, downcast,
Fall into a coma, at the prey of your pneumonia
Which will last for weeks, and may cause you to breathe your last.
And I am overwhelmed by a world-sadness,
Your projects worked, but your being locked-out from them won't cease.
I am melancholy, and, at eighty-four,
Ready to end my writings and enjoy some peace,
Irremediably sad, and my future now seems hollow
As you linger in life and could die tomorrow.

22 June, 2 September 2023

9. 'World-sadness', cf. '*Weltschmerz*', "feeling of pessimism; an apathetic or vaguely yearning outlook on life [German *Welt* world + *Schmerz* pain]" (*Concise Oxford Dictionary*).

13. 'Irremediable', "that cannot be remedied" (*Concise Oxford Dictionary*).

31
Guard

Since you've been diagnosed as prone to infection
Visitors must be restricted to close family.
Your immune system may not cope with flu
Brought in by strangers to this ward's sanctuary.
You're as defenceless as when you were a child
And went to bed with your "rinnun", a silk ribbon
You held to your cheeks while I read you a story
Before I turned out your light, your lips silken.
I guarded your health when you were little
And now I'm doing the same as I stand guard
By your bed amid germs and medical threats,
Of your pneumonia which will last many weeks and is hard-
Pressed by your coma and your epileptic fits,
Aware I can't shield you from infection's multiple hits.

23 June, 2 September 2023

32
Level-One Rehab

There's better news, you were sat in a special chair
For half an hour, and you're off all monitoring,
And the physio's starting the paperwork
For level-one rehab in a unit coming
Up first with a vacant bed, in Norwich or Putney,
That will accept you. Now therapists will assess
Your speech and movement, and all your abilities.
They're not sure of the level of your awareness
And understanding, but the paperwork's begun,
It's no longer palliative care but a long-term plan.
It's all been exhausting and you've fallen asleep.
But they've roused you to sit for tests and have begun their scan.
It will take time, but I'm pleased I can see
A way forward, and the start of your recovery.

23 June, 3 September 2023

33
Pain

A four-hour journey through queuing traffic, I see
You lying, eyes closed, pale, breathing on your own with sighs.
I say I'm here, and you open and close your eyes.
I ask, "If you can see me, open your eyes."
You do, and groan. I say everything will be
All right, I've spoken to the doctors, you have done
Well. I say speech therapists are assessing if you
Can understand, and say, "Can you hear me? One
Opening of eyes means yes, and two mean no."
You open your eyes once, and groan. Nurse comes through
In a Muslim hood, and asks me to ask you,
"If you're in pain, open your eyes," and you do.
She pours into your drip liquid paracetamol
Between your groans, and, now tired, you sleep like a doll.

24 June, 3 September 2023

34
Drawing to a Close

I have sat in several stroke wards and have seen
How many aged struggling to breathe suffer
With pneumonia on their chest and no swallowing
Like my daughter in her stroke ward, and now her mother
Is having a hip replaced in the same hospital –
Near my Otley Hall and my cousin's Coggeshall Abbey
(Near my daughter's some-time second home) that's being sold –
And I, sad, struggling to visit and tired at eighty-
Four from my conflicts, feel my life's drawing to a close
And that I may be joining them both in a palliative ward
And may also be unresponsive to nurses' words
And, now caring for her who looked after us with such concord,
Know I must finish my works and not waste a day or fail,
And that I have to be strong but know I am growing frail.

25 June 2023

6. Otley Hall. Nicholas Hagger owned Tudor Otley Hall from 1997 to 2004, see volume 36, pp.70–71, 79 and 84.
12. 'Concord', "harmony" (*Concise Oxford Dictionary*).

35
Sleeping Beauty

I think of the Princess who fell asleep
For a hundred years, and you've been two weeks asleep
But I am like the Prince who looked at her
And wondered how he could rouse her from her deep.
I said to you earlier, "One day I hope you will say,
'Hi, Dad'," but the muscles that make you swallow and stare
Are paralysed, as is your tongue that cannot speak,
And so you must sleep on, beauty, and repair
Parts of your shattered brain, like an archaeologist
Piecing together a broken vase, make them stir
In your skull so you partially function again.
And I, the Prince who will wake you from your coma,
Wear shirts and pyjamas you bought, your gifts that make
Me remember you as I wait for you to wake.

25 June, 3 September 2023

36
Wounded Deer

You bought me so many things, and I recall
How you and Ian brought huge wrapped gifts I'm fond
Of, a bronze metal stag with antlers and a deer
Which graze near the bushes by our carp pond,
And I knew I was the stag (two seven-branched antlers
My disciplines and genres) and you were the deer.
As we grazed and fed the fish we looked at the pair.
The day of your stroke I found near the pond here
The deer lying on the grass with a snapped-off leg.
The gardener had hit it with my tractor. I found
Superglue and he stuck it together and now the pair
Are still together, the deer with a great wound.
O my daughter, keep going and we can still graze
Near the fish-pond and forget your wounded daze.

26, 27 June 2023

2. Ian Gibbons, her husband, a musician – keyboard player – who played with The Kinks (see 'Limbo', pp.263–264).

37
Recovery

You've been sitting in a chair since one (your eyes
Open three and a half hours by the time I went).
The physio comes by, and moves your arms.
She says the paperwork for rehab has been sent
To the Norwich unit that's assessing. The speech
Therapist says you're more alert, she's finding ways
To communicate with you, and she writes on the wall chart,
"Blink once, yes; Blink twice, no." All must say each phrase.
A doctor comes and tells me the PEG tube
Will be installed next week, all have agreed,
And the seizure may be ischaemic, not epileptic,
But you have oedema (fluid), a new need.
Now alone with you, I ask if you recognise me.
You blink, and I hope you've begun your recovery.

27 June 2023

9. See 'PEG' in note to line 7 on p.276.

38
Desperation: Shaken

A report from your mother, you were in bed,
Quiet, staring ahead, your left eye fixed and at rest,
Your right eye moving, the left side of your mouth drooped.
She mentioned your friend Janette, and you were distressed,
Cried out in "desperation, misery, despair",
Which she found harrowing. She tried to calm
You, fearing your distress would bring on another stroke.
She said firmly, "Stop," and you did and came to no harm.
She said, "Calm down," and you calmed; and then she wiped
Cherry blossom from your washbag on your forehead,
And you seemed to like that. She was with you for two hours.
Shaken, she left when you slept, tucked up in your bed.
Your mother's finding it hard, she's barely coping.
I have to be strong and soothe your desperate crying.

28, 30 June 2023

39
Calm

You're in a new nightdress and they've washed your hair.
You've sat in the special chair and been put into bed.
You are drowsy, you close your eyes and sleep.
Today is going to be a lighter day, the physio's said.
Then you look at me: a normal right eye, dilated left eye.
You move your head to one side, and your left arm.
I share positive memories of our walks and our fish.
You begin to wail, I soothe you with Shh, my balm,
And reassure you, say you will be all right
And lull you into a peaceful drowse, your soul.
O my daughter, I held the universe in my hand
From creation to dark, and saw it all as a whole,
But would swap this knowledge to bring you back from all harm.
I soothe you and stroke your hand, lull you into calm.

28, 29, 30 June 2023

40
Resetting

You're having your mouth swabbed and your teeth cleaned
When I arrive at your bedside. The therapist hints
You've been in the chair and are tired, but have been more calm.
She's been moving your hands, your feet are in splints.
I say you've been breathing so much better, and your lips
Are moving more, and I turn to you: "Your brain
Is resetting in sleep, the time you're asleep is good."
Jill says: "I move your hands again and again
To remind your brain to carry on what it did."
You look as if you're about to groan, I tell
You, "Each week's better than last week, all will be OK."
And I think of Julian of Norwich's "All shall be well,
And all manner of thing shall be well," and I know I trust
The universe and its power to shield us from dust.

3, 4 July 2023

4. 'Splints' are to keep the joints in place and to protect them.
12. The meaning of Julian of Norwich's "All shall be well, and all shall be well, and all manner of thing shall be well" is: "All will be well, and all manner of things will be well."

41
Infection

You are asleep, your head is on one side,
A monitor bleeps, feeding-bags and tubes siphon.
You're breathing calmly, your mouth no longer droops.
I let you sleep, knowing you have an infection
That stopped you from having a PEG tube inserted
Into your stomach. A nurse comes by to say
Your temperature's down, it's now 37.7.
It was in the Covid zone yesterday.
The nurse says saliva's infected your chest,
You're on antibiotics, your blood pressure's low.
Your potassium and sodium are high,
There's to be a review of when your PEG's go.
You open your eyes and look, I say "Back to sleep"
And stroke cream on your swollen hands as you peep.

6 July 2023

42
Distressed

Now I hear that your temperature's risen
And your infection's back. I was hoping
Your sleep yesterday helped the antibiotics to work
But you've been distressed in waves as if you're reacting
To pain. You may now have a urinary tract
Infection, and your immune system may
Be weak, and it may have spread to your kidneys,
With pain in your back and sides, and you can't say.
I can only wait and see how you are each day,
And hope you're clear of infection ten days from now
When your PEG's to be installed, if you're well enough.
I trust the medics but must reassure you somehow.
I can't visit until Tuesday, and now await
Daily bulletins as you struggle with this turn of fate.

7 July 2023

14. 'Turn of fate', an unexpected change of circumstances.

43
Crying Out

A report from your mum, you're "not in a good way at all".
You're clearly in pain, you're crying out every
Minute, you've a urinary tract infection
That's, wave after wave, hurting your tummy.
Your temperature's down – that's good – but you are flushed
And dehydrated: nurse brought you water.
You've had paracetamol and a new antibiotic,
And they've turned off your bleeping monitor.
You're worse than a week ago, your mother said "Calm down"
And I said "It's all right" and stopped you crying
Out by reassuring you. Now a day later
You're in a deep sleep, peacefully sleeping,
Breathing relaxed, this news has a better feel.
You've a chance of getting back on an even keel.

8, 9 July 2023

44
Counting, Memory, Hearing

You're over your infection now, and you're in
Your own room as you were distressed this morning,
But are now calm. I sit and talk to you
And notice your eyes are co-ordinating.
A therapist now moves your arms and legs
And asks "Is your name Nadia, blink five times if so",
And you do, and "Were you born in April, blink once if not"
And you do, then "In December, blink twice if so", and you know
And do, proving you can count and understand
And have a memory of your birthdays.
She raises your arm and your eyes follow it upwards.
She claps loudly and you jump, you can hear each phrase.
Later I sit with you, you squeeze my fingers – a goal –
With your right hand, your brain's resuming control.

11 July, 20 August 2023

45
Key

Your mother comes to her door in an arch of leaves,
Eighty-one with a bloodshot eye, in pain but erect,
And gives me a key on a coloured-bead ring she's found
In your boxes, perhaps to where your storage is decked.
I will go to your storage and check if your furniture
Is in with my books, and will cut the padlocks
To the two self-storage rooms if necessary
And replace them with combination locks (new blocks).
Two weeks today your mother is going in
To the hospital you're in to have her hip replaced
And I, the oldest of the three of us,
Will have the two of you under lock and key, encased.
And she is old to be having a hip bespoke
And you are young to have had a brain-stem stroke.

11 July, 20 August 2023

4. 'Decked', "set out" (*Shorter Oxford English Dictionary*), hence 'located'.

8. ‘Block’, “an obstruction” (*Concise Oxford Dictionary*), hence ‘blocks’, ‘blocking or obstructing devices’.

12. ‘Encased’, “put in a case; surrounded as with a case” (*Concise Oxford Dictionary*), with a suggestion of being under lock and key.

13. ‘Bespoke’, “(of goods, especially clothing) made to order” (*Concise Oxford Dictionary*).

46
Bleak

Your mother has found you worn out and distressed.
She saw the consultant who’s concerned at the high
Level of your anguish, that seems to mix physical
Discomfort and mental awareness that you might die.
He’s changed your medication, and says that despite
Indications of improvement you will require
Full and long-term care for the rest of your life.
It’s a bleak assessment based on past dire
Events and the severe damage in your brain.
It’s a likelihood not written in stone – it’s hard
To express – you’ll be institutionalised as I’ve long thought.
The therapist wants us to move from blinks to a card
Whose top says Yes, bottom No, and moves your eyes.
It’s a small improvement within a bleak future that cries.

12 July, 20 August 2023

47
A Beacon of Hope

So what can I do except relate to you
Within your new normal, steer clear of fright,
Not show despair, glad of any improvement,
A reassuring father in your plight.
If you are institutionalised I must visit
Regularly, adjust to your new way of life
As you will have to, be constant, just there,
A beacon of hope where bleakness is rife.
I must calm you, reassure you I’ll always be there
Till – now eighty-four – I meet my own end,
And make sure you’re looked after till you depart

As a valued family member and friend.
O my daughter, you've shown me so much kindness
In my long life and now I must return no less.

12 July, 20 August 2023

48
Encouragement

Your consultant's looking long-term but that
Doesn't exclude more progress as the medics sort
Out ways to communicate and lessen your distress.
All I can do is reassure and support
Without displaying the worries I have.
It's not easy but we'll do it, you and me.
A therapist says the brain resets and finds
New pathways, and we have to wait and see
How you progress. We're impressed by the care
You've had, all the care teams have one intent –
Your best interests – at heart, which is comforting.
We'll keep going with gentle encouragement,
And set an example that there's no condition or harm
That cannot be handled within a smiling calm.

12 July, 20 August 2023

49
Crying from Pain

My thoughts of calm are shattered, your mum's been
And had a stressful time. You'd been hoisted
Into the chair so physios could assess how you sit
On a wooden seat, but they put you back into bed
When they found you had a temperature, and you cried
For two and a half hours, you were distressed and tearful.
She tried chatting and reading, but couldn't stop you.
Your pain seems deep-seated, mental and physical.
It's heartbreaking, you're exhausted but can't sleep.
I've asked to see the consultant tomorrow,
But the junior doctors have just gone on strike
For five days, and there may be a no-show.

And now I think of the happy little girl
And laughing woman you became, and my mind's in a whirl.

13 July, 19 August 2023

50
Keeping You Calm

It's a dreadful situation. Parents want to make
Their children's sufferings better. We grapple,
But can't do this for you as you're so full of anguish,
And no one knows if it's physical or mental.
Chatting can awaken thoughts of what can't now be done,
Reading aloud's all right when you're lying in bed.
Familiar creams, smells, sounds are a good idea.
Listening to music is good, but not to your dead
Husband's, which may awake anguished memories.
You're in hospital, we must consider what is best.
You can't use earphones or turn a radio off.
It's impractical at present. If you're distressed
I'll do all I can to keep you calm in this mess
When I visit you tomorrow, and control your distress.

13 July, 19 August 2023

51
Harrowing

I find you crying from a wave of pain
And try to calm you, a nurse comes into your gloom
And swabs off yellow matter from your tongue.
Then the consultant takes me to an empty room
And we sit on chairs and discuss your distress
And how he's changed your medication to control
Both physical and mental pain, and post-stroke
Epilepsy, and then looks ahead to your PEG, the next goal,
Then to rehab somewhere, and then full long-term care:
He doesn't expect you'll be moving your limbs – we can't roam –
Or swallow or control your bodily functions,
You'll need round-the-clock nursing in a care home.

I return and try to calm your groans, and know
Your despair's as you may never move your limbs or swallow.

14, 16 July 2023

52
Understanding Too Well

You have a better understanding of your plight
Than many around you, and you seem to know
That you will not move your arms and legs again,
And see through the hopes of a recovery, even slow,
Of those who cannot tell you the stark truth,
Which is too cruel to contemplate, that you have years
Of lying quadriplegic, unable to speak,
Your hopes in ruins, your life ahead full of fears
And a pale shadow of what it could have been
If this dreadful stroke the consultant's encountered
Once every ten years, had not come from nowhere
To lay you low paralysed and sepulchred.
You planned to look after your parents in our last pell-mell,
Now we're looking after you, and you understand too well.

14, 16 July 2023

13. 'Pell-mell', "confusion" (*Concise Oxford Dictionary*).

53
Care Home

I ring your mum on what the consultant said:
That the PEG's a box rehab wants ticked, a facilitator,
And that when rehab's over you'll need full care
In a home as you've no control of your saliva
As you can't swallow, and of your bodily functions;
And to fit a hoist would mean reinforcing a beam.
Your parents are over eighty and can't perform
The day-and-night service by a care-home team.
Your house, which you worked so very hard to buy,
May have to be sold as a contribution to your care
Which your mum says will be palliative, alleviating pain
And anxiety as you know, hence the anguish you bear.

Your mum's shocked the physios push you about roughly
To move your limbs, and infringe your modesty.

15, 16 July 2023

54
Tears

I hear you lying groaning as if in pain.
The ward clerk says you're like it all the time.
I sit and talk to you, you seem in despair.
You've no tube in your nose and a plastered belly. I'm
Thinking of your PEG, I bring a nurse and say
"If you've pain in your stomach, blink five times," and, calm,
You do, and before you have two doses of pain relief
I heal you with four surges down my right arm.
Now you're calm as the physios cream your hands and feet.
You blink five times that you feel your hands and toes.
You open your mouth at will, and when they move
Your head from its side you blink comfort and repose.
Now you're at peace, healed. Have the surges expelled your fears?
I creep out of your room, eyes wet with tears.

18 July, 19 August 2023

55
At Cromwell's House, Ely

I sit in Cromwell's parlour in Ely, and see
Him receive would-be beheaders around the hearth,
And note the wooden panelling was pale yellow,
Since browned by smoke from burning logs. My path
Passes through the cold larder to the kitchen,
And I note the oven's now without a door,
Then go upstairs to the bedrooms where he, his wife,
Two sisters and six children slept, note the floor;
Then the blacked-out 'haunted room' (Cromwell's bedroom)
Where the ghost of Cromwell's been sensed for ages,
And my flesh creeps at a presence; then downstairs
The tithe office where Cromwell received taxes

From farmers, until, from high-church practices seething,
He organised the beheading of his King.

20, 24 July, 19 August 2023

Written in room 17 of Poets House, Ely with Cromwell's house visible through the window. Cromwell lived there from 1636 until he surrendered the lease on the house in 1641, and perhaps continued to live there as a tenant until 1649, when he moved to London at the time of the execution of Charles I.

13. 'High-church practices'. Charles I imposed semi-Catholic rituals on all churches including the church next to Cromwell's House, especially after he appointed William Laud Archbishop of Canterbury in 1633.

56
At Ely Cathedral

I sit in the nave amid 1100s
Norman arches, three-tiered for the Trinity,
And then beneath the octagon, whose first tower
Collapsed seven centuries ago into debris,
One of the medieval world's seven wonders;
Visit the Gothic Lady Chapel, then saunter
To the choir and the Presbytery of 1252,
Take in St Etheldreda, the founder
Of this Cathedral in Anglo-Saxon times.
In the aisles are tombs and reclining statues
Of the Cathedral's Deans and Bishops – who served
And were immortalised in a hundreds-of-years' snooze.
I pass the 1100 Prior's door
And in the Galilee porch, want to go back in for more.

20, 24 July, 19 August 2023

Written in room 17 of Poets House, Ely with the Cathedral visible through the window.

1. '1100s', pronounced 'eleven hundreds'.
4. The first tower of the octagon collapsed in 1322.
7. '1252', pronounced 'twelve fifty-two'.
8–9. St Etheldreda founded Ely Cathedral in 673.
13. '1100', pronounced 'eleven-hundred'.

57
Walled-In Wellness

In Ely Cathedral I picked up a book
On Julian of Norwich, who lived in a walled-in cell
And wrote when ill in 1373
"Sin is behovely, but all shall be well
And all shall be well and all manner of thing shall be well"
In her *Revelations*, which Eliot quotes on a tab
In 'Little Gidding', and now I think of you
Waiting to go to Norwich for rehab,
Walled-in within your body, not a cell.
O my daughter, who smiled so vivaciously,
I am looking to find wellness behind your pain
But it seems you're trapped in a catastrophe
And all I can see is: you can open to the Light
Which pours through me in healing and may 'well' your plight.

20 July, 19 August 2023

2. The walled-in cell at the church of St Julian in King Street, Norwich (which has survived) had three windows to comply with the *Ancrene Riwle*: one that opened to the church; one to an inner room for food; and one to the outer world so locals could seek advice.
3. '1373', pronounced 'thirteen seventy-three'. *Revelations*, *Revelations of Divine Love*. Julian of Norwich had her visions, her revelations of divine love, on 8 May 1373.
6. 'Tab', "a small strip of material attached… for identification" (*Concise Oxford Dictionary*).
14. 'Well', here used as a verb: "make well".

58
Eternal Soul

You are groaning as I arrive, I tell
A nurse, and a doctor examines you in bed
And agrees you need pain relief, and while we wait
I heal you with four surges into your head,
The third one very strong, and as you lie
I say, "Close your eyes and look for the Light that stole
In and sent these healing surges through me just now."
Suddenly, I see you as an immortal soul,
And glimpse you as an eternal being.

Then I know that Julian saw wellness subsist
In all as they would enter eternity.
Then your way opens, I'm told you're twelfth on a list,
And the ward clerk asks me to come on Monday at three
As the rehab assessor from Norwich wants to see me.

20 July, 19 August 2023

10. 'Subsist', "be kept alive; remain in being, exist" (*Concise Oxford Dictionary*).

59
Cleansing

And now I see that your groaning is the brain's
Way of getting rid of blockages and re-routeing.
As it resets it releases emotional waste,
As if putting out its refuse, and cleansing.
I have been saying "Shh", but now I see
After Abigail said the brain has to clear and spout
That you are preparing for a new life as a soul,
Getting rid of the clutter it can do without.
The healing process you're going through looks dire,
But the brain can re-route itself within the first
Three months from a stroke, and further in the next nine months,
And what was spared in your brain stem's behind each burst
Of groaning. And so, as you cry and groan
I see all's well as you're being cleansed with each moan.

20 July, 19 August 2023

60
Return to Otley Hall

On the way from Ely to the hospital,
We pass Otley Hall, see the gardens are open
With a café-restaurant that's full, people sitting outside.
The moat's green-flecked in an overgrown garden.
There's a marquee on the lawn. In the restaurant
I see the guidebook I wrote, piled up for sale,
And, told the new owner's sitting at a table
With a laptop, show her a picture of me and regale
Her. She says it's been hard finding cultured people

And she's living in a village and comes in to 'work'. I
Roam round the grounds to the knot-garden and gaze
At the rickety roof that's tumbling down. Wry-
-ly I survey the Tudor glory I restored
And made a million from and reflect I'm now ignored.

21, 24 July, 19 August 2023

8. 'Regale', "entertain or divert (with talk)" (*Concise Oxford Dictionary*).

61
Body like a Cell

On Monday you're being assessed for Norwich rehab
And I'm meeting the assessor to hear his verdict, that's good.
Twenty-seven years ago, I went to St Julian's church
And cell, which were bombed in the war, and rebuilt, and I stood
In the restored cell with three windows: to the church
For Mass; to an inner servant's room, so her two
Sisters could hand in food and take her chamber-pot;
And to the street, where plague victims could queue
And be counselled about their dreadful lives, and she'd say
All would be well as God, the Light, loved them totally
And would take each immortal soul to eternity.
You embody the human condition: soul within body.
She lived through her soul, you're living through your soul as well,
Trapped in your body as she was in her cell.

22 July, 14 August 2023

3–4. Nicholas Hagger went to St Julian's church, Norwich and to Julian of Norwich's rebuilt cell, on 29 February 1996. Julian of Norwich was born in 1342.

8. Plague. The Black Death pandemic arrived in England in 1348 and until 1665 there were only four years with no recorded cases.

62
Legal Consent

It seems you can't consent to a Power of Attorney.
By Zoom with a solicitor I authorise
An application to the Court of Protection:
To fund utilities for your house is wise.

Later I visit your hospital, and am told
The assessor's unwell: Thursday. My face is a mask.
I sit with you and the speech therapist comes in
And shows me a 'letter-box' I now peep through and ask
You a question – eyes up for Yes, down for No. A laugh?
That'd be new. We talk, she says I should go slow on the Court
As you will improve and with professionally-monitored blinks
Consent to a Power of Attorney can be taught,
And Norwich rehab can fix this as it's their bent
To progress patients so they can give legal consent.

24 July, 14 August 2023

63
Arcady

You loved walking in my garden in Arcady,
We'd saunter to the pond and feed the fish,
Go down to the gate to the left of the far oak,
Walk the first green field as would be your wish
Amid buttercups, clover and starry stitchworts,
And saunter to the bottom of the second green
Field. We'd come back and look at the heather bed
And go up to the knot-garden and stand between
Statues of Summer holding a sheaf of corn
And Winter holding a scythe, and look at the knot,
See how, from a point, life came to our universe
And spread into twenty-five civilisations' plot.
Now you can't walk there, I tell you the garden news
So your imagination's there to recall the views.

25 July, 14 August 2023

12. 'Plot', "a defined and usually small piece of ground [such as the 25 beds of the knot-garden]; the interrelationship of the main events" (*Concise Oxford Dictionary*).

64
Possessions

I stand before grey self-storage containers
On Canvey Island, ascend wobbly steps, feel
And try the key I was given at reception

And unbolt the first-floor door to at last reveal
Your furniture, the contents of your old home
Which you lived in as a widow for three years to adjust,
Then sold, and were going to move this furniture
Into your new home you'd already exchanged on, robust
Before you were struck down. Now I am here.
I take photos to send to your relatives, and, bold,
Measure the twenty-by-eight-by-eight-feet space,
And plan the delivery of these piled-up household
Possessions – chairs, tables, beds, sofa – to try
And assemble a home I hope you'll occupy.

26 July, 14 August 2023

8. 'Robust', "strong and sturdy" (*Concise Oxford Dictionary*).

65
Grimace

Today I've heard that a therapist thinks your stroke
May have damaged the emotional control behind your brain's stare,
And your groaning may be random, not at something said.
I ponder and see your groaning as despair
At your locked-in predicament, frustration
At not being able to say what you want to say
Or ask questions that burn: 'Will I get better?'
And 'Am I stuck for life in my locked-in dismay?'
And 'Will I have a second stroke any time?'
I feel so sad for you and your damaged brain,
And your mum, who's elsewhere in your hospital, having had
Her hip replaced and is grappling with her pain.
And at eighty-four, I would gladly take your place
But must keep going to get you both through this long grimace.

26 July, 14 August 2023

2. See 'PBA' (pp.297–298) and its note to lines 7–8.

66
Bizarre

If I had received a message in Japan
From my deep source that both you and your mum would be bent

On living in Suffolk after I had restored
(And then sold) Otley Hall there where the Jamestown Settlement
Voyage that founded America was planned,
And that you'd both be patients in Ipswich Hospital
At the same time and you'd be looked after by me
At the elderly age of eighty-four, feeble,
And that you'd be a locked-in quadriplegic
And I'd still be going to a gym, my heartbeats now true,
I wouldn't have believed it, it's too bizarre
And tormentingly sad that I would be caring for you,
Not you for me, during my closing years,
Which I do gladly, wanting to wipe away your tears.

27 July, 14 August 2023

67
Aware Crying

The assessor did not come today, and it's not known
When or if you'll go to rehab one day.
You're crying as I enter your room, and this time
You don't stop to listen to what I say.
I see the therapist who wondered if your stroke
Has damaged your brain's emotional control in your gloom.
She says you're not crying when you're alone,
Only when staff or visitors enter your room.
At first you were in a coma in your ward,
Then in wakening unconsciousness, and now through your eyes
You've a new level of responding consciousness,
You're aware of your situation, and blink replies
And show you're aghast at your plight with endless crying.
And I wish you were an unaware baby wailing.

27 July, 14 August 2023

14. 'Wail', "(noun), a prolonged plaintive inarticulate loud high-pitched cry of pain, grief; (verb) utter a wail" (*Concise Oxford Dictionary*).

68
Fragile

At any time there may be an urgent call
And I may have to rush to your room, "Please come quickly" –
I may need a driver if it can't be planned –
As you may have had another stroke or maybe
A seizure that has ebbed away your life
As three of your four brain arteries are still blocked
And a new event may release new blood clots.
And if your life's an endless crying, locked-
In inability to talk or move
Your limbs, I would say "It's a blessing" (with a smile
Of disbelief), "a merciful release, you're now at peace."
Your present existence is tenuous, fragile.
But as your dad I can't entertain this thought
And I know I must look for a cure as a father ought.

27 July, 13 August 2023

12. 'Tenuous', "slight, of little substance; thin, slender, small" (*Concise Oxford Dictionary*).

69
PBA

I think I understand what's been making you cry.
Your right-brain, brain-stem stroke disconnected
Your frontal lobe, which controls emotions,
And your cerebellum and brain stem, where, it's said,
Reflexes are mediated, form a connecting link,
The cerebro-ponto-cerebellar pathway,
A disconnect involving bouts of crying,
Called pseudobulbar affect (PBA).
You need to be on an additional US drug,
Dextromethorphan and quinidine sulphate tablets,
Which the UK and EU do not accept
As they speed up a heart into arrhythmic heartbeats' 'fits'.
Somewhere, is there a safe cure without side-effects
That will manage your disconnect so it reconnects?

27 July, 13 August 2023

7–8. PBA, pseudobulbar affect, is a neurological condition that causes outbursts of uncontrolled crying. It is a neurological impairment and is not considered a mental illness.

12. 'Fit', "a sudden brief attack of an illness or of symptoms; a sudden short bout or burst" (*Concise Oxford Dictionary*).

70
Hospitality

I watch the last Ashes Test at the Oval.
England lead by two hundred and fifty at tea.
I leave my seat and walk up steps and go
To the hospitality suite and hurriedly
Munch cream tea and cakes, and return as the players come out.
The floor has circles saying 'Ashes Suite
Hospitality' every yard, and I'm transported
To your hospital's one-room suite and the feared defeat
That turns all to ashes, where you're perhaps crying
At your predicament, when I'm here and sit
Enjoying my eldest son's birthday present:
Hospitality tickets for five of us to watch cricket.
And I am forlorn amid the evening crowd
As I think of you, alone and crying aloud.

29 July, 13 August 2023

71
Assessor

The physio Abi greets me, "I've just come off the phone
To the assessor, he's coming on Friday
At 2pm and will see us all, and you.
She's ninth on the list" – down from number twelve. I say
I will be there. "She's been sitting to be washed."
That's what rehab's assessor has been hoping.
I leave her and find you sitting in a chair.
I say, "Your eyes are moving better, shh your groaning,"
Then have to leave as you're hoisted back into bed,
And then watch your PEG's weekly clean from your chair.
And watching you, I wonder if your crying

Indicates a damaged brain rather than utter despair
At your predicament, and I long to get you moving
Into rehab and new drugs that can end your crying.

1, 13 August 2023

72
Athens

A grandson's going to Athens. I say,
Forgetting my heartache in Arcady,
"Persia was like Russia, and Greece Ukraine
At the start of the 5th century BC.
The Athenians repelled Persian invasions –
A runner brought word of one from Marathon
And collapsed and died after blurting the news – and their
Defence of the city-state and islands became the Aegean
Athenian Empire, its treasury on Delos.
Athens, now supreme, was challenged by Sparta
And lost the Peloponnesian War when plague
Decimated its army, and declined further
Into a province in the Empire Rome would create,
Just as Britain would decline into an American 'state'."

3, 13 August 2023

73
Unexpected

A message, the assessor's not coming,
He's unwell again. I arrive at the hospital
On Friday, and the physio says, "The assessor…."
I say it's the third time he's let us down, gabble:
If he rejects her he'll have held her up a month
Within the three months new pathways are fast and get through.
She nods. I sit with you and comb your scalp.
Abi comes in and says to you, "You know I told you
We're trying to place you in specialist care,
A bed's come up and you're moving there on Monday."
It's so unexpected, I ask, "To Norwich?" She nods.

The physio told her I'd mentioned a month's delay
And she rang Norwich and by-passed the assessor.
So you're leaving, and, wet-eyed, I'm full of rapture.

4, 13 August 2023

10. 'Rapture', "ecstatic delight" (*Concise Oxford Dictionary*).

74
Goldfinch

Now Norwich is taking you, your way forward is known.
Rehab will manage your physical and mental pain
And open new pathways in the next ten months.
They'll change your medication, work on your damaged brain:
Your temporal lobe may be severed from your brain stem.
They'll do their best, but you may still be quadriplegic.
And I've done my best for you, now is a good time
To consider, like Julian, walled-in stoic,
Your spiritual unity with the mystic Light
As your dad once did in his youthful 'The Silence'.
I have registered your house's utilities,
If you can't move in you must let it, if that makes sense.
Like Fabritius's chained goldfinch you have survived
The collapse of your plan to live there, please don't feel deprived.

23, 27 July, 4, 12 August 2023

13. *The Goldfinch* is a painting by the Dutch Golden-Age artist Carel Fabritius of a life-sized chained goldfinch, signed and dated 1654. It may have been in Fabritius's workshop in Delft when a gunpowder explosion killed him and destroyed much of the city. The painting was lost for two centuries and rediscovered in Brussels.

75
Unthankful Hell

You are now in Norwich where Heavenly Julian
Wrote "All manner of thing shall be well" – even in
Stroke after-care in level-one rehab.
I find you in Caroline House within
Colman Hospital in Unthank Road, room 6.
You're asleep, the consultant comes. In the garden

He says he'll review your medication
And stop your groaning, perhaps with serotonin,
And in four to six weeks he'll tell me the way forward
And work towards giving you the capacity,
With the speech and psychological therapists I meet,
To consent to a Power of Attorney.
He'll work to release you from your unthankful Hell
Locked in your body, like Julian walled in her cell.

8 August 2023

76
Sunset

I watch on a rocking-chair as the dazzling sun
Slides down behind the trees of Arcady
And in the stillness of the early dusk
I think of you in your place of recovery
And of your new consultant who is aware
You have low blood pressure and asked, what if your heart
Gives way and you need resuscitating,
Which would leave you worse off, what do I think? I start.
I want you to have the best chance of surviving
And through new pathways become able to move,
And time will tell if you are going to be
Quadriplegic for good, or if you can improve.
Now all is dark with a distant glow in the sky
That recalls all you did before your darkening drew nigh.

9, 12 August 2023

77
Raw in Arcady

I sit in Arcady, in this paradise,
The morning sun fills the blue sky, and green
Trees throw shadows on grass, where there used to be
Roman or Saxon roundhouses that can be seen
In LiDAR below-surface images,
Once occupied by Henry the Eighth's deer park;
And my thoughts are filled with this peaceful pastoral,

This bucolic countryside, and yet within their arc
Are my thoughts of you lying motionless in your bed,
Unable to speak or swallow food, and cast
Into waves of distress that come out as groaning
Or crying all the time, and I contrast
This timeless rural idyllic scene with your
Wordless locked-in distress that leaves me raw.

10, 12 August 2023

Title 'Raw in Arcady', when spoken could be "roar in Arcady".

78
Mangled

I am in anguish in my Arcady,
An agony that wrings poems from my soul
Like the mangle that squeezed wet washing in my childhood
Kitchen, before it was hung on a line with a forked pole
In the garden to dry in the wind, poems of wet
Experience of every emotion hung out to dry.
I am old now, and face a slow decline, and you
Lying still, unable to move your limbs or try,
Or speak or swallow, are an image of what awaits
As I order my papers and complete my life's work's thread
To become what you are now, when it should be me
With *you* visiting *me* in my hospital bed.
You've confronted me with the human condition I'm
Going to become at the end of this Arcadian time.

10, 12 August 2023

10. 'Order my papers', put my papers in order.

79
Lightning Strike: Oak Tree and Split Branch

I look out at the four oaks on the lawn beneath
My window, in this paradisal Arcady,
And at the nearest oak tree with a box for owls,
And I suddenly realise: *I* am an oak tree,
My life has been a tree growing branches
And you are a branch growing from my trunk alone,

And now I'm an oak tree and you are a lopped branch.
But no, *you* were an acorn and have grown
Into an independent oak with a brain-stem trunk
And branches out into your brain, which a lightning
Strike from a black cloud in the sky split off
In places, leaving you damaged and fracturing.
However I look, a branch has split from your oak:
Who you were has gone, I see the damage and choke.

10, 11 August 2023

80
Gone For Ever

Your mum, Caroline, tells me about your house,
How the grass will be mown and the hedges will be sheared.
I say it was your project, and you may be
Following what we do from your walled-in world. Seared,
She says sadly, "The old Nadia's gone for ever,"
And I'm haunted by these words, for if she's right
You've died as a personality with your laughter,
Your organising flair, your caring for all plight.
I'm happy that during your time in level-one
Rehab at Caroline House you'll have new pathways
In sleep that can turn the silence of your damaged brain
Back into the old Nadia's vivacious gaze.
I hope new pathways will restore your soul
And that your skull won't become an empty bowl.

10, 11 August 2023

4. 'Seared', in great anguish.
8. 'Plight', a condition that is unfortunate. Here, all misfortune.

81
Agape

I walk about with a cloud around my soul
Amid Arcady's green grass and thriving trees,
For though I am at peace apart from the court
I am constantly thinking of you in your locked-in 'disease',
Unable to move any limb, speak or swallow,

Lying among your excretions till nurse is about
And comes to change you, unable to call her, just groan.
I am haunted by your crying, it's a crying-out
For things to be done, and I'm present in your room
And looking for nurse to carry out your will
Rather than here in Arcady among birds and flowers
Where we walked every time you visited me, down our hill.
I walk in paradise but can't escape
Thoughts of you quadriplegic, your eyes, like my thoughts, agape.

12 August 2023

14. 'Agape', "gaping, open-mouthed"; also (pronounced 'agapay') "Greek = brotherly love" (*Concise Oxford Dictionary*). Hence 'family love'.

82
Kinks

You looked after your husband as he died,
You slept at his bedside, on the hospital floor.
At the funeral at Southend Crem, you greeted all –
Including all the main Kinks – at the door,
Men your husband played with, who you organised,
Booking their theatres, hotels, equipment
So their concerts happened with all back-ups.
I'd spoken to Ray Davies at the Ipswich Regent.
You'd given me a framed 'Sunny Afternoon', which he'd signed.
He came to the funeral and told me, standing near flowers,
"Nadi was the best thing that happened to Ian."
So many spoke of your organising powers.
I hope new pathways will bring you back so
You can meet all those Kinks-lovers you'd got to know.

12, 13 August 2023

3. Nadia's husband Ian Gibbons, the Kinks' keyboard player, died on 1 August 2019, and his funeral was held on 28 August 2019.
8. In May 2010 Ray Davies asked Nadia for a signed copy of Nicholas Hagger's *Collected Poems, 1958–2005*. According to Nadia, he carried it about with him and it lived on the floor by his bed.

83
Eyegaze Machine

Inside your room staff are doing "observations".
You scream as you're hoisted into your wheelchair.
I sit in the garden and wait until
A nurse wheels you out to sit in the fresh air.
You're crying and spoiling the serenity.
Then the consultant takes me to a room and lays
Out the way forward: you'll be on an eyegaze machine
Like Stephen Hawking's, when by your eye gaze
You'll have a voice and speak short sentences,
Take control for requests (subject to assessors)
And he's tackling your groaning – and helping your recovery –
With selective serotonin reuptake inhibitors
(SSRIs), which I raised with him last week.
This machine and the pills will make your future less bleak.

15, 18 August 2023

84
Low Blood Pressure

When I return you've been moved back into your bed
As your blood pressure was too low to be in the garden.
The consultant said again to me that if
Your heart fails there will be no resuscitation
As that would leave you worse off than before,
And your mum has confirmed that is also her view.
You're with the speech and language therapist.
She asks if you know where you are and explains that you
Are in Norwich undergoing rehab.
She asks if you know why, and explains you've had a stroke
And that all the team are trying to get you back.
You listen, no groaning while she explains, you soak
It in. Outside she says you're progressing, there's more movement
In your mouth, and your head, and more swallowing's evident.

15, 18 August 2023

85
Escaping from Locked-In: Talking

I considered Hawking as I worked out
The first-ever Theory of Everything
In my *Algorithm of Creation*, and saw
Him on stage and heard his machine's voice speaking.
I was sceptical of some of his research –
That the universe had no beginning – but admired
His theory of radiation from black holes,
Known as "Hawking radiation", which he'd inspired.
And now you're to be taught to use this machine,
Which will speak with a more natural voice than his and surprise.
Everything in my life is somehow connected.
You can talk again as you track with your up-down eyes.
I'd rather you talked as the old you with a grin,
But eye tracking may get you out of being locked-in.

15, 18 August 2023

86
Wildfire

The consultant said to me, "There are billions –
I mean billions – of brain cells, and each connects
With the others in ways we do not know.
No one knows what reconnections this process effects
When Nadia sleeps. She's taking melatonin,
It draws from her body and gives her sleeps in long spells,
The conditions her brain needs to repair itself
And reconnect to cope with the damaged cells."
Your stroke was like a wildfire that burnt out
A large part of your home town, cut power – it's dead –
And plunged you into darkness without services.
But life goes on, power's being reconnected.
When that's happened your head, arms, legs may move
And you may speak words and your outlook may improve.

18 August 2023

87
Cornish Hermitage

Online I join the camera that gives a live view
Across the misty harbour where waves toss
To our pink Cornish house. It's high tide, I see
People in shorts walking to and fro, some across
The bridge which can be winched down to let boats
And ships go in and out, and it strikes me:
They are all walking, perhaps twenty, moving their feet,
Holiday-makers and tourists all doing naturally
What you can't do as you can't wiggle a toe
Till your billions of brain cells can re-link, and renew.
My pink hermitage looks so calm above the waves,
I can't go there as I'm up here to be near you.
I knew when you'd watch, and would wave from the harbour wall,
But sadly now you can't watch or go there at all.

18 August 2023

88
Suffolk Fair Maid

I have come across your last Valentine's card,
Coloured hearts shaped into larger hearts, there must be
Eighty hearts on the card, and when I opened it
Tiny hearts showered my lap, taking the tally
To over a hundred hearts; and inside you wrote,
"Dad, sending all my love on Valentine's Day,
Today and always.... Lots of love" (I'm smiling),
"Your Suffolk Fair Maid." I see my screen say
That Thomas Fuller in *Worthies of England*
(1662) wrote of Suffolk Fair Maids
As that county's women were legendary
For their beauty in the late medieval decades.
Suffolk fair maid, your Fairmead dad misses
You, and from Arcady sends kisses as best wishes.

18 August 2023

89
Involuntary Groaning

My key worker rings: the speech therapist
Had a long Yes-No session with you today
And asked more complex questions, including
"Can you control your groaning in any way?"
And you were correct in all your answers, logical,
With a clear understanding of your predicament
And replied "No" to that fundamental question,
Which may confirm you've got PBA to some extent
And need the SSRIs you may have started.
I ask her to request the consultant
To review if the right medication has been prescribed
To control your involuntary crying's torment.
You must now be given medical control
Over waves of emotion that are swamping your soul.

18, 19 August 2023

90
Belief

I've found an article by Kate Allatt,
Who was nine weeks in intensive care, and then, wide awake,
Eight months in rehab, with a brain-stem stroke,
Not as bad as yours, but good to have her take
As there are only seven hundred who are locked-in.
It was like being buried alive. She did not know
About neuroplasticity, when the brain is rewired
So neural networks can reorganise and grow –
And change with growth. She emphasises belief,
Fighting to move a toe to run and roam,
Practising movements four hundred and fifty times a week
Until it moved, motivated by going home.
You must persist with will-power to move your limbs, and blaze
With belief as your brain rewires for new pathways.

18, 19 August 2023

91
Turning a Corner: Donkeys

They've moved you into a different room, I watch
You move your head, squeeze my fingers – sublime! –
With your right hand and wiggle your right toe.
Then your groaning starts, not as bad as last time.
A physio asks if you'd like to see the donkeys
And (with help) hoists you in a sling into a wheelchair deftly
And pushes you outside amid patients in wheelchairs
And parks you near Pippin, a miniature donkey
That (bribed with ginger-nuts) rests its nose on your knees
And, as I move your hand to touch it, chews your pillow.
You squeal with laughter, and you're turning a corner,
You're laughing like the old you we used to know.
Your brain's found new pathways to restore your power.
Your house – tell your limbs to move several times each hour.

22 August 2023

14. 'Your house' etc. Think of your house and get your limbs moving so you can live in it, tell them to move several times each hour.

92
Rehabilitating

The consultant's watching, we walk to a nearby seat.
He says you're on a small dose of SSRI,
And he'll increase it after three weeks, and you're now groaning less.
All this addresses the physio's saying you've said by
Your eye-raising you can't control your groaning.
He says there will be a review when we will see
How you've been assessed in just over two weeks' time.
Then the chief occupational therapist comes, she will be
My key worker from now and ring me at home.
She says she sees your care in Norwich lasting
Three to six months, probably more like six months.
And as your vision can't read the edges of the lettering
She'll prove that consent for a Power of Attorney has been
Given without starting you on an eyegaze machine.

22 August 2023

2. 'SSRI', "selective serotonin uptake inhibitor", an antidepressant.

93
Laughing

In your room the physio's saying that you laughed
At the donkey eating your pillow, and the deal
Was that if you saw the donkeys you'd ride on her 'bike'
As you did this morning: two pedals and one wheel.
She straps on your feet and the wheel moves and cycles you,
It looks as if you're pedalling from your wheelchair in style.
I say you're doing so well you could double the speed.
Physio jokes I'm not helping, you raise eyes in Yes and smile.
Now I'm wheeling you back to the donkeys. I say
I've mistaken the tilt for the brake and have nearly fired
You and you laugh, and now you don't groan at all
But sit with the donkeys, intent till I ask if you're tired.
You raise your eyes in a Yes, and I wheel you back in
And you're still laughing and have not groaned through your grin.

22 August 2023

3. 'Bike', the MOTOmed in the gym that pedals a patient's legs. See p.328, note to line 14, for a fuller explanation.

94
Nursing Care

The key worker rings on a post-rehab way forward.
I say there's a negative narrative that foretells
Certain quadriplegia and institutional living,
And a more positive one that sees billions of cells
That link, no one knows how, and reset themselves
To create new pathways which, aided by willpower, improve,
Unlock or facilitate movements that I want.
She says that in six months' time there may be a move
To a nursing or residential home, or level-two rehab
Or a family home with a reinforced joist
Or a combination. Your parents are in their eighties
And can't provide full-time nursing care with a hoist
And relief staff known to cancel and cause a scare.
The post-rehab way forward's through full-time nursing care.

23, 24 August 2023

95
Conflict
(+A + –A = 0)

A sunny morning in peaceful Arcady
And birds are singing and flitting in August's largesse,
And I am in conflict between this paradise
(+A) and the room you occupy and your distress
(–A), and I realise that I am living half
My life thinking of you and your agony that pines,
Your walled-in silence that jars with my peace,
A conflict I've caught in my rhymed and unrhymed lines.
I am here in harmonious Arcady in sun
But part of my mind's in your darkened room in shade
And I am with you in what your nurses are doing
And am in disharmony I need to reconcile, abrade.
Somehow I must unify my daily conflict –
Arcady v. Norwich – but my thoughts still contradict.

26, 27 August 2023

2. 'Largesse', "generosity, beneficence" (*Concise Oxford Dictionary*).
6. 'Pine', "decline or waste away, especially from grief, disease" (*Concise Oxford Dictionary*).
12. 'Abrade', "scrape or wear away by rubbing" (*Concise Oxford Dictionary*).

96
Debilitating

I sit in The George, Norwich over hot soup
And smoked-salmon sandwiches and say I've grown old,
And no longer walk in a straight line and don't want to walk
In our garden as it's getting beyond me to be that bold.
It's as though I've suddenly at eighty-four
Moved into a new phase in my slow declining.
Ann says I've been like it since you had your stroke,
An event that has proved debilitating.
I say I need two years to finish my work on my books,
Tidy my room, put my affairs in order, engage,
And if I'm disabled may have to enter a care home,
I have two years to resist this creeping old age.

This toing and froing may have taken its toll on my fate
And a bell may be tolling if I can't de-debilitate.

28 August 2023

8. 'Debilitating', "enfeebling, enervating" (*Concise Oxford Dictionary*).
10. 'Engage', "come into battle, take part" (*Concise Oxford Dictionary*).
13. 'Taken its toll on', "caused harm or danger to".

97
Triggering Regret

You're waiting unsmiling in a black wheelchair.
The nurse invites me to push you round the garden.
I steer you under the honeysuckle arch
And past gladioli, fuchsia and sun roses. Then
We sit in the sun with your head in the shade.
You turn your head impressively from left to right
And move your right toe, and there's been no crying.
Back in your room I park you so your cards are in sight
And I read out the therapies on your timetable. You cry,
And you cry when I show you a bird feeder through your window.
You cry when I leave. I've tried to motivate you
But have reminded you of therapies you would forgo.
And the bird feed that you can no longer get.
I've tried to be positive but somehow triggered regret.

28 August 2023

12. 'Forgo', "abstain from, decline to take" (*Concise Oxford Dictionary*).

98
Unheeded Pain

I hear from a physio you may have been months in pain
On your paralysed left side from your right-brain stroke,
And your groaning from this pain you couldn't (or wouldn't) declare
When we were trying to fathom how much was a mental choke
Rather than physical distress. But now you're having
Pain-relief 'injections' squirted into your PEG's zone
And I need to ask if your pain's under control.
Your stroke's effect on you's been only partly known.
There are other mysteries at present, all wild flowers have gone.

There are no buttercups, daisies or dandelions out.
Your pain went unheeded, like the cause of Nature's pain,
Something's happened we haven't been told about,
Which may be wildfire smoke falling as poison rain
Or (more sinister) weapons polluting the winds from Ukraine.

30 August 2023

99
Statues on Hope's Pedestal

Your mum's taken your stroke hard, she says you look drugged
And you've lost everything – your life and your dignity –
And they're doping you with experimental drugs
And the physios are pulling you about recklessly.
I sympathise with her misery, which we all share,
But I look ahead: I didn't want you struck down,
But your stroke's happened and I must encourage
You, make the best of a bad job and not frown.
And above all I must tell you you're doing well
And the physios are doing their best, and give you hope.
I must notice your progress and praise each move of your head
And wiggle of your toes as signs you're beginning to cope.
Your mum says such improvements are negligible,
But I see them as landmarks, statues on Hope's pedestal.

30 August 2023

100
World-Unity and World-Sadness Reconciled in the One

In Japan I was given a positive philosophy
Of life, a conception of the world, a 'world
Perception': my Universalist *Weltanschauung*
Which I set out in sixty works I unfurled.
It was optimistic, incorporated all knowledge,
Saw the unity of humankind and the universe
And led to my Theory of Everything.
But since your stroke I have shifted within to immerse
My soul in a negative *Weltschmerz*, 'world pain' or sorrow,
World sadness, the pessimistic view of the Romantics

Of the human condition and the meaning of life.
Now I must reconcile these two opposites,
World-unity and sadness, in the One for I know
And live by: 'plus A' plus 'minus A' equals 'zero'.

2 September 2023

3. '*Weltanschauung*', "a particular philosophy or view of life; a conception of the world [German, from *Welt* world + *Anschauung* perception]" (*Concise Oxford Dictionary*).
4. 'Unfurled', "spread out (a sail, umbrella etc.)" (*Concise Oxford Dictionary*).
7. 'Theory of Everything'. This can be found in Nicholas Hagger's *The Algorithm of Creation* (2023).
9. '*Weltschmerz*', "a feeling of pessimism; an apathetic or vaguely yearning outlook on life [German, from *Welt* word + *Schmerz* pain]" (*Concise Oxford Dictionary*).
14. Cf. the algebraic formula +A + −A = 0.

101
Hope

I find you sitting in a wheelchair in your room
And show you the dog my son's brought, and sprayed,
And you smile as I put your hand on his head.
I wheel you round the garden and park in the shade.
The speech and language therapist comes and says
She's been testing you and from your replies has found
You've full understanding of language, but are without speech,
You have dyspraxia, which must be worked round.
I say I've said new pathways are being made,
And you'll practise moving your head and feet as you sit.
I say how well you're doing, there's hope, and you cry.
She says they've had you in early, they usually admit
After four months, it will take time, it's not bleak.
And your swallowing's improving, and you may soon speak.

5, 7 September 2023

102
Not Fully Locked-In: Walking Again

It's a positive narrative, you're moving your arms
And feet, and I can see you shuffling along
Like the woman outside your door, edging with a crutch.
You're alert and are not locked-in and are strong.
You're turning your head and are acting unlocked.
The key worker says there's movement in your right hand,
You can press a button for a buzzer near your fingers.
She puts the button on your knee-pillow near where I stand,
And you buzz and a voice says, "Can I have some help, please?"
It's wired to the system and heard in the corridor.
The physio says, "We did tilt-table standing today,
And she stood at forty-five degrees, and wanted to do more."
You're not going to be quadriplegic, with new routes in your brain
You're going to move arms and feet, and walk again.

5, 7 September 2023

103
Wisdom and Feeling Unite in Stillness

Your mum is pained that you're being kept alive
By drugs for a locked-in, quadriplegic life that you'll grouse
You don't want and she feels you shouldn't have,
With worthless 'improvements', you'll never move into your house.
I resist an emotional reaction, and look for the best.
I didn't want your paralysis, but now that it's rife
I must accept it and improve it from here,
Get you making progress even though your old life
Will never come back. I see you escaping
Locked-in quadriplegia, and standing intense
And walking where wisdom and feeling unite
Into a new-found stillness, a deep silence.
You're the silence of my best-known poem, in your plight
You act it out, and can now look within for the Light.

7 September 2023

2. 'Grouse', "grumble or complain pettily" (*Concise Oxford Dictionary*).
6. 'Rife', "spread, abounding" (*Concise Oxford Dictionary*).
13. 'Best-known poem', 'The Silence' (1965–1966).

104
Escaping

I was banned from seeing you by the secret State
And, when I refused to sign, banned from publicity
So my works would be surrounded by silence.
I got on with it and brought out books, more than sixty.
I escaped, now you must likewise escape from your life-threatening
State. You came to Norwich in locked-in quadriplegia
And can escape by speaking and walking.
It's as if you'd been banned from all further
Communication and movement, and must follow your dad
In by-passing the ban and recovering what you may.
In this you'll have my full support as you will
Be following my example in your own way.
You're going to speak and walk, and stand up straight,
And escape a locked-in quadriplegic's fate.

8 September 2023

105
120 Billion Connecting Brain Cells

I leave you in your bed and join your mum
For the review meeting. The consultant tells
His team of five to greet us, and then speaks
Of the brain's hundred-and-twenty billion cells'
New pathways, PBA and your medication
Which has made your body less prone to infection.
The speech therapist says you may soon be speaking again,
But you have dysarthria (when speech muscles weaken).
The physio says you have head control and balance,
The psychologist says you feel sadness and anger.
The nurse says you will need two nurses' care.
Can you escape locked-in quadriplegia?
No one knows what pathways billions of brain cells can take
And what trillions of new connections allow them to remake.

8, 10 September 2023

5. PBA, pseudobulbar affect, see note on pp.297–298.

106
Blocked Motorway

The consultant gives me a diagram
Of the brain's circle of Willis, and he has crossed through
The middle cerebral artery on its right side
And its link to the pontine arteries in you,
And on the left the vertebral artery.
He says all these are gone in your brain, leaving a shell,
And if they're still blocked is not an issue
So long as you continue to be well.
And he does not want to send you to hospital
For a new MRI when nothing can be done.
You have had very severe damage to your brain
And many brain cells died when they were overrun.
If a motorway's blocked you must find a new route and fend.
It may take longer but can still get you there in the end.

8, 10 September 2023

13. 'Fend', "look after oneself" (*Concise Oxford Dictionary*).

107
Care Home Ahead

I say to the team, there's a chance your improvements will work
And you'll escape, be able to speak and walk and amaze.
I say, as your father I can't say to you, 'Despair,
You'll be a locked-in quadriplegic for the rest of your days,'
As I have to give you hope and say, 'Will-power
And new pathways can bring improvements that are sweet,
So practise moving your head, arms, legs when alone,
You're a fighter, be determined and get back on your feet.'
The consultant says you'll be here for at least six months,
Then at Ipswich, the level-two Sue Ryder home there,
Or for more level-one at All Hallows, Bungay,
For full-time long-term two-nurse ongoing care.
The NHS will take care of you, I'm relieved.
Your future's assured, your escape can be achieved.

8, 11 September 2023

108
On the Right Path

So that's as far as I can take you now.
I've seen you through hospital and into five weeks spent
In level-one care at sixteen-thousand a month
And, urged by your consultant to write to his management,
Another six months, and now I've found you a care home
If you can't move into the house where you'd like to dwell.
On my way out your consultant catches me and says,
"Thank you for your email, it went down very well,
And for being positive and motivating the staff."
So where you go next may be due to the email I sent.
I say Caroline House's reputation will rise
If they get you out of locked-in quadriplegia's torment.
You're now on the right path of pathways for an escape,
And I must draw comfort from Arcady's landscape.

8, 11 September 2023

109
Assimilated Agony, Transcending

I sit in Arcady in the sweltering sun
And take stock of three months of agony:
The shock of the news of your right-brain stroke
And your brain-stem paralysis and your locked-in palsy.
I think of how it was forecast you'd be dead within
Two days, then three weeks, and how you display
Rapid progress this last week, so the dour narrative
Of locked-in quadriplegia can give way
To a narrative of escape with motivated staff
And the prospect you'll speak and walk independently
Even though the old humorous Nadia may have gone;
And to a positive view that's at one with my Arcady.
I have assimilated my agony and transcend,
And can now concentrate on preparing for my own end.

8, 11 September 2023

4. 'Palsy', "paralysis, a condition of utter helplessness" (*Concise Oxford Dictionary*).

13. 'Transcend', "be beyond the range or grasp of (human experience, reason, belief, etc.); excel, surpass" (*Concise Oxford Dictionary*).

110
Preparing to Go

And so I sit and gaze at my four oak trees
And the fields and sweep of the Forest above Fairmead,
My Tudor deer park, where I can make my peace
With all the events in my life, some of which still bleed:
From being banned from seeing you to my distaste for the court,
The plague and mystic glimpses, the Oneness I know
Of Nature and the universe, my Tudor times
And my final life as I prepare to go.
I look back on a life in Japan that you witnessed,
The Light and the birth of my Baroque vision and art
In 'The Silence', which you saw from my knee in my study,
Then my sixty books, and now with a heavy heart
I know I must prepare to go, but have placed you
In care that will see out your days, and in that I've been true.

8, 11 September 2023

111
Avoiding Reporting

You're lying in bed and jump when I come in.
I want to report you're here for three months more,
Then there'll be an assessment on those three months,
And you'll be consulted, but I can't say either for
You may groan and cry out at the prospect
Of continuing your stay, and if asked your intent,
If you want your medication to continue,
You may look down and reject further treatment
And, despite what I've negotiated, quietly
Stop taking the medication that keeps you alive.
I say I could take you out in your wheelchair.
You press the buzzer, a voice asks for help to arrive.
Nurse comes. I say, "She's asking you to throw me out."
And you laugh. I go out to the garden, there's rain about.

12 September 2023

112
Sixty-Degrees Standing

The main physio waves me in and says, "Come to the gym."
Two wheel you in your wheelchair, you're crying.
They strap you to your harness and hoist you,
Crying, not in pain, to the tilt table, placing
Your feet on the foot-rest and, having strapped you, raise
Your head to thirty degrees and then to fifty,
Crying, and then to sixty degrees. You stand.
The main physio, pleased, says, "Next time, ninety."
I stand before you and say, "Just as at the hospital
They hoisted you into a chair and now you can sit
In your wheelchair, so tilting you like this can lead
To your standing, perhaps taking a step? That's the spirit."
"In a few months' time," the physio says doubtfully,
But I know you'll one day take a step boldly.

12, 13 September 2023

113
Three-Month Crying Blight and Plight

You don't cry as we process down the corridor.
Your consultant stops me and says, tilting his head,
"I've spoken to Dr Chowdhury about the three
Blocked arteries and seizure, and I'll include what he said
In the emailed minutes, so you and her mother hear
The same information at the same time" – equally.
I ask what the management said to my email.
He says, "They told me, 'You're doing a good job, carry
On doing it'" – hence three, perhaps more, months
I say your crying in the gym was harrowing.
There's a thunderstorm, you cry as we prepare to leave.
I hold your hand, you squeeze my fingers, crying.
Your raised dose may be flushing out your blight's sadness and anger,
And your three-month crying plight may soon be over.

12, 13 September 2023

13. 'Blight', "any obscure force which is harmful or destructive" (*Concise Oxford Dictionary*).

14. 'Plight', "condition or state, especially an unfortunate one" (*Concise Oxford Dictionary*).

114
Arcady Paralysed, Now Paradisal

Again I'm in Arcady and, with my staff, my long
Shepherd's crook I hold below its curve, saunter
Across grass to the pond and feed the fish,
Then see buttercups, daisies and clover
Growing back with stitchwort. They disappeared three months ago
When your crying blight and my crying sonnets began.
Arcady was blighted by a polluted rain,
Perhaps from Ukraine, blown by wind that ignored a ban.
This year no swallows have come, migrating birds
Have known not to come to Arcady out of fear,
But now Paradise is back and the wild flowers
Look healthy, and the swallows will come next year.
Three months you were paralysed as I was, and Nature.
Now Arcady's back, your crying and my sonnets may be over.

12, 13 September 2023

6–7. 'Blight', "any plant disease caused by mildews, rusts, smuts, fungi, or insects; any obscure force which is harmful or destructive" (*Concise Oxford Dictionary*).

115
Infirm and Involuntary

I went to the gym yesterday, but am still unsteady
On my feet, I'm told I've aged since your stroke, have gone
From nimble to showing-my-age, infirm eighty-four,
Mind preoccupied, not one with my work, and wan
From thinking of you in Norwich, unsure how long before
The arthritic hands that drive me must be
Replaced. It would help me if you could stop your involuntary,
Infirm crying, I must continue to visit and see
If tweaking your medication will bring it to an end.
And I must stop my involuntary pouring out
Of my emotions in sonnets as if there's a disconnect
Between my brain stem and occipital lobe, and must shout.

I must regain my infirm calm in this Arcady
As you regain yours in your infirmary.

14 September 2023

3, 13. 'Infirm', "physically weak, especially through age" (*Concise Oxford Dictionary*).
4. 'Wan', "(of a person's complexion or appearance) pale, exhausted, worn" (*Concise Oxford Dictionary*).
14. 'Infirmary', "a hospital; a place for those who are ill" (*Concise Oxford Dictionary*).

116
Capacity

The speech and language therapist now writes
You've demonstrated you understand what's aired
To you, and the team will now ask you if you consent
That information about you can be shared.
You've been assessed on whether you understand questions –
And have demonstrated you understand correctly –
On granting a Power of Attorney for finances
And have said you want me to hold your Power of Attorney
In conjunction with my eldest son, no one else,
And have been consistent across sessions in your choice.
You've correctly identified the difficulties with your house
And want the paperwork done now so I'm your financial voice.
You have demonstrated you have legal capacity
And reports can now grant me your Power of Attorney.

15 September 2023

7, 14. 'Power of Attorney', "the authority to act for another in legal or financial matters" (*Concise Oxford Dictionary*).
13. 'Capacity', "legal competence" (*Concise Oxford Dictionary*).

117
Moving, Swallowing, Laughing, Balancing, Cycling – Escaping

You're lying in bed when I arrive. I ask
If you've been read the minutes of the meeting,
You eyes-up yes. I show you two books and say
They're about two women with locked-in syndrome escaping –
You eyes-up yes – within eight months. Now you cry.

I say they advise moving your hands and feet
Every ten minutes. You move your right toes, knee
And fingers, and are swallowing, and you laugh from your sheet.
We're taken to the gym, and you sit and balance,
Head down, therapists not touching you, you don't slump;
Then cycle, your leg muscles pushing, for twenty minutes.
Then you sit in the chilly garden where flowers clump.
You're moving, swallowing, laughing, balancing and cycling
After thirteen weeks, and by Christmas can be escaping.

19, 23 September 2023

118
Glassing-In Arcadian Landscape

I survey my Arcadian landscape, holding my crook
Like Strephon, the Arcadian shepherd, and each landmark,
And absorb the lush late-summer green of the grass
And the sweep of the trees round Henry the Eighth's deer park,
Towards which I walked each day during lockdown,
Revelling in the rustic wildlife and pasture,
The deer, foxes, birds, butterflies and wild flowers.
I open my post-box, from the Council a letter:
The Indian owner of the house behind the sloping field
Seeks planning permission to glass that grass near his home
With a thousand ground-based solar panels
In this historic green-belt Fairmead where deer still roam.
Now my Arcadian landscape, blighted by war and your stroke,
May be glassed-in for eco-profit, and I'm asked to be woke.

19, 23 September 2023

2. Strephon is an Arcadian shepherd in Philip Sidney's *Arcadia* (1580) and in his later *Countess of Pembroke's Arcadia* (1590). He reappears in Gilbert and Sullivan's *Iolanthe* (1882).
14. 'Woke', "alert to racial prejudice and discrimination".

119
Arcady's New Blight

There was billowing smoke in Arcady last week,
And my neighbour rang to ask if I could find out why.

I sent my gardener down to check, alarmed
There might be a wildfire in the tinder dry.
A sofa was on fire beyond our bottom gate.
I wrote to the land's owner over the hill,
And now I'm speaking to my neighbour about
Solar panels, not wildfires, and he's asked if I will
Join a local group who are engaging
A planning consultant to see off this vandalising
Of Arcady that was recovering from its blight,
And was Paradise again, wild flowers were returning.
And now there's another blight that must be seen off without strife,
With resolute protection of our pastoral life.

19, 23 September 2023

120
War in Arcady

And now there's deep division in Arcady.
The absentee owner of the house over the hill
Beyond my bottom field has applied to install
A thousand three-metre-high solar panels that will
Feed forty homes, twenty-five panels per home.
Where these forty homes will be has not been said.
It seems he intends to build a housing estate
And transform Arcady, and I've contributed
Six hundred pounds for a planning consultant
To defend us locals' peace that's already died.
There's war in Arcady to reject his plan.
I was at peace in this pastoral countryside
Till your stroke, then the absence of blighted wild flowers
And now glassing the grass have blighted my rustic hours.

22, 23 September 2023

121
Atrophy: Faltering Together Following our Fall

I am old and can't walk in a straight line
Due to atrophy in my cerebellum, found
On my MRI, that's been mild and's becoming severe

As it's atrophying control of my movements, bound
In a disconnect with my occipital lobe.
As your PBA disconnect pours crying mine pours verse,
It wrings sonnets past my paralysed gatekeeper.
Your disconnect's more severe than mine, far worse,
And's stopped your throat muscles from speaking, whereas mine's
Parted my cords so my husky voice finds it hard to engage.
You're worse than me, but I'm on the same spectrum,
You're further on, but I falter as I age.
We walked together when you were very small,
Now we're faltering together, following our fall.

22, 23 September 2023

10. 'Cords', "vocal cords".

122
Harmony in the Soul: The Music of the Spheres

"When you get old, soul sings" I was once told.
It's true. As I go about my daily pottering
I hear distant music in my mind, especially
In air conditioners' or car wheels' humming.
Up, down, the pleasant music goes, and I
Anticipate each mellifluous chord in peace,
And I think back to the Greeks' *musica universalis*,
The music of the spheres' harmony that does not cease,
The music of the celestial bodies
Taught in the medieval quadrivium's prong,
Whose speeds Kepler turned into tones, seeing
It as a continuous and ever-changing song.
I live in harmony with the universe and hear
The universe's harmonies in each ear.

26, 28 September 2023

6. 'Chord', "three or more notes sounded together, as a basis of harmony" (*Concise Oxford Dictionary*).
7. 'Greeks'. The 'universal music' of Pythagoras and Aristotle.
8. 'Sphere', "each of a series of revolving concentrically arranged spherical shells in which celestial bodies were formerly thought to be set in a fixed relationship" (*Concise Oxford Dictionary*).
'Music (or 'harmony') of the spheres', "the natural harmonic tones supposedly produced by the movement of the celestial spheres or of the bodies fixed in

them" (*Concise Oxford Dictionary*).

10. 'Quadrivium', "a medieval university course of arithmetic, geometry, astronomy and music" (*Concise Oxford Dictionary*).
'Prong', "each of two or more projected pointed parts at the end of a fork, etc." (*Concise Oxford Dictionary*). Here four pointed ends of the fork of the medieval university course.

11. 'Kepler'. Johannes Kepler (1571–1630) is known for his laws of planetary motion.

13–14. 'Harmony', "a combination of simultaneously sounded musical notes to produce chords and chord progresses, especially as having a pleasing effect" (*Concise Oxford Dictionary*).

123
Rescuing from Harm

I send my email to your solicitor
Following your choice of me as your attorney,
And ask her to prepare the legal documents
For finance, with my eldest son alongside me,
And perhaps health, with your mum, who I've rung. She was critical
Of the therapist who found you have capacity
And has sought independent advice questioning
Your capacity and POA, and's in no hurry.
You're crying from pain, nurse gives you pain relief.
You're crying a lot. You're too unwell to go out
Into the garden. I stroke your hair with the scalp brush,
Say you're escaping, you look up at me, then cry, what about?
Today's been a setback, nurse straightens your right arm,
Then I tell you I'm rescuing you from all harm.

26, 28 September 2023

8. 'POA', Power of Attorney.

124
Fountain

I am like the fountain in my Arcadian garden,
I pour a flow of words like its water.
I gush an effortless spurting energy
From within I barely understand, stronger

At eighty-four than I should be, coping
With bringing out four books and the proofreading,
A solar farm, getting you through your difficulties
Set out in the latest update, battling:
My computer's Sent Items are full so my emails
Are stuck in my Outbox, and incoming are out of sight.
My shredder's cable looped my ankle, I fell
And its box has cracks, its top an unchanging red light.
Through it all I fountain works, flow, gush and spew,
And all the while I pour words about you.

28, 29 September 2023

7. 'Solar farm', see sonnets 118–120: 'Glassing-In Arcadian Landscape', 'Arcady's New Blight' and 'War in Arcady'.

125
Eyewitness: Overcoming

You toddled into my study in Japan,
Nearly three, and I lifted you onto my knee so you
Could see my penned writing laid on my desk:
'The Silence' I thought my masterpiece, a new
Baroque Age being born from my centre-shift.
You were an eyewitness of my early poetic life,
You were there as my images poured in during
The great heat of a Tokyo summer, along with my wife.
You stood near me when I first saw the Light,
And I wrote to you on my way to see Pound, that same day
That turned me from Modernism to the Baroque,
And you witnessed the milestones on my long Mystic Way.
Now I'm an eyewitness of your battling
Being locked-in, and *your* long overcoming.

28, 29 September 2023

1. 'Toddle', "walk with short unsteady steps like those of a small child" (*Concise Oxford Dictionary*).
10. Pound, Ezra Pound. Nicholas Hagger visited Pound in Rapallo, Italy on 16 July 1970.

126
Incapacity

I've had an email from my solicitor,
She's rung your mum and is saying there should be
An independent assessor she will appoint
To question your unspoken capacity,
And that she must visit you and receive your instructions –
And confirm your incapacity as you're dumb.
I visit in a mask as there's one case of Covid,
And read in the blue book you've said the word 'mum'.
The speech and language therapist comes in,
We converse across your bed with you listening.
I ask if they've ever had an independent assessor.
She says No, it must be a medic assessing.
I watch two physios fix you to your bike
And you machine-pedal with a capacity I like.

3 October 2023

6. 'Incapacity', i.e. there can be no Power of Attorney.

14. 'Machine', MOTOmed, a sloping steel frame with two pedals in which the machine and human inputs can be graduated between zero and all.
'Capacity', ability to understand information and make decisions about one's life.

127
Fifty-Year-Old Pain

Now I'm taken away by the consultant's assistant.
I say your mum's questioning your capacity
And wants an independent assessor.
She confirms that Caroline House has definitely
Never had this situation until now.
She will take it back to the team and suggest my
Way forward when I visit you next week.
When I leave, you mouth (nearly verbal), 'Bye.'
I reflect on how fifty-three years ago your mum
Agreed to deprive you of my fatherhood and, fraught,
Blocked my reconciliation attempt,
Then sought to block my access to you in a court,

So I was asked to sign I'd never see you again….
In Arcady I relive a fifty-year-old pain.

3, 4 October 2023

128
Determined Intent

I hear – as I leave for a birthday meal
With my two sons, who are back from a visit
To watch Europe trounce America at golf
In Rome – that my composer brother has been hit
In his face in Spain by a golf ball that broke his nose
And bloodied an eye that now sees only shade and light.
I am shocked and sad that no one called out "Fore",
And say he has a piece of organ music to write:
Tranquillity in hot sun, striking of the ball,
An explosion of pain, then slow recovery
As the brain's healing brings overcoming,
Universal music that ends in serenity
About enjoyment and a sudden accident
And how all traumas are healed by determined intent.

3, 5 October 2023

7. 'Fore', "golf, a warning to a person in the path of a ball" (*Concise Oxford Dictionary*).
8. 'Organ music'. See 'A New Age of Light' (pp.211-213) for Jonathan Hagger's organ composition.

129
Peace in Arcady: Stag

No, I say, I will not be tormented
By these agonies that befoul my Arcady –
Your stroke that has left me haunted by the bans
On my seeing you and on my works; planning calumny.
I'll again be at peace at the heart of the universe.
I walk past four oaks to my first field where
Turf's been removed to probe for roundhouses caught
In a LiDAR picture that de-grassed the earth bare,
And with my shepherd's crook recall my joys

Amid skimming swallows and grasshoppers, and my glee
At a stag caught by its antlers in my wire fence.
I return to the bronze stag and deer you gave me,
And am now at peace by Arcady's carp pond,
An old man amid memories, awaiting the beyond.

3, 5, 6 October 2023

4. 'Calumny', "malicious representation" (*Concise Oxford Dictionary*).

130
In Arcady: Old Man in a Circle

In Arcady I'm at peace with the universe
And its Year that includes each cyclic spiral
(Day-night, life-death, rise-fall, the cosmic cycle)
And's represented by an old man in a circle
That contains the months, their work and the zodiac.
I have become that old man who resets
At the heart of the universe that revolves round him
The orbitings of the sun, moon and planets
That arrive back in their same positions today
After what Plato called a Great Year, whose span
He, Newton and modern astronomers have calculated
At more than twenty-five thousand years. I can
Be at peace within Arcady's Great Year,
And now *am* the old man in its circle's cyclic sphere.

5, 6 October 2023

2. 'Year', "the year is, as it were, the prototype of all cyclic processes (the day, the span of human life, the rise and fall of culture, the cosmic cycle, etc.).... The year is usually represented by the figure of an old man in a circle, with two or three outer rings containing such items as: the names of the months, the cycle of work appropriate to each month, the signs of the Zodiac and so on." J.E. Cirlot, *A Dictionary of Symbols* (1962).
   'Spiral', adjective, "winding about a centre in an enlarging or decreasing continuous circular motion"; noun, "a three-dimensional spiral curve, a spiral galaxy" (*Concise Oxford Dictionary*).
4. Nicholas Hagger's poem 'Old Man in a Circle' (1967), which was based on Cirlot's old man in a circle who controls the Great Year and in particular shifts from an old age to a new age, is about the end of an old imperial and colonial age and the beginning of decolonisation (see his *Collected Poems 1958–2005*, volume 6, pp.116–128). Now 56 years later, an old man himself,

he writes of the old man in a circle who controls the whole of the Great Year and the unity of the universe.

10. Plato, see his dialogue 'Timaeus'.

'Great Year'. Plato hypothesised that winding the orbital motions of the sun, moon and planets that can be seen with the naked eye forward or back in time would arrive at a point where they are in the same positions as they are today. Plato called this time period a Great Year, which he calculated would take place every 36,000 years. Newton understood that from the earth's point of view the sky is really moving in one huge circle, and that it takes 360 times 72 years for celestial bodies to return to their original posts. A Great Year to Newton was 72 x 360° = 25,920 years. The Great Year has been defined by scientific astronomy as the period of one complete cycle of equinoxes around the ecliptic, which takes about every 25,800 years.

13. 'Arcady's Great Year', i.e. the workings of the universe in Arcady.

131
Wilderness: Magpie, Free

I wander in my wilderness in October.
Roses bloom, but no buttercups enthral,
No clover in my clover fields. I listen
To splashing water from the waterfall
As I feed my carp, holding my shepherd's crook,
And notice red holly berries, and black
Elderberries, and reflect that although the leaves
Have not turned yellow, the flowers are gone, all's slack.
It's just green trees and jackdaws on the grass.
The year has grown old and like me's now slow,
And I, its old man, view its stifled growth
In the knowledge we're both approaching our time to go.
Arcady is still, a magpie flies to a tree.
From my wilderness and old age I'll soon flit and be free.

7 October 2023

132
Independent Capacity Assessor Declined

A nurse is taking your blood pressure. You stare at me
And cry. I apply lip balm. The consultant
Looks in and chats: after speaking to your mum
Our solicitor's requested an independent

Assessor of your capacity, and as their
Assessment's been questioned the hospital
Won't get involved, I should find a POA assessor
But no Court-of-Protection deputies can meddle
As the experts have found you *have* capacity.
I say I will go slow on a POA.
I return as you're wheeled outside in your wheelchair.
I sit on the wall with you. The therapist comes out to say
You were asked several times if you consent to meet an assigned
Independent assessor and each time you declined.

10, 29 October 2023

7. 'POA'. Power of Attorney.
8. 'Deputies'. A stroke victim who is locked-in, quadriplegic and cannot speak or write who is found not to have capacity is placed under the Court of Protection and cannot have attorneys with Powers of Attorney, only deputies who operate under instruction from the Court of Protection, which has the power to decide in what care home he or she will live.
Deputyship under the Court of Protection in accordance with the Mental Capacity Act 2005 is for those who have not been found to have capacity, which is based on understanding regardless of ability to verbalise in speaking or writing.

133
Crying Despair

So what it means is you want me to be
Your attorney without involving an outside assessor
But approval would take eight months to implement
And approval's been slowed by your mum's adviser.
We'll soon learn that you should be discharged to nursing care,
Not to your house with a carer (who'd have time off as well),
And if it's level-one the NHS will pay
But if level-two *you* have to pay, we should sell
Your house and dispose of your furniture that's now
In store, and set up a lifelong fund to go
Towards paying for your care, but we'll have no POA.
As I cream your fingers and brush your scalp I know
You'll need full-time lifelong permanent care
And sadly won't escape quadriplegic crying despair.

10, 30 October 2023

3. 'Eight months'. Three months to complete the legal process, assessment of capacity by an assessor recognised by the hospital, legal visits to the hospital and signing of the Last Powers of Attorney (LPAs), and five months for the LPAs to be registered by the Office of the Public Guardian.

134
Court: Caught

My solicitor rang your mum and agreed with her
In questioning whether you have the capacity
To choose me as your attorney as you can't
Verbalise, we're back to being equal deputies. She
Has offered an independent assessor that you
Have declined, and learning this the consultant has been
To Safeguarding, who've said the therapist
Could be taken to court if she signs your capacity's clean.
Fifty years ago I was caught, I was to be outed
In court to deny my access to you, that's why
I left my secret work, they too steered clear of court.
So fearing court, the hospital won't certify
You've capacity so I can be your chosen attorney.
But you'll soon be verbal, sending emails on a MegaBee.

10, 29 October 2023

3. 'Attorney'. The attorney has a Power of Attorney.
4. 'Deputies'. With Court of Protection deputyships.
14. 'MegaBee'. An electronic e-tran board operated by eye gaze and making possible the sending of verbal emails that demonstrate capacity.

135
Fall

I drive to the dental hygienist's surgery
And am forced to park above the cricket ground,
At the top of The Uplands, and as I walk back
Down the sloping uneven pavement I avoid – walk round –
Two bins and my left foot treads on jagged tarmac
With a plunge of three inches hidden by weeds, and twists
Near the kerb, and suddenly I'm flying through the air
And land on my left hand and knee – no, on my wrists,
And am dragged. I get up, there's a tear in my right trouser leg

And blood beneath, and my left ankle's been twisted.
I carry on and at the surgery receive
First aid on my knee: gauze and plaster where I've bled.
It's my first fall, at eighty-four, a sign
I could fall again and break my hips and spine.

12, 30 October 2023

5. 'Jagged', "with an unevenly cut or torn edge; deeply indented; with sharp points" (*Concise Oxford Dictionary*).

136
Silent

My wife speaks out. She's not coping with your news,
Nor is our first son, who's floundering at work
With high blood pressure and the extra of you.
I must think of your effect on them, does it irk?
And on me as my health is perceived as being on
A downward spiral, my fall a symbol I may croak.
And your mum is barely coping, as well. I must recover,
Revert to how I was before your stroke.
For the good of our family I must be silent
About you, keep you to myself, be normal again.
I must visit you in Norwich on my own
Though I'm not able to drive, and protect all from the strain.
You look to me for improvements in your health,
I must protect my family from heart attacks by stealth.

12, 30 October 2023

4. 'Irk', "irritate, bore, annoy" (*Concise Oxford Dictionary*).

137
Expectations like a Sea-Swell's Foam

The weekly update says the therapist
Is working on communication aids that tend,
E-tran frames and oromotor mouthing of words.
The team have agreed you'll stay until the end
Of January. You were upset. On your discharge
You would like to live in your house and feel homely.
They'll assess the equipment and adapting it will need.

The caring was not discussed, or agency
Reliefs not turning up, leaving you in the lurch,
Or a Power of Attorney to access your bank account.
You've no control of your bodily functions
And are fed via PEG tube and need an amount
Of long-term full-time care in a nursing home
And your expectations may fade like a sea-swell's foam.

13, 23 October 2023

2. 'Tend', "take care of, look after (a person, especially an invalid)" (*Concise Oxford Dictionary*).

138
Broken Ankle-Bone

I visit the Junior School I founded to see
The finished Senior School we've been building
That will add a hundred and twenty pupils a year.
I wander through decorated rooms, noting
Clusters of microscopes and lab test-tubes,
Leaning on the stick my father last used quite
Sixty years ago, following my fall and the pain
In my left ankle that kept me awake last night.
Now my wife drives me to Cheshunt Community
Hospital's walk-in clinic that X-rays my swollen
Ankle, and I come out with a black boot.
My medial malleolus bone's broken.
So, driven, I will hobble to you with my input
On your discharge, despite a broken foot.

14, 21 October 2023

1. Junior School. Coopersale Hall School, Epping, Essex, which Nicholas Hagger founded in 1988.

139
Frustration

I hobble in and sit, and show you my boot,
And (you in your chair) say an ankle-bone's broken,
And the key worker comes in and I say that I've brought
Non-alcoholic wine for you to taste when

It's frothed to foam that will melt in your mouth.
She confirms that your mum will soon have agreed
To meet her at your house so she can inspect
And assess the equipment it would need
To be ready as an option for your discharge, and you cry
For it means you'll be in rehab for three months more.
Then nurses come to hoist you back into bed.
I hear you crying as I sit outside your door.
I'm inured to it now, it's no longer heart-rending.
Your PBA's frustration's never-ending.

17, 18 October 2023

13. 'Inured', "accustomed to something, especially unpleasant" (*Concise Oxford Dictionary*).
'Heart-rending', "very distressing" (*Concise Oxford Dictionary*).

14. 'PBA'. In pseudobulbar affect (emotional incontinence), the gatekeeper that controls emotion partially ceases to work.

140
Chill in the Air

There's a chill in the air in this peaceful Arcady.
We've lurched into a time of nationalist war
That's spread from Ukraine to the Middle East
As Israel destroys terrorist Hamas for
Attacking and butchering Jewish civilians.
War's a rumbling background in the daily news
And may again be above this paradise,
Bringing destruction from the air. I muse
In dismay after a busy week, and look
At the update on your fatigue, locked-in syndrome,
Weak upper limbs that can't maintain sitting.
It signals you'll be discharged to a nursing home,
Not your house, as you need round-the-clock nursing care,
And I sense a new chill in this Arcadian air.

21 October 2023

141
The Way Forward

Yesterday your mum found you distressed and in despair,
Unable to cope with your trauma, and was horrified.
Today you smiled when I arrived, and signed
Your council-tax form with a cross (your mark) beside
Your witnessing consultant so they can deal with me.
In the gym you were cycled for twenty minutes to acclaim,
And, back in your room in your wheelchair, you eye-
Gazed coloured letters on an e-tran frame
That spelt out your message to me, "Lovely to see you."
You will soon have an electronic machine from CASEE
And will be able to send emails to your friends.
"It is what it is," you used to say to me.
So improve where you are with your old determination,
The way forward's just opened, and's your salvation.

24, 26 October 2023

10. 'CASEE', Communication Aid Service East of England.

142
Recovering: Again at Peace in Arcady

And now I can end my crying, groaning sonnets.
You're recovering and your path will wind and roam.
Your life will not return to how it was
And you may be discharged to a nursing home
To continue your recovery for a while until
You move into your house, or for the rest of your living.
I am recovering from my agony
At your hopelessness and despair, and my foot's healing;
And Arcadia's recovering from its blights, its flowers
Will return in the new year, its solar-panelled sore
Will be seen off as endangering its sweep of trees.
I will saunter in my Arcady as before.
I will email and visit you and you will email me,
I'll again be at peace in my last days in Arcady.

24, 26 October 2023

143
In Arcadia: The Oneness of the Universe

I walk to my meadow with my shepherd's crook
And gaze in sunshine at blackberries in the breeze
And see a deer watching me as in the Tudor time,
And look back at my hermitage surrounded by trees
And feel the Oneness of the universe
Beneath transient conflicts – your rehab pain,
The fall-out from depleted uranium
Munitions supplied by the US to Ukraine
In rain, aspirations to turn that field to glass –
And rustic peace, in timeless Arcadia glow.
In my last days I see *yang* and *yin* balance:
Plus A plus minus A equals zero.
I embody the union of ephemeral agony
And timeless ecstasy in this serene Arcady.

24, 26 October 2023

6. 'Transient', "in short duration; momentary; passing; impermanent" (*Concise Oxford Dictionary*).
12. The algebraic formula in Nicholas Hagger's works: +A + −A = 0, *yang* + *yin* = Great Nothing.
13. 'Ephemeral', "lasting or of use only for a short time; transitory" (*Concise Oxford Dictionary*).

144
Difficult

You smile a greeting, and the consultant comes in
And confirms you'll have a Covid jab, and tells
Me you're having Fluoxetine for mood
(Your involuntary crying). Now in the gym, in short spells
You're hoisted to stand on a Quest 'standing machine'
But cry at the pain in your ankles and knees
Taking your weight after months of lying in bed.
Back in your room the speech therapist confirms she's
Working with you on an electronic e-tran frame,
A MegaBee that can send an email by eye gaze
And an on/off switch for a TV and light, and you cry.
Are you crying because you can't do what you're asked, in a daze?

I know it's difficult, and your discharge seems a nightmare,
But you'll have tried to improve before moving to nursing care.

31 October, 1 November 2023

145
Strike

My TVs had no signal here in Arcady.
I rang the company that looks after them and was told
To switch Sky to terrestrial – still no signal –
And then see if the top Sky box in the loft had holed
Green lights next to it, it hadn't – and then find a switch
Down in a fuse board. In the airing cupboard I found
A switch down and pushed it up and the power returned,
And now the televisions are working and sound.
I rang this news through and was told, "There were storms last night,
You may have had a lightning strike." Ann's confirmed
There were rumblings of thunder and lightning I slept through.
A strike must have struck out our power, and I never squirmed.
And I think of the stroke that struck your energy that hour.
If only I could push up a switch and restore *your* power.

3 November 2023

4. 'Hole', "an empty space in a solid body" (*Concise Oxford Dictionary*). 'Holed lights', 'lights in a solid box with holes or slats in it'.

146
Flemish Characteristics: Nothing's Certain

Like my Flemish ancestor Carolus Haggar
Who left plague-ridden Bruges for Chelmsford and trust
In life under near-Flemish Queen Philippa of Hainault,
I – *we* – have the Flemish characteristics to adjust
To what has happened to you: I am tolerant,
Flexible, open-minded, disciplined and hard-working,
And express my emotions openly in poems
As the great Rubens did in each painting
Within the Flemish Baroque – my Baroque vision
Came from my Flemish roots, or so it would seem.

But my tolerance and openness are challenged
By your sudden reversal of fortune and collapsed dream.
In life, nothing's certain, in one moment we can lose
Speech, movement and expectations, even during a snooze.

5, 7 November 2023

5, 7 November 2023. The first 10 lines were drafted earlier, undated, and then put aside.

3. 'Near-Flemish Queen'. Philippa of Hainault was born in Valenciennes in Hainaut, France, which bordered Flanders (and ruled it in 1067-1071 and 1191-1246), and married Edward III in 1328.

8–9. Flanders in the Middle Ages included a large part of Belgium, a part of Holland and some territory in North-West France. The Flemish towns most known for Flemish painting included Bruges, Ghent, Antwerp, Brussels and Utrecht. These passed to the Spanish Habsburgs in 1556. Rubens was born in 1577 in Siegen, Germany, but worked in Antwerp, which was previously in Flanders but then in the Spanish Netherlands, and is known as the greatest exponent of Flemish Baroque painting.

9. "My Baroque vision". This was anthologised in Nicholas Hagger's *A Baroque Vision*, which has a painting by Rubens on the front cover.

147
Speechless and Still, like an Infant

I watch my infant granddaughter attempt
To press a toy's buzzer, and then sit, leaning,
Held by my younger son, her head bowed, and then stand
With her hands on a coffee-table, knees buckling,
And watching her hands, bowed head and sagging knees
I think of you being held by a physio
And encouraged to do the same things in your gym.
O cruel life to return a retired widow
To the helpless postures of an eight-month-old child,
And a mind with latent words like an infant's dark.
We live on the assumption that we will reach old age
But many things can befall us before that landmark.
But there the parallel stops: babies progress,
Whereas you may stay speechless and still, filled with distress.

5, 7 November 2023

148
Palliative Care

There's talk of your discharge to level-two Sue Ryder
Home in Ipswich, if you can swallow and prepare
By then, when your house has been assessed for hoist equipment
To exclude its suitability for full-time care;
And I now have to face the possibility
That, after five months of the best rehab regime, you're
Not going to improve and at the next meeting
Will be declared to be quadriplegic except for
Twitches in your right toes, knee and fingers
And head's left-right movement when on a pillow,
And (urged by your mum) in need of palliative care
To optimise quality of life without 'ordeal by physio'.
I've hoped you'll speak and move, but they're not happening.
I'd be sad if they now just mitigate your suffering.

7 November 2023

2. 'Prepare', i.e. make the preparations necessary for acceptance.

149
Death Setting You Free

I am back to the second day after your two strokes
When in a deep sleep – *coma* – you had lost your powers,
And a young doctor knelt by me at your bedside
And said you might live another forty-eight hours.
Your stroke was so severe, they had made you comfortable,
You were having palliative, not intensive, care contrived
To cope with your pain, nausea, breathing and trauma.
A large part of your brain was not working, and if you survived
It would mean one-to-one caring, but that was unlikely.
Two days later I was shown a CT scan that tells
Of your brain, with a dark area from the top down,
And an older doctor said, "Those are dead brain cells."
So now it's proposed, five months later, you should be
In palliative care so death can at last set you free.

7 November 2023

1. 'The second day'. Tuesday 13 June 2023.
10. 'Two days later'. Thursday 15 June 2023.

150
Defying or Accepting Fate

Time was when it was good to struggle with fate;
"Fate often preserves the undoomed warrior when
His courage is strong." I've urged will-power and struggling
Against your speechless, motionless fate by often
Cycling in the gym, being hoisted to the standing
Machine or raised by the tilt table, to a laugh,
Or eye-gazing the e-tran frame into words.
Now your mum's telling the consultant and staff
You hate being pushed by the physios and demeaned
By your incontinence when you're in pain or in gloom,
Still grieving, and should now have palliative care,
Be made comfortable and accept your impending doom.
A victorious defying that overcomes is good.
Is it more ignoble to accept your victimhood?

8 November 2023

2–3. From *Beowulf*: "*Wyrd oft nereð unfaegne, eorl, þonne his ellen deah.*" (NB, *nereð* is pronounced nereth, and *þonne* is pronounced thonnie.)

151
Caring for All 'Yous' or 'Old You'

You're not the person you once were, I agree.
You were poised, vivacious, confident and well-bred,
An accomplished organiser of your husband's band
And of his funeral, where you stood at the door and greeted
The dozens of music-lovers who would speak with you.
And now, as I brush your scalp so your hair's styled
And lip-salve your lips and cream your fingers,
You look up at me like a trusting, wordless child.
Your personality's been taken by your stroke,
You silently answer yes-no questions with your eyes.
Is it kinder to make you comfortable and free of pain
And let you die as the 'old you' is gone or in disguise?
I've cared for you in all your ages and 'yous' and why,
If one 'old you' has gone, should the new 'you' have to die?

8 November 2023

152
Phases of 'One You'

I've loved different 'yous' at different ages:
The toddler in Japan who each day held my hand
And walked with me to Edogawa bridge:
The table-learning eight-year-old who'd stand
And be dodged in Libya; the boarding-school girl who stayed
With me each holidays; the school-leaver
In a caravan in a Scottish garden, who I
Helped to buy a flat and comfort near Edinburgh;
The air-hostess who looked so smart when I
Flew to Scotland with you, who helped others to lift
And bundle a steward onto a luggage rack;
And the concerned housewife who always came with a gift.
And these were phases of one 'you', and I view
Your current silence as another phase of 'one you'.

8 November 2023

153
Occultation

I sit in my window above this Cornish sea
Far from Arcady and the hospital, squinting –
To the west of the sun that's dazzling
And blinding this fine November morning –
For the occultation that's about to happen
When the moon will pass in front of Venus, a dot.
Now the sun's too bright to see even the moon.
But just as I know of this celestial event – and what
Is happening out there in the wider universe
When Jupiter has been high, visible all night,
Feeling so well in this sea air, nasal passages clear –
So something's happening to my co-existence with your plight.
My sometime moon is obscuring my Venus's love.
I am at peace under the now clouding sky above.

9, 10 November 2023

Title 'Occultation'. The moon obscured Venus in an event known as an 'occultation' at 9.45am on 9 November 2023.

154
Heroic Endurance

Your mum's rung Sue Ryder Home, Ipswich, they've offered
You a vacant bed but the hospital's keeping you
As planned. It seems you won't move into your house.
You'll be at the coming meeting and can choose what you'll do,
But on Tuesday I'll say you need full-time long-term
Nursing care in a care home that won't impact
On your elderly family, who'll still visit you
Without having to manage your hoist and your wheelchair, act
On your incontinence, splints, PEG-feeding and pills.
It will be a looser set-up, there'll still be
Rehab, but your friends can visit and you'll be kept
Comfortable with pain relief and some therapy.
Your heroic endurance has led to improvements
And now you must not depend on elderly parents.

10 November 2023

4. At the review meeting on 15 December 2023 Nadia was offered an extension of her stay to at least the end of March as she was deemed still in need of level-1 care and as improving enough to warrant this.

155
Harmony and Bliss in Arcady

In November sun I walk in my Arcady's wild
Down the sloping lawn with my shepherd's crook
And reflect that all conflicts have at last been reconciled:
Glassing-over refused, Tudor deer parks with a good look,
Birds flitting and fluttering as I survey the fish,
The red holly berries portending Christmasing.
Next year the wild flowers will be back as I wish,
And the swallows, and after the winter a warm spring.
There's discord out there, protests against Israel,
And the Third World War may already be spreading fast,
But I've withdrawn from the troubled court and its tale.
You'll soon be settled, so the agony has now passed.
I have reconciled all conflicts in this harmony,
And am again blissful in my Arcady.

10, 11 November 2023

4. 'Glassing-over', application to install 1,000 solar panels.
11. 'Tale', 'narrative'.
14. 'Blissful'. The harmonious bliss is reflected in the first fully-rhymed sonnet in this sequence.

156
The Vivid Greens of Arcady

I'm wheeled to the theatre ignoring my heart's pain, keen
For my second cataract in a week to be liquidised.
I tell the anaesthetist my green tea's already as green
As the tea in Japan sixty years back. He says Monet prized
His later, splodged paintings of his water lilies
He did after his excised cataracts, Nature's new impact –
Should I now swoon out dozens of new sonnets to fizz
With my new perception of colour…? After my cataract
Is washed out as tears and the new lens is in I am wheeled
To recovery, a one-eyed Cyclops in a wheelchair – like you;
Half my face plastered, on the same battlefield
As you, and, at one with you, will soon, amid greenery, review
The triumph of our heroic endurance, and I'll blissfully
Sip in the vivid greens of my wonderful Arcady.

15–17 January 2024

1. Nicholas Hagger had two cataracts removed at Moorfields Eye Hospital, London on 8 and 15 January 2024 by Professor David Gartry, who performed the first femtosecond laser-assisted cataract surgery in the UK in 1989. Nicholas Hagger was woken by a pain in his heart at 3.15am on 15 January, but ignored this for most of the day to get the procedure done.
2. 'Liquidised'. A cataract is when the eye's natural lens that throws an image on the retina becomes cloudy or opaque. Under Professor Gartry's technique the cloudy lens is removed by ultrasound energy that makes an incision, liquefies and then washes out the natural lens and inserts an artificial lens that unfolds and transmits clear images to the retina.
5. Claude Monet had surgery on his cataracts in 1923, and then produced many of his 250 paintings of the water lilies in his garden which link Impressionism to modern abstract art.
7. 'Swoon', "faint; fall into a fainting fit" (*Concise Oxford Dictionary*). 'Swoon out', "write sonnets whose intensity would make the poet swoon, i.e. faint". This sonnet, like sonnets 155, 157 and 158, is fully rhymed and opens the possibility of a new volume of vividly colourful poems within Arcady.

10. 'One-eyed Cyclops'. Homer's Odysseus encountered Polyphemus, the one-eyed giant, in Sicily, where he was shut up with 12 of his companions in the Cyclops' cave.

13–14. 'Blissfully/Sip'. As in sonnet 155, the harmonious bliss is reflected in the second fully-rhymed sonnet in this sequence.

157
The Old You's Back

"If you want to skip a week because of snow"
You spell out on your e-tran board, and I see
The old you who always thinks of others and I know
Is back. You've been watching the weather forecast on TV
And noticing where the frosty cold spell sits.
You want to avoid inconveniencing
Us though you look forward to our weekly visits.
The old you's back, and now I read you're coping
With a switch to turn on a lamp, radio, call bell
And TV. You're to control a wheelchair and sign
Your name. "All manner of thing shall be well."
You're moving forward, and soon you'll be fine,
Find you can swallow and speak words and move,
And sit and balance with neck posture that will improve.

Date 20, 21 January 2024

Title This sonnet is before no.158 in event order, though written later. It is fully rhymed like sonnets 155, 156 and 158.

3–4. "The old you…/Is back." Compare no.80 (p.303) when the fear was that the old Nadia had gone for ever.

11. "All manner of thing shall be well." Julian of Norwich, see nos.40 and 57 (pp.282 and 291).

158
Dream: Stag and Deer Grazing in Heaven's Arcady

I see the bronze stag through the frosty glass
With white antlers by the white-backed wounded deer,
They're grazing together on the frozen grass
When the carp are cowering from the Arctic cold, in fear.
All Nature is sheltering from minus-seven frost, as we
Graze together, I remind you that, despite the white glow,
Summer will soon be here in Arcady

And the hawthorns round the field will have blossom like snow
In sunshine that will have budded the trees, and I dream
Of a time beyond our stoic endurance when we will
Always graze together near a pastoral pond and stream
And you'll alert me to the hounds that kill
And you'll be moving again; and this dream may be
That one day we'll graze together in Heaven's Arcady.

18, 19, 22, 23 January 2024

This is the 158th sonnet in 'Agony in Arcady: Stroke', to a "fair maid" (see pp.261 and 307). Shakespeare wrote 154 sonnets, the first 126 to a "fair youth". It is fully rhymed to reflect the bliss in Arcady, as are sonnets 155, 156 and 157.

2. 'Wounded deer', see no.36 (p.280) 'Wounded Deer' for the deer's wound (a snapped leg).

12. 'The hounds'. The hounds that killed Actaeon, here representatives of those who wanted to stop Nicholas Hagger from ever seeing Nadia again from 1973, over 50 years previously.

14. On 22 January 2024, the date this poem was dictated, there had been a storm like a mini-tornado in Fairmead during the night, and the stag and deer were both felled, and the stag was lying on top of the deer. The deer's leg had again been snapped.

Coda on Overcoming

'Coda' (music), "the concluding passage of a piece or movement, usually forming an addition to the basic structure" (*Concise Oxford Dictionary*).

159
Guard of Honour: Tribute to Heroic Endurance and Overcoming

I visited you for the last time at Caroline House.
You'd just passed the 'test' to have an eyegaze machine
That turns eye gaze into words like Hawking's.
Two days later a bell rang and all staff were seen
To form a guard of honour in the corridors
And clap as you were wheeled out on a stretcher
As a tribute to your heroic endurance
And overcoming. You waved a right finger
Like the Queen as you headed for the front door.
Now you have settled in your care home quietly,
And I find you in a large ground-floor room

With a high ceiling, that is named 'Daisy'.
The staff are attentive and took you on a tour.
Now you're in a royal palace, and we're all in awe.

25 May, 3 June 2024

160
Care Home, Struggling

From the corridor I reach your sunless room
In the eighteenth-century care home with a high ceiling
Founded by the uncle of Wolsey (who brought
From Hampton Court Otley Hall's linenfold panelling).
Your head is leaning leftwards, you are grim.
Your left arm's stiff and swollen, with a finger-
Pointer you spell out it will only move
In the evening, you're staring into the future.
Your more relaxed, level-2 regime's stiffened
Your limbs, I wheel you to the reception hall,
And as it's still raining we look at the hearth,
And the blue-and-white Delft tiles. You're struggling with it all.
You're overcoming, keep doing your best
Even though you've gone backwards since you moved to more rest.

30 May, 3 June 2024

12. Delft. From the 1600s the most famous tiles were made in Delft, South Holland, where the style originated. The blue tiles appeared c.1620 and were inspired by porcelain imported from China.

161
DNR: Heroic Limit

And now I'm in Cornwall by the sea. The front
Lawn's covered with daisies, and I think of your room,
Daisy – the downstairs rooms are named after flowers –
And brood on your plight in your daily sunless gloom.
The less intense therapies mean you're longer alone,
And you could get depressed. And I recall a new
Care assistant introducing herself
And asking if your DNR should continue.
You spelled out, pointing with your finger-stick at

Letters on the e-tran frame, a grim – I froze –
"Up to doctors", heroically putting your life in their hands
As if you did not mind which course they chose.
And I am filled with sadness by the sea's flow
As if you'd said you've reached as far as you can go.

30 May, 3 June 2024

8. 'DNR'. "Do not resuscitate."

162
Overcoming like Sisyphus

Driving home Ann says, "I hate this A12 road.
There are always roadworks and queues, I question my fate,
If I did something dreadful in a former life.
Who was punished in Hell and had to repeat his hate?"
And I say Sisyphus, who rolled a boulder
Bigger than himself up a hill in Tartarus, in pain,
And when it rolled back down to the bottom
Willed himself to return and roll it back up again –
Just as I finish a work and the task rolls back down
So I have to struggle, push, get another one done,
And again find I have to go back to the start;
Like my sonnets: an endless rolling-up, then the next one.
And we struggle uphill each time we see you, and cope,
And will gladly repeat it next week, to give you hope.

30 May, 3 June 2024

Title. Sisyphus, King of Corinth, hubristically killed guests and thought himself more clever than Zeus, who, angered, punished him by making him endlessly push a boulder uphill in the depth of Hades until it rolled back down and he had to go back and start rolling it up all over again. (See picture on p.xxxix.)

9. 'Work', "a literary or musical composition" (*Concise Oxford Dictionary).*

163
Sisyphus, and a Better World

My whole life has been like Sisyphus and his boulder,
As Silberrad remarked the last time I saw him greet.
I hew a large rock into a manageable boulder
And heave it uphill, then return and repeat.

I am free to operate but denied publicity
By a secret State, so I push as if it's been hurled,
Ignored by all others, a solitary forcing-up,
Motivated by will to bring in a better world.
And while I push upwards and pant and shove
My heavy boulder to where it should be, I pause
And inform those who have cared on my progress
In letters describing what each rock does and its cause.
Like Sisyphus, I've been condemned to this fate,
And have endured and overcome this secret State.

4 June 2024

2. John Silberrad remarked to Nicholas Hagger shortly before he died in 2005: "You'll never finish your work. You'll be like Sisyphus who rolled his boulder up to the top of the hill – and then he was fated to have it fall down again and go back to the beginning." See *My Double Life 2: A Rainbow over the Hills*, p.257.
5. See Preface, pp.xxxii–xxxv, xxxviii.

164
Overcoming like Shakespeare: Find a Way or Make a Way

While I am in Cornwall I read newsletters'
Articles saying that the great Shakespeare – lo! –
Was not the Stratford man, but de Vere's pseudonym,
A secret that all who prepared the First Folio
Allegedly kept as Elizabeth the First had given
Spendthrift de Vere a thousand pounds when he
Became bankrupt, in return for two plays a year.
There's no proof, only speculation, and I see
In *Shakespeare's Book*, which arrived with your stroke,
That Shakespeare rose in his Stratford grammar school's care
To heights of knowledge and wrote the thirty-six plays
Which were brought out after his death by the "incomparable paire";
Just as I've written more sonnets than him, by following a rule –
Overcome without noble birth – that I learned at school.

30 May, 3 June 2024

1–2. "Newsletters'/Articles": The Shakespeare Oxford and The De Vere Society newsletters.
9. Nadia Hagger had her stroke immediately after receiving a delivery, which seems to have been of Chris Laoutaris's *Shakespeare's Book*, her present to her

father for Father's Day, 2023.

12. The "incomparable paire". William, Earl of Pembroke and Lord Chamberlain, and his brother Philip, Earl of Montgomery, who were addressed as such by the two actors, John Hemmings and Henry Condell. (These were the four main preparers of the First Folio published in 1623, see line 4.)

13. "A rule", "*Aut viam inveniam aut faciam*", "Find a way or make a way", the motto of Chigwell School, Essex bequeathed by its founder in 1628, Archbishop Samuel Harsnett (whose papers are kept as a Special Collection in the Albert Sloman Library at the University of Essex together with Nicholas Hagger's archive).

165
Overcoming Two Hundred and Ten Resurrections

I sit above the tranquil sea and brood.
My CPAP machine says my stop-breathings last night were rife:
More than two hundred times I was saved by its air hiss
Through my nasal-prong mask and jolted back to life.
Seven hours – four hundred and twenty minutes – of sleep,
And it says I had 29.7 events hourly –
Two hundred and ten events. Half my time as I slept
I stopped breathing for a minute, then air hissed in and breathed me
For a minute, then immediately I stopped again.
I died for seven hours, and was resurrected
Every minute, for me to sleep is to die.
I tighten my chin-strap and mask, overcome being dead.
But one of these nights there'll be no resurrection.
A gull flutters down among green rocks and is gone.

1, 3 June 2024

2. Nicholas Hagger was diagnosed as having sleep apnoea in 2017 and was forced to sleep in a mask attached to a CPAP machine to keep him breathing. Having averaged 29.7 stop-breathings an hour, bordering on 'severe' apnoea, he tightened his chin-strap and mask (in defiance of specialist advice) and got back to 'normal' apnoea, under five events per hour.

166
How to Overcome Locked-In Quadriplegia

I think of what the last year must have been like for you:
Lying on your back, quadriplegic stereotype –
Unable to move your arms, legs, head, in need

Of a hoist, unable to swallow, speak or wipe
Dribble from your lips but able to understand,
Locked-in, eyes-upping Yes, No's eyes-downing,
Incontinent, PEG-fed, mouth for tasting from teaspoons,
And at first, pain in your limbs from your stroke, waiting
For nurse to bring your pain relief. But now
You can finger-button call nurse, change TV. Hooray.
You've some independence but need two nurses' care.
The care home's quiet and lonely for chunks of the day,
And, brooding, you're asked, "Do you still want 'Do not resuscitate?'"
O, how can you overcome your trapped fate?

1, 3 June 2024

2. 'Stereotype', "a person or thing that conforms to an unjustifiably fixed, usually standardised, mental picture" (*Concise Oxford Dictionary*).

167
Overcoming: Oval Soul Reflecting the Light like a Puddle

I see the Light each night now reflected,
As in a puddle, in my lit oval soul. Wow!
I gaze before I sleep and the words of a hymn
Come into my mind, "How silently, how
Silently the wondrous gift" – of the Light – "is given,"
And I think you too could see your soul's puddle
If you look behind your closed eyes before sleep.
Would it comfort you to know you're eternal
In part as you endure your dreadful ordeal?
You could then see we are not only our limbs
Which may or may not move, and that within
The confines of our paralysed bodies' dims
There's an oval brightness that transcends our strife –
Your striving – and takes us to the next stage of our life.

2, 3 June 2024

This poem suggests that the oval cloud Nicholas Hagger saw repeatedly in volume 38 was his soul that reflects the Light.

168
Overcoming Gloom with Soul's Brightness

We have both overcome in our own different ways.
You've been working hard to improve your hand and your gaze
And have struggled to practise movements when you're alone.
You're finding a way, and your brain's making new pathways
And you're making a way by willing yourself to move forward –
The clapping staff hailed your response to their ask.
And I, though eighty-five now, am like Sisyphus,
Keep going to complete the never-ending task,
Tread worn paths but also make my own way
By healing via channelling my soul's Light from the One,
And while I amass a mound of words I look
Every night for the brightness of my oval soul and its sun.
And I hope you'll overcome your limitations and address
Your gloom by spending hours in your soul's brightness.

3 June 2024

12. 'Sun', the Light.

169
All Overcomings: Mind over Matter in Heaven's Arcady

I am back in Arcady, and near the pond
Where the stag is grazing alongside the deer
Amid summer green and burgeoning flowers,
And I know that all overcomings, when we peer,
Have in common: determination, will
And a strong belief in mind over matter,
A resolve and discipline that improves one's lot
By repeated control of feelings and behaviour.
It's like going to a gym and getting fit,
Mind willing body forward, keeping going.
So it is with us, and with your making a way
For your brain to find new pathways and goal-setting.
Actaeon-like, the stag's urging the deer on as they graze,
And in Heaven's Arcady their souls will be bright to their gaze.

4 June 2024

(Above) Actaeon with two seven-branched antlers, etched by Jean Mignon in the 1550s?, shown after being turned into a stag by Diana after surprising her bathing/discovering information that should have remained secret; and (below) Actaeon shown in a sculpture by the late-Baroque Italian sculptor Paolo Persico, 1786–1789, at the Royal Palace at Caserta, Italy, still with the head of a stag, being killed by some of his 50 hounds, in Nicholas Hagger's interpretation of the myth on account of the secret knowledge contained in some of his 63 books. (See p.89, note 14, for details of Ovid's account of the myth of Actaeon.)

Nicholas Hagger's crest and coat of arms awarded by the College of Arms. The Patent is dated 22 May 2019, his 80th birthday. The crest shows a stag with two seven-branched antlers and one hoof on a roundel in Libyan colours with a spying poet's and writer's eye near four acorns, against a seven-banded rainbow. The coat of arms shows the three Flemish lions from the Hagar 1605 coat of arms brandishing quills, and two oak trees with endless knots, representing time and infinity/eternity. The motto has the globe of the earth and the sun at each end, suggesting Nicholas Hagger's Universalist perspective.

The Tree of Tradition of all civilisations, showing their writings, traditions and influences on the branches of their nation-states which come out of a common trunk. This can also be seen as the Tree of European civilisation, *Geschichtsbaum Europa*, with its writings, traditions and influences on the eventual 50 branches of its nation-states. (See Nicholas Hagger, *The Tree of Tradition*.)

INDEXES

CHRONOLOGICAL ORDER OF POEMS

Chronological order in which all poems in volumes 35–41 were conceived and written

(Dates indicate when poems were written and revised. They reflect the dates at the end of each poem but are listed here in the order in which the poems were created.)

	Date
Time's Mower and the Buttercups	19 June 2010
Knot-Garden	7 October 2010
The Mountain Range and Time	16 October 2010
Berlin: City of the One	4, 12 December 2015
Berlin Wall	4, 12 December 2015
The Oak Tree and the Branch: The UK Referendum on the EU, 'Brexit'	14–15 August 2016
New World	18–19, 21 August 2016
Distant Lights	18–19, 21 August 2016
Peace: Grandchildren, Aleppo	18–19, 21 August 2016; 4 June 2023
New World Tapestry	18, 21 August 2016; 4 June 2023
Bridge	19, 21 August 2016
Bomb	19, 21 August 2016; 4 June 2023
NATO	20–21 August 2016; 4 June 2023
Wonderment	20–21 August 2016; 4 June 2023
Oneness	21 August 2016; 4 June 2023
Conviction	22 August 2016; 4 June 2023
Purpose	22 August 2016; 4 June 2023
At Delphi	17–18 October 2016
The Tick of Time	18 October 2016
Leaves like Faces	18 October 2016
Lyre and Pipes	18 October 2016
Epping Forest Stag (For Ambassador Gusi)	22 October 2016
Rock	2–3 November 2016; 1 June 2023

	Date
Energy	30 April, 23 August 2017
Brexit Election	11, 13, 24 June, 1, 3, 8–9 July 2017
Within Dark Tunnels	24 June, 13 July 2017
Sea Stirred	16, 23 August 2017
White Crests: Motion and Stillness	22–23 August 2017
Christmas Cherry (A Metaphysical Poem to my Dutch PA)	26–27 October 2017
A Vaseful of Flowers (To my Dutch PA)	26–27 October 2017
Warm Sun on Cheeks: How the Universe Works	13 November, 16–17 December 2017; 17 February, 5 June 2018
A Dozen Jackdaws	30 November, 15–16 December 2017
Nesting-Box	11 January, 17 February 2018
My Books Heaped like Raspberries	6 February 2018
Diving Birds	15, 17 February 2018
Fifty-Nine Years Ago in the Hotel Miramar, Malaga	6, 12 April 2018
Among Grandchildren on Gibraltar	10, 12–14 April, 5 June 2018
Ancestral Tree	14–15 April 2018; revised 11 December 2022
A Split Cedar	25 April, 30 May, 3 June 2018
Dove Supreme	25 April, 30 May, 3 June 2018
Fountain: Newts	1, 30 May, 3 June 2018
Royal Harmony (On the Wedding of Prince Harry and Meghan Markle, 19 May 2018)	28–30 May, 3 June 2018
The Setting Sun	27, 28 June 2018
Like a Bee Crawling	29 June 2018
The Deep	29 June 2018
Siskins	30 June 2018
Hovering Bird	16 August 2018
A Deluge of Light	17 August 2018
A Harmony of Orange Lights	20 August 2018
Fountain: Water Lilies	26 August 2018
Sparrowhawk and Reality	11 September 2018
Ragged Tulip (For Ian)	29 September 2018

	Date
We are like Trees	29 September 2018
In Front of the Fireplace	30 September 2018
Magical Moonlight	28 October 2018
Oak Tree	15 November 2018
Plasters and Bandages (A Far Memory)	28 November 2018
Blown Spume	18 December 2018
Being like a Puddle	22 December 2018; revised 11 December 2022
Soul like a Puddle	10 February 2019
Hearts like a Shout	14 February 2019
Orange Sun	12 May 2019
Farewell to my Europe	14–27 May 2019
Kestrel	10 June 2019
A Great Illusion	17 July 2019
Triathlon	27 July 2019
Wildness	29 July 2019
A Squall	30 July 2019
A Life Draws to a Close (For Ian)	31 July 2019
Breakers	9 August 2019
Full Moon and Reality	12 August 2019
Destiny at the G7	25 August 2019
Rose Garden like a Union Flag	21 September 2019
Our Expanding Universe	3 November 2019
Feeding Time	9 November 2019
The Message of the Fireworks	10 November 2019
Autumn	17 November 2019
Falling Apart: Atrophy in Cerebellum, Vocal Cords (A Fragment)	30 November 2019
Hail	14 December 2019
Shoreline	15 January 2020
Abednego	30 January 2020
Another Sparrowhawk	30 January 2020
Snakes	9 February 2020
Promised Land	1 March, 2–3 September 2020
Bedouin Tent	5 March 2020

	Date
All-Looking Among Bedouins	5 March 2020
Three-Tiered Fountain	5 March 2020
Sunset: Ra	5 March 2020
In the Roman Theatre at Aspendos	13 March 2020
Ramesses the Second's Concubine	16 March 2020
Jellyfish	Mid-March 2020; 10 December 2022
Solitude	30 March 2020; revised 16 December 2022
Rejoicing Amid a Deadly Virus	30 March 2020; revised 25 December 2022
'Old People's Home'	7 April 2020
Virus	10 April 2020
Romantic Isolation	10 April 2020
Pink Supermoon	10 April 2020
Bees in the Rosemary	11 April 2020
A Cluttering of Jackdaws	11 April 2020
Thinking Jackdaw	13 April 2020
Coronavirus: A *Memento Mori*	20 April 2020; revised 26 December 2022
Oval Cloud: Sculptures	25 April 2020; revised 15 December 2022
Oval Cloud: Swansdown	25 April 2020; revised 15 December 2022
Oval Cloud: Shapes	25 April 2020; revised 16 December 2022
Oval Cloud: Amanuensis of All the Muses and Tenth Muse	25 April 2020; revised 17 December 2022
Oval Cloud: Messages	25 April 2020; revised 17 December 2022
Oval Cloud: Muses' Amanuensis	25 April 2020; revised 17 December 2022
Oval Cloud: Outside Time	25 April 2020; revised 27 December 2022
Drooping Daisies	28 April 2020
Oval Cloud: Enduring	28 April 2020; revised 17 December 2022

	Date
Dragonfly	30 April 2020
Cuckoo	1 May 2020
Sea and Rocks	1 May 2020
Oval Cloud: Slide Show	6 May 2020; revised 17 December 2022
Oval Cloud: Soul and Halo	9 May 2020; revised 19 December 2022
Smiling Buttercups	18 May 2020
Two Potted Geraniums and a Blind Down	25 May 2020
Lesser Stitchwort	26 May 2020
Small Tortoiseshell	29 May 2020
Buttercup: Provinces and Disciplines	29 May 2020
Stars	30 May 2020
Meadow Brown and Purple Clover	31 May 2020
Goldfinches	1 June 2020
Buttercup	3 June 2020
Oval Cloud: My Comforting Cloud Returns	22 June 2020; revised 21 December 2022
Blackberry Brambles	23 June 2020
Swallows	27 June 2020
Swallow, Companion	28 June 2020
Oval Cloud and Swallows	29 June 2020; revised 21 December 2022
Oval Cloud: Cloud like a Woolsack	29 June 2020; revised 21 December 2022
Treading Round Flowers	6 July 2020
Clover	9 July 2020
A Swallow's Circle	24 July 2020
Sky on Fire	31 July 2020
Wistful Orange Moon	3 August 2020
Sheep Huddled	5 August 2020
Lights in the Dark	5 August 2020
Splashes of Light	8 August 2020
Fluttering Moth	9 August 2020
Sunlight Rains	10 August 2020
Honey-Bee	10 August 2020

	Date
Sparrow	12 August 2020
A Speedy Swallow Pities a Slow Human	26 August 2020
Elm	29 August 2020
Goldfinch on a Flowerpot	29 August 2020
A Tilted Head	5 September 2020
Second Childhood	7 September 2020
Crow and Water Lilies	8 September 2020
Dandelion Clock Nearly Blown by the Wind	13 September 2020
Sowing by the Moon	Between 13 September 2020 and 10 October 2020
Flashing Lights Across the Sea	10 October 2020
Cormorant	13 October 2020
Flaming Elm	25 October 2020
Veiled Mist	5 November 2020
Sparrowhawk Still	19 November 2020
Crepuscular	22 November 2020
Shadow on the Sea	10 December 2020
Clouds like a Spider's Web	8 January 2021
Plague	16 January 2021
Flocks	28–29 January 2021
Sparrowhawk Not Welcome	5 February 2021
Sparrowhawk's Claws	9 February 2021
Moth	9 February 2021
Fox	12 February 2021
Icicle	13 February 2021
Buttercups	15 February 2021
Ladybird	15 February 2021
Sun on Sea	18 February 2021
Moon like Cheese	1 March 2021
Cherry	5 April 2021
Blossom like Frost	10 April 2021
Oval Cloud: Nine Muses	10 April 2021; revised 21 December 2022
Sparkling Sea and Gulls	14 April 2021
Daisies, Stars	15 April 2021

	Date
Herring Gull	15 April 2021
Sparkling Sea, Sneeze	16 April 2021
Smiling Night	17 April 2021
The Funeral of the Duke of Edinburgh: The Elizabethan Age Drawing to a Close	17, 24–25 April 2021
Two Foxes	23 April 2021
Death Staring, Waiting	6 May 2021; 28–29 December 2022
Last Call to the Afterlife	6 May 2021; 28–29 December 2022
The Tapestry Room in Henry the Eighth's Second Hunting Lodge	22 May, 1 June 2021
Tapestries in the Soul	22 May 2021; revised 7 January 2023
A Tapestry on the Fall of the West	24 May, 1 June 2021
What my Tapestries Won't Show	24 May 2021; revised 7 January 2023
Connaught House's Knot-Garden	25 May 2021
England as in Henry the Eighth's Day	25 May 2021
Owls Hooting	25 May 2021
Achilles' Shield	25 May 2021; revised 8 January 2023
Moon	26–27 May 2021
Downpour from the Sun	30 May 2021
Henry the Eighth's Copped Hall	2 June 2021
Henry's Third Hunting Lodge	2 June 2021
Otley Hall's Knot-Garden	2 June 2021
Knot-Garden: The One at a Glance	2 June 2021
Stitchwort Stars	16 June 2021
Swallows Back	5 July 2021
Bee in the Lavender	18 July 2021
Seckford's Head	20 July 2021; revised 8 January 2023
Muse's Slave	20 July 2021; revised 8 January 2023
Sparkling Sea	4 August 2021; revised 10 December 2022

	Date
Sea Storm and Mind	5 August 2021
The Evening Star is Bright	7 August 2021
Fallen Leaves	9 August 2021
Shooting Star	9 August 2021
A Calm Sea	12 August 2021
Moth Drawn by Light	12 August 2021
Pecking and Picking	2 October 2021
Soul Sings	11 October 2021
Shimmering Gold	21 October 2021
Rock Pipit	22 October 2021
Between Moon and Star	24 October 2021
The Power of the Sea	24 October 2021
Nuthatch	9 November 2021
Squelching Heart	10 November 2021
Fox Sniffing	17 November 2021
Carrion Crow	19 November 2021
Black Crow and Plague Victim	19 November 2021
Blood-Red Sun	16 December 2021
Surging Waves like a Virus	18 December 2021
The Fall of the West	9 February 2022; revised 13–14 January 2023
Reddening Sun	11 February 2022
Storm	13 February 2022
After the Storm	18 February 2022
War and Spring	26 March 2022
Waiting on a Clot	30 March 2022
On a Precipice	30 March 2022
Reprieve	30 March 2022
Game (or Gammy) Heart	1 April 2022
Leaning Daisies	1 April 2022
Daffodils	1 April 2022
Nothing's Changed: All Fools	1 April 2022; revised 14 January 2023
Wagtail	7 April 2022
Fall like a Tall Tree	9 April 2022

	Date
Years like Foaming Waves	10 April 2022
A Shadow in Time	10 April 2022
Pipit and Reflection	13 April 2022
Bats	13 April 2022
A Peacock Butterfly	16 April 2022
A Heavenly Garden	8 May 2022
Devout Anne Boleyn	14 May 2022
Clarity	14 May 2022
Swan, Delving	14 May 2022; revised 14–15 January 2023
Glorification	14 May 2022; revised 15 January 2023
Tapestries: Actaeon	14 May 2022; revised 22 January 2023
The Return of the Prodigal	14–15 May 2022
Stop-Breathings	17 May 2022
Swallow	8 June 2022
A Small Tortoiseshell's Salute	14 June 2022
Mist	30 June 2022
Wasps and Bees	12 July 2022
Oblivion	1 August 2022
Black-Headed Gull	1 August 2022
At Portsmouth: Leaving Port	1 August 2022
Gong	1 August 2022
Trawled	1 August 2022
Night-Sea Voyage	1 August 2022
Raindrops like Early Stars	3 August 2022
Decius Mus's Sacrifice	4 August 2022
A Hermit and Solitude	6 August 2022
Death: Coach	6 August 2022
Hag's Head and God	8 August 2022
Under Ben Bulben: Grave and Boat	9 August 2022
Rocks like Sheep	9 August 2022
Back from my Grave	9 August 2022
House Martins and Sheep	9 August 2022

	Date
In Mount Stewart's Sunken Garden	12 August 2022
From Waterloo to Peterloo	12 August 2022
Clouds and Foam	18 August 2022
Work and Universe	28 August 2022
A Tudor Outlook	22 August 2022
Bayeux Tapestry Revisited	22 August 2022
Past Lives	22 August 2022
Zodiac	22 August 2022
Death of the Queen: The End of the Elizabethan Era	8–9 September 2022
Last Buttercup	14 September 2022
Pilgrimage	17 September 2022
What If?	18 September 2022
The Funeral of Queen Elizabeth II (On the Ambivalence of Revival and Decline)	19 September 2022
Sheep	20 October 2022
Turbulent Sea	20 October 2022
Tide	21 October 2022
Planets and Shadow	22 October 2022
Full Moon and Fireworks	6 November 2022
COP27: Bettering the Lot of Humankind	7 November 2022
Anarchy: A Nightmare	16 November 2022; revised 2 April 2023
Time's Ticking	7 December 2022
Night Sea	8–9 December 2022
Full Moon	9 December 2022
Screaming Gulls	10 December 2022
Chaotic	13 December 2022
Oval Cloud: Cloud of Knowing	18 January 2023; revised 19–20 January 2023
On my Own	18 January 2023; revised 21–22 January 2023
Healing Power	20 January 2023; revised 22 January 2023
Actaeon's Fate	22 January 2023; revised 25 January 2023

	Date
Oval Cloud: Envelopment	7 February 2023
Oval Cloud: Texts in Code	8 February 2023
Oval Cloud: Message from Eternity	9 February 2023
Oval Cloud: Peace Plan and Wi-Fi	12 February 2023
Anaximander's Cosmos: The Boundless	12–13 February 2023
Sparrowhawk	5 March 2023
Oval Cloud: Death, Soul Packed and Ready to Go	5 March 2023
Oval Cloud: Soul like a Pouch	5 March 2023
Aging	6 March 2023
Wild Nature	Mid-March 2023
A New Age of Light	12–15 March 2023
Shoal	31 March 2023
Calm Sea	1 April 2023
Coronavirus	1 April 2023
Forgetfulnesses	2 April 2023
Scudding, Changing	2 April 2023
Sea and Mind	4 April 2023
At Coldridge: An Unspeakable Truth	5–6 April 2023; first drafted 29 December 2021
The Painted Hall, Greenwich	8 April 2023
In Fairmead in Arcadia	14–15 April 2023
My Tapestry	16, 20–21 April 2023
The Bayeux Tapestry	16, 20–21 April 2023
What Wyatt Saw	17, 23 April 2023
The World Falling Apart: An Unspeakable Secret	14 April 2023
Shelley and the One	18–20 April 2023
Brexit Blunder	21, 23 April 2023
Roots in Bruges	23 April 2023
The Oak Tree and the Fallen Branch	27–30 April 2023
Epistle to a Civil Servant (Epistle to a Civil Servant who Keeps the Official List of Writers Allowed to Operate but with Limited Publicity)	3–4 May 2023

	Date
The Coronation of King Charles III and the True Poet	5–7, 20 May 2023
Leaving Court to End my Days in Arcadia	13 May 2023
In the Wilderness in my Arcady	14, 16, 21 May 2023
Heart Murmur	15–16, 20 May 2023
A Deer in Arcady	16, 20 May 2023
Tudor Deer-Hunting	17, 20 May 2023
Oval Clouds: Muses	17, 20 May 2023
Time's Up	17, 21 May 2023
Oval Cloud: Ideas Bag	18, 20 May 2023
Withdrawing into the Invisibility of my Arcady	19, 21 May 2023
Gonging my Hearse	22 May 2023
Waiting: Legacy	25, 29 May 2023
Everything Helps	25 May, 8 June 2023
Oval Cloud: Ancient Letters	27, 28 May 2023
A Robot's View of my Works 2	27 May, 5 June 2023
A Robot's View of my Works 1	27 May, 8 June 2023
Body and Brain: Design that's Meant	28 May, 6 June 2023
In the Now	29 May 2023
A Remarkable Life	29, 30 May, 1 June 2023
An Extraordinary Life	29, 30 May, 1 June 2023
A Fulfilled Life	30 May, 1 June 2023
Sent Down with a Message by the Light	30 May, 2, 3 June 2023
A Providential Life	30 May, 2, 3 June 2023
A Providential Life and the Light	30 May, 2, 3 June 2023
Providence's Deep Mystic Way, Unitive Vision, Baroque and Universalism	30 May, 2, 3 June 2023
A Rewarding Life	30 May, 2, 3, 6 June 2023
Direction and Destiny: Mission to Bring Peace to Humankind	30 May, 3 June 2023
There is a Providence: Fulfilling our Destiny	30 May, 3 June 2023
Providence and Influences: Key People arrive at the Right Time	30 May, 3 June 2023
Providential Life and Works	31 May, 7 June 2023
Pattern in Episodes	31 May, 7 June 2023

	Date
Pattern like a Pine Cone	31 May, 7 June 2023
Hermit in the Wilderness	31 May, 7 June 2023
Shown my Future Direction and Destiny	31 May, 7 June 2023
Slave of the Muses	31 May, 8 June 2023
Keep Going	31 May, 8 June 2023
Doing Good	31 May, 8 June 2023
Family and All We Knew	31 May, 8 June 2023
England and Europe	31 May, 8 June 2023
The West in Decline	31 May, 8 June 2023
The Light of the World	31 May, 8 June 2023
Renaissance Man	31 May, 8 June 2023
Old Age	31 May, 8 June 2023
Booming Out	31 May, 8 June 2023
Providential Light and New Powers	31 May, 8 June 2023
Polymath	31 May, 9 June 2023
End of Life	31 May, 9 June 2023
Death	31 May, 9 June 2023
Postscript, Gratitude: 23 Sonnets Sent Through in a Day	31 May, 9 June 2023
A Tapestry of a New World Order: A Coming Golden Age	4, 5 June 2023
Tapestry of Oneness and Peace	4, 5 June 2023
Knowing my End	5 June 2023
Tapestry that Draws on the Tradition and Reveals Oneness	6 June 2023
The Oak Tree's Bubbling and Groaning	6 June 2023
Looking Back on my End	6 June 2023
The Oak Tree and the Healing Branch	10 June 2023
Blood Clot	12, 25 June 2023
Brain Stem, Locked-In	13, 25 June 2023; 30 April, 1 May 2024
Nightmare	14, 26 June 2023
Postponing	14, 26 June 2023
Limbo	14, 27, 30 June 2023
Quadriplegic	14 June, 1 July 2023
Deep Sleep	14 June, 1 July 2023

	Date
Project	14 June, 1 July 2023
Not Long to Live	15 June, 1 July 2023
Reunited	15 June, 2 July 2023
Eyewitness: Bungalow	15 June, 2 July 2023
Pneumonia	15 June, 11 July 2023
Communication: Howl	17 June, 2 July 2023
Crying	17 June, 2 July 2023
New House	17 June, 2 July 2023
Rose's Floor	17 June, 3 July 2023
Genetic Flaw	17 June, 3 July 2023
Shallower Breathing	17 June, 8 August 2023
Despair	17 June, 20 August 2023
Speechless	17 June, 23, 24 August 2023
Stroking Beauty	17 June, 24, 25 August 2023
Living in Uncertainties	18 June, 25 August 2023
Tiredness and Quiet Despair	19 June, 25 August 2023
Banned from Seeing You	20 June, 25 August 2023
Walled-In Silence	20 June, 26, 27 August 2023
Coma	20 June, 26 August 2023
MRI	21 June, 29 August 2023
New Spin	21 June, 30 August 2023
Seizure	22 June, 1, 2 September 2023
Melancholy	22 June, 2 September 2023
Guard	23 June, 2 September 2023
Level-One Rehab	23 June, 3 September 2023
Pain	24 June, 3 September 2023
Drawing to a Close	25 June 2023
Sleeping Beauty	25 June, 3 September 2023
Wounded Deer	26, 27 June 2023
Recovery	27 June 2023
Calm	28, 29, 30 June 2023
Desperation: Shaken	28, 30 June 2023
Resetting	3, 4 July 2023
Infection	6 July 2023

	Date
Distressed	7 July 2023
Crying Out	8, 9 July 2023
Counting, Memory, Hearing	11 July, 20 August 2023
Key	11 July, 20 August 2023
Bleak	12 July, 20 August 2023
A Beacon of Hope	12 July, 20 August 2023
Encouragement	12 July, 20 August 2023
Crying from Pain	13 July, 19 August 2023
Keeping You Calm	13 July, 19 August 2023
Harrowing	14, 16 July 2023
Understanding Too Well	14, 16 July 2023
Care Home	15, 16 July 2023
Tears	18 July, 19 August 2023
Walled-In Wellness	20 July, 19 August 2023
Eternal Soul	20 July, 19 August 2023
Cleansing	20 July, 19 August 2023
At Cromwell's House, Ely	20, 24 July, 19 August 2023
At Ely Cathedral	20, 24 July, 19 August 2023
Return to Otley Hall	21, 24 July, 19 August 2023
Body like a Cell	22 July, 14 August 2023
Legal Consent	24 July, 14 August 2023
Arcady	25 July, 14 August 2023
Possessions	26 July, 14 August 2023
Grimace	26 July, 14 August 2023
Fragile	27 July, 13 August 2023
PBA	27 July, 13 August 2023
Bizarre	27 July, 14 August 2023
Aware Crying	27 July, 14 August 2023
Hospitality	29 July, 13 August 2023
Assessor	1, 13 August 2023
Athens	3, 13 August 2023
Unexpected	4, 13 August 2023
Goldfinch	23, 27 July, 4, 12 August 2023
Unthankful Hell	8 August 2023

	Date
Sunset	9, 12 August 2023
Lightning Strike: Oak Tree and Split Branch	10, 11 August 2023
Gone For Ever	10, 11 August 2023
Raw in Arcady	10, 12 August 2023
Mangled	10, 12 August 2023
Agape	12 August 2023
Kinks	12, 13 August 2023
Eyegaze Machine	15, 18 August 2023
Low Blood Pressure	15, 18 August 2023
Escaping from Locked-In: Talking	15, 18 August 2023
Wildfire	18 August 2023
Cornish Hermitage	18 August 2023
Suffolk Fair Maid	18 August 2023
Involuntary Groaning	18, 19 August 2023
Belief	18, 19 August 2023
Turning a Corner: Donkeys	22 August 2023
Rehabilitating	22 August 2023
Laughing	22 August 2023
Nursing Care	23, 24 August 2023
Conflict (+A + −A = 0)	26, 27 August 2023
Debilitating	28 August 2023
Triggering Regret	28 August 2023
Unheeded Pain	30 August 2023
Statues on Hope's Pedestal	30 August 2023
World-Unity and World-Sadness Reconciled in the One	2 September 2023
Hope	5, 7 September 2023
Not Fully Locked-In: Walking Again	5, 7 September 2023
Wisdom and Feeling Unite in Stillness	7 September 2023
Escaping	8 September 2023
120 Billion Connecting Brain Cells	8, 10 September 2023
Blocked Motorway	8, 10 September 2023
Care Home Ahead	8, 11 September 2023
On the Right Path	8, 11 September 2023
Assimilated Agony, Transcending	8, 11 September 2023

	Date
Preparing to Go	8, 11 September 2023
Avoiding Reporting	12 September 2023
Sixty-Degrees Standing	12, 13 September 2023
Three-Month Crying Blight and Plight	12, 13 September 2023
Arcady Paralysed, Now Paradisal	12, 13 September 2023
Infirm and Involuntary	14 September 2023
Capacity	15 September 2023
Moving, Swallowing, Laughing, Balancing, Cycling – Escaping	19, 23 September 2023
Glassing-In Arcadian Landscape	19, 23 September 2023
Arcady's New Blight	19, 23 September 2023
War in Arcady	22, 23 September 2023
Atrophy: Faltering Together Following our Fall	22, 23 September 2023
Harmony in the Soul: The Music of the Spheres	26, 28 September 2023
Rescuing from Harm	26, 28 September 2023
Fountain	28, 29 September 2023
Eyewitness: Overcoming	28, 29 September 2023
Incapacity	3 October 2023
Fifty-Year-Old Pain	3, 4 October 2023
Determined Intent	3, 5 October 2023
Peace in Arcady: Stag	3, 5, 6 October 2023
In Arcady: Old Man in a Circle	5, 6 October 2023
Wilderness: Magpie, Free	7 October 2023
Independent Capacity Assessor Declined	10, 29 October 2023
Court: Caught	10, 29 October 2023
Crying Despair	10, 30 October 2023
Fall	12, 30 October 2023
Silent	12, 30 October 2023
Expectations like a Sea-Swell's Foam	13, 23 October 2023
Broken Ankle-Bone	14, 21 October 2023
Frustration	17, 18 October 2023
Chill in the Air	21 October 2023
The Way Forward	24, 26 October 2023

	Date
Recovering: Again at Peace in Arcady	24, 26 October 2023
In Arcadia: The Oneness of the Universe	24, 26 October 2023
Difficult	31 October, 1 November 2023
Strike	3 November 2023
Flemish Characteristics: Nothing's Certain	5, 7 November 2023
Speechless and Still, like an Infant	5, 7 November 2023
Palliative Care	7 November 2023
Death Setting You Free	7 November 2023
Defying or Accepting Fate	8 November 2023
Caring for All 'Yous' or 'Old You'	8 November 2023
Phases of 'One You'	8 November 2023
Occultation	9, 10 November 2023
Heroic Endurance	10 November 2023
Harmony and Bliss in Arcady	10, 11 November 2023
The Vivid Greens of Arcady	15–17 January 2024
Dream: Stag and Deer Grazing in Heaven's Arcady	18, 19, 22, 23 January 2024
The Old You's Back	20, 21 January 2024
Guard of Honour: Tribute to Heroic Endurance and Overcoming	25 May, 3 June 2024
Care Home, Struggling	30 May, 3 June 2024
DNR: Heroic Limit	30 May, 3 June 2024
Overcoming like Sisyphus	30 May, 3 June 2024
Overcoming like Shakespeare: Find a Way or Make a Way	30 May, 3 June 2024
Overcoming Two Hundred and Ten Resurrections	1, 3 June 2024
How to Overcome Locked-In Quadriplegia	1, 3 June 2024
Overcoming: Oval Soul Reflecting the Light like a Puddle	2, 3 June 2024
Overcoming Gloom with Soul's Brightness	3 June 2024
Sisyphus, and a Better World	4 June 2024
All Overcomings: Mind over Matter in Heaven's Arcady	4 June 2024

CHRONOLOGICAL ORDER WITHIN VOLUMES

Chronological order in which unnumbered poems in volumes 35, 37 and 39 were written, listed under each volume

(Dates indicate when unnumbered poems were written and revised. They reflect the dates at the end of each poem but are listed here in the order in which the poems within each volume were created. Numbered poems have their dates but are still in numbered event order.)

	Date
Volume 35: *The Oak Tree and the Branch*	
Time's Mower and the Buttercups	19 June 2010
Knot-Garden	7 October 2010
The Mountain Range and Time	16 October 2010
The Oak Tree and the Branch: The UK Referendum on the EU, 'Brexit'	14–15 August 2016
At Delphi	17–18 October 2016
The Tick of Time	18 October 2016
Leaves like Faces	18 October 2016
Lyre and Pipes	18 October 2016
Epping Forest Stag (For Ambassador Gusi)	22 October 2016
Energy	30 April, 23 August 2017
Brexit Election	11, 13, 24 June, 1, 3, 8–9 July 2017
Within Dark Tunnels	24 June, 13 July 2017
Sea Stirred	16, 23 August 2017
White Crests: Motion and Stillness	22–23 August 2017
Christmas Cherry (A Metaphysical Poem to my Dutch PA)	26–27 October 2017
A Vaseful of Flowers (To my Dutch PA)	26–27 October 2017
Warm Sun on Cheeks: How the Universe Works	13 November, 16–17 December 2017; 17 February, 5 June 2018
A Dozen Jackdaws	30 November, 15–16 December 2017
Nesting-Box	11 January, 17 February 2018

	Date
My Books Heaped like Raspberries	6 February 2018
Diving Birds	15, 17 February 2018
Fifty-Nine Years Ago in the Hotel Miramar, Malaga	6, 12 April 2018
Among Grandchildren on Gibraltar	10, 12–14 April, 5 June 2018
Ancestral Tree	14–15 April 2018; revised 11 December 2022
A Split Cedar	25 April, 30 May, 3 June 2018
Dove Supreme	25 April, 30 May, 3 June 2018
Fountain: Newts	1, 30 May, 3 June 2018
The Setting Sun	27, 28 June 2018
Like a Bee Crawling	29 June 2018
The Deep	29 June 2018
Siskins	30 June 2018
Hovering Bird	16 August 2018
A Deluge of Light	17 August 2018
A Harmony of Orange Lights	20 August 2018
Fountain: Water Lilies	26 August 2018
Sparrowhawk and Reality	11 September 2018
Ragged Tulip (For Ian)	29 September 2018
We are like Trees	29 September 2018
In Front of the Fireplace	30 September 2018
Magical Moonlight	28 October 2018
Oak Tree	15 November 2018
Plasters and Bandages (A Far Memory)	28 November 2018
Blown Spume	18 December 2018
Being like a Puddle	22 December 2018; revised 11 December 2022
Soul like a Puddle	10 February 2019
Hearts like a Shout	14 February 2019
Orange Sun	12 May 2019
Farewell to my Europe	14–27 May 2019
Kestrel	10 June 2019
A Great Illusion	17 July 2019
Triathlon	27 July 2019

	Date
Wildness	29 July 2019
A Squall	30 July 2019
A Life Draws to a Close (For Ian)	31 July 2019
Breakers	9 August 2019
Full Moon and Reality	12 August 2019
Destiny at the G7	25 August 2019
Our Expanding Universe	3 November 2019
Feeding Time	9 November 2019
The Message of the Fireworks	10 November 2019
Autumn	17 November 2019
Falling Apart: Atrophy in Cerebellum, Vocal Cords (A Fragment)	30 November 2019
Hail	14 December 2019
Shoreline	15 January 2020
Abednego	30 January 2020
Another Sparrowhawk	30 January 2020
Snakes	9 February 2020
Poems written in Jordan, Egypt and Turkey	
Promised Land	1 March, 2–3 September 2020
Bedouin Tent	5 March 2020
All-Looking Among Bedouins	5 March 2020
Three-Tiered Fountain	5 March 2020
Sunset: Ra	5 March 2020
In the Roman Theatre at Aspendos	13 March 2020
Ramesses the Second's Concubine	16 March 2020
Jellyfish	Mid-March 2020; 10 December 2022
Volume 36: *The Tapestry* (50 Sonnets)	
Part One: Tapestry, The New World and the One	
1. My Tapestry	16, 20–21 April 2023
2. The Bayeux Tapestry	16, 20–21 April 2023
3. New World Tapestry	18, 21 August 2016; 4 June 2023
4. Berlin: City of the One	4, 12 December 2015

	Date
5. Berlin Wall	4, 12 December 2015
6. Brexit Blunder	21, 23 April 2023
7. New World	18–19, 21 August 2016
8. Peace: Grandchildren, Aleppo	18–19, 21 August 2016; 4 June 2023
9. Distant Lights	18–19, 21 August 2016
10. Bridge	19, 21 August 2016
11. Bomb	19, 21 August 2016; 4 June 2023
12. NATO	20–21 August 2016; 4 June 2023
Part Two: The Tapestry Room: Tudor Living and the One	
1. The Tapestry Room in Henry the Eighth's Second Hunting Lodge	22 May, 1 June 2021
2. Tapestries in the Soul	22 May 2021; revised 7 January 2023
3. Roots in Bruges	23 April 2023
4. A Tapestry on the Fall of the West	24 May, 1 June 2021
5. What my Tapestries Won't Show	24 May 2021; revised 7 January 2023
6. Connaught House's Knot-Garden	25 May 2021
7. Achilles' Shield	25 May 2021; revised 8 January 2023
8. England as in Henry the Eighth's Day	25 May 2021
9. What Wyatt Saw	17, 23 April 2023
10. Henry the Eighth's Copped Hall	2 June 2021
11. Henry's Third Hunting Lodge	2 June 2021
12. Otley Hall's Knot-Garden	2 June 2021
13. Knot-Garden: The One at a Glance	2 June 2021
14. Seckford's Head	20 July 2021; revised 8 January 2023
15. Muse's Slave	20 July 2021; revised 8 January 2023
16. The Fall of the West	9 February 2022; revised 13–14 January 2023
17. Nothing's Changed: All Fools	1 April 2022; revised 14 January 2023

	Date
18. Swan, Delving	14 May 2022; revised 14–15 January 2023
19. Devout Anne Boleyn	14 May 2022
20. Glorification	14 May 2022; revised 15 January 2023
21. Tapestries: Actaeon	14 May 2022; revised 22 January 2023
22. Actaeon's Fate	22 January 2023; revised 25 January 2023
23. Clarity	14 May 2022
24. The Return of the Prodigal	14–15 May 2022
25. Decius Mus's Sacrifice	4 August 2022
Part Three: Tapestry, Hunt to Find the Oneness of the Universe and of all Humankind	
1. Wonderment	20–21 August 2016; 4 June 2023
2. Oneness	21 August 2016; 4 June 2023
3. Conviction	22 August 2016; 4 June 2023
4. Purpose	22 August 2016; 4 June 2023
5. Rock	2–3 November 2016; 4 June 2023
6. A Tapestry of a New World Order: A Coming Golden Age	4, 5 June 2023
7. Tapestry of Oneness and Peace	4, 5 June 2023
8. A Tudor Outlook	22 August 2022
9. Bayeux Tapestry Revisited	22 August 2022
10. Past Lives	22 August 2022
11. A Deer in Arcady	16, 20 May 2023
12. Tudor Deer-Hunting	17, 20 May 2023
13. Tapestry that Draws on the Tradition and Reveals Oneness	6 June 2023
Volume 37: ***A Plague in Arcadia: Oneness with Nature and the Universe***	
Poems Influenced by Coronavirus	
Solitude	30 March 2020; revised 16 December 2022
Rejoicing Amid a Deadly Virus	30 March 2020; revised 25 December 2022

	Date
'Old People's Home'	7 April 2020
Virus	10 April 2020
Romantic Isolation	10 April 2020
Pink Supermoon	10 April 2020
Bees in the Rosemary	11 April 2020
A Cluttering of Jackdaws	11 April 2020
Thinking Jackdaw	13 April 2020
Coronavirus: A *Memento Mori*	20 April 2020; revised 26 December 2022
Drooping Daisies	28 April 2020
Dragonfly	30 April 2020
Cuckoo	1 May 2020
Sea and Rocks	1 May 2020
Smiling Buttercups	18 May 2020
Two Potted Geraniums and a Blind Down	25 May 2020
Lesser Stitchwort	26 May 2020
Small Tortoiseshell	29 May 2020
Buttercup: Provinces and Disciplines	29 May 2020
Stars	30 May 2020
Meadow Brown and Purple Clover	31 May 2020
Goldfinches	1 June 2020
Buttercup	3 June 2020
Blackberry Brambles	23 June 2020
Swallows	27 June 2020
Swallow, Companion	28 June 2020
Treading Round Flowers	6 July 2020
Clover	9 July 2020
A Swallow's Circle	24 July 2020
Sky on Fire	31 July 2020
Wistful Orange Moon	3 August 2020
Sheep Huddled	5 August 2020
Lights in the Dark	5 August 2020
Splashes of Light	8 August 2020
Fluttering Moth	9 August 2020
Sunlight Rains	10 August 2020

	Date
Honey-Bee	10 August 2020
Sparrow	12 August 2020
A Speedy Swallow Pities a Slow Human	26 August 2020
Elm	29 August 2020
Goldfinch on a Flowerpot	29 August 2020
A Tilted Head	5 September 2020
Second Childhood	7 September 2020
Crow and Water Lilies	8 September 2020
Dandelion Clock Nearly Blown by the Wind	13 September 2020
Sowing by the Moon	Between 13 September 2020 and 10 October 2020
Flashing Lights Across the Sea	10 October 2020
Cormorant	13 October 2020
Flaming Elm	25 October 2020
Veiled Mist	5 November 2020
Sparrowhawk Still	19 November 2020
Crepuscular	22 November 2020
Shadow on the Sea	10 December 2020
Clouds like a Spider's Web	8 January 2021
Plague	16 January 2021
Flocks	28–29 January 2021
Sparrowhawk Not Welcome	5 February 2021
Sparrowhawk's Claws	9 February 2021
Moth	9 February 2021
Fox	12 February 2021
Icicle	13 February 2021
Buttercups	15 February 2021
Ladybird	15 February 2021
Sun on Sea	18 February 2021
Moon like Cheese	1 March 2021
Cherry	5 April 2021
Blossom like Frost	10 April 2021
Sparkling Sea and Gulls	14 April 2021
Daisies, Stars	15 April 2021
Herring Gull	15 April 2021

	Date
Sparkling Sea, Sneeze	16 April 2021
Smiling Night	17 April 2021
Two Foxes	23 April 2021
Death Staring, Waiting	6 May 2021; 28–29 December 2022
Last Call to the Afterlife	6 May 2021; 28–29 December 2022
Owls Hooting	25 May 2021
Moon	26–27 May 2021
Downpour from the Sun	30 May 2021
Stitchwort Stars	16 June 2021
Swallows Back	5 July 2021
Bee in the Lavender	18 July 2021
Sparkling Sea	4 August 2021; revised 10 December 2022
Sea Storm and Mind	5 August 2021
The Evening Star is Bright	7 August 2021
Fallen Leaves	9 August 2021
Shooting Star	9 August 2021
A Calm Sea	12 August 2021
Moth Drawn by Light	12 August 2021
Pecking and Picking	2 October 2021
Soul Sings	11 October 2021
Shimmering Gold	21 October 2021
Rock Pipit	22 October 2021
Between Moon and Star	24 October 2021
The Power of the Sea	24 October 2021
Nuthatch	9 November 2021
Squelching Heart	10 November 2021
Fox Sniffing	17 November 2021
Carrion Crow	19 November 2021
Black Crow and Plague Victim	19 November 2021
Blood-Red Sun	16 December 2021
Surging Waves like a Virus	18 December 2021
Reddening Sun	11 February 2022

	Date
Storm	13 February 2022
After the Storm	18 February 2022
War and Spring	26 March 2022
Waiting on a Clot	30 March 2022
On a Precipice	30 March 2022
Reprieve	30 March 2022
Game (or Gammy) Heart	1 April 2022
Leaning Daisies	1 April 2022
Daffodils	1 April 2022
Wagtail	7 April 2022
Fall like a Tall Tree	9 April 2022
Years like Foaming Waves	10 April 2022
A Shadow in Time	10 April 2022
Pipit and Reflection	13 April 2022
Bats	13 April 2022
A Peacock Butterfly	16 April 2022
A Heavenly Garden	8 May 2022
Stop-Breathings	17 May 2022
Swallow	8 June 2022
A Small Tortoiseshell's Salute	14 June 2022
Mist	30 June 2022
Wasps and Bees	12 July 2022
Oblivion	1 August 2022
Black-Headed Gull	1 August 2022
At Portsmouth: Leaving Port	1 August 2022
Gong	1 August 2022
Trawled	1 August 2022
Night-Sea Voyage	1 August 2022
Raindrops like Early Stars	3 August 2022
A Hermit and Solitude	6 August 2022
Death: Coach	6 August 2022
Hag's Head and God	8 August 2022
Under Ben Bulben: Grave and Boat	9 August 2022
Rocks like Sheep	9 August 2022

	Date
Back from my Grave	9 August 2022
House Martins and Sheep	9 August 2022
In Mount Stewart's Sunken Garden	12 August 2022
From Waterloo to Peterloo	12 August 2022
Clouds and Foam	18 August 2022
Zodiac	22 August 2022
Work and Universe	28 August 2022
Last Buttercup	14 September 2022
Pilgrimage	17 September 2022
What If?	18 September 2022
Sheep	20 October 2022
Turbulent Sea	20 October 2022
Tide	21 October 2022
Planets and Shadow	22 October 2022
Full Moon and Fireworks	6 November 2022
COP27: Bettering the Lot of Humankind	7 November 2022
Anarchy: A Nightmare	16 November 2022; revised 2 April 2023
Time's Ticking	7 December 2022
Night Sea	8–9 December 2022
Full Moon	9 December 2022
Screaming Gulls	10 December 2022
Chaotic	13 December 2022
On my Own	18 January 2023; revised 21–22 January 2023
Healing Power	20 January 2023; revised 22 January 2023
Anaximander's Cosmos: The Boundless	12–13 February 2023
Sparrowhawk	5 March 2023
Aging	6 March 2023
Wild Nature	Mid-March 2023
Shoal	31 March 2023
Calm Sea	1 April 2023
Coronavirus	1 April 2023
Forgetfulnesses	2 April 2023

	Date
Scudding, Changing	2 April 2023
Sea and Mind	4 April 2023
Heart Murmur	15–16, 20 May 2023
Body and Brain: Design that's Meant	28 May, 6 June 2023
The Oak Tree's Bubbling and Groaning	6 June 2023
In Fairmead in Arcadia	14–15 April 2023
Shelley and the One	18–20 April 2023
Volume 38: ***An Oval Cloud*** (24 Sonnets)	
1. Oval Cloud: Sculptures	25 April 2020; revised 15 December 2022
2. Oval Cloud: Swansdown	25 April 2020; revised 15 December 2022
3. Oval Cloud: Shapes	25 April 2020; revised 16 December 2022
4. Oval Cloud: Messages	25 April 2020; revised 17 December 2022
5. Oval Cloud: Outside Time	25 April 2020; revised 27 December 2022
6. Oval Cloud: Muses' Amanuensis	25 April 2020; revised 17 December 2022
7. Oval Cloud: Amanuensis of All the Muses and Tenth Muse	25 April 2020; revised 17 December 2022
8. Oval Cloud: Enduring	28 April 2020; revised 17 December 2022
9. Oval Cloud: Slide Show	6 May 2020; revised 17 December 2022
10. Oval Cloud: Soul and Halo	9 May 2020; revised 19 December 2022
11. Oval Cloud: My Comforting Cloud Returns	22 June 2020; revised 21 December 2022
12. Oval Cloud and Swallows	29 June 2020; revised 21 December 2022
13. Oval Cloud: Cloud like a Woolsack	29 June 2020; revised 21 December 2022
14. Oval Cloud: Nine Muses	10 April 2021; revised 21 December 2022

	Date
15. Oval Cloud: Cloud of Knowing	18 January 2023; revised 19–20 January 2023
16. Oval Cloud: Envelopment	7 February 2023
17. Oval Cloud: Texts in Code	8 February 2023
18. Oval Cloud: Message from Eternity	9 February 2023
19. Oval Cloud: Peace Plan and Wi-Fi	12 February 2023
20. Oval Cloud: Death, Soul Packed and Ready to Go	5 March 2023
21. Oval Cloud: Soul like a Pouch	5 March 2023
22. Oval Clouds: Muses	17, 20 May 2023
23. Oval Cloud: Ideas Bag	18, 20 May 2023
24. Oval Cloud: Ancient Letters	27, 28 May 2023
Volume 39: ***Court Poems: More Royal Classical Odes***	
Royal Harmony (On the Wedding of Prince Harry and Meghan Markle, 19 May 2018)	28–30 May, 3 June 2018
Rose Garden like a Union Flag	21 September 2019
The Funeral of the Duke of Edinburgh: The Elizabethan Age Drawing to a Close	17, 24–25 April 2021
Death of the Queen: The End of the Elizabethan Era	8–9 September 2022
The Funeral of Queen Elizabeth II (On the Ambivalence of Revival and Decline)	19 September 2022
A New Age of Light	12–15 March 2023
At Coldridge: An Unspeakable Truth	5–6 April 2023; first drafted 29 December 2021
The Painted Hall, Greenwich	8 April 2023
The World Falling Apart: An Unspeakable Secret	14 April 2023
The Oak Tree and the Fallen Branch	27–30 April 2023
Epistle to a Civil Servant (Epistle to a Civil Servant who Keeps the Official List of Writers Allowed to Operate but with Limited Publicity)	3–4 May 2023
The Coronation of King Charles III and the True Poet	5–7, 20 May 2023
Leaving Court to End my Days in Arcadia	13 May 2023

		Date
In the Wilderness in my Arcady		14, 16, 21 May 2023
Withdrawing into the Invisibility of my Arcady		19, 21 May 2023
The Oak Tree and the Healing Branch		10 June 2023
Volume 40: ***In Arcady: A Gong and Padded Stick*** (40 Sonnets)		
1.	Time's Up	17, 21 May 2023
2.	Gonging my Hearse	22 May 2023
3.	Waiting: Legacy	25, 29 May 2023
4.	Everything Helps	25 May, 8 June 2023
5.	A Robot's View of my Works 2	27 May, 5 June 2023
6.	A Robot's View of my Works 1	27 May, 8 June 2023
7.	In the Now	29 May 2023
8.	A Remarkable Life	29, 30 May, 1 June 2023
9.	An Extraordinary Life	29, 30 May, 1 June 2023
10.	A Fulfilled Life	30 May, 1 June 2023
11.	A Rewarding Life	30 May, 2, 3, 6 June 2023
12.	Sent Down with a Message by the Light	30 May, 2, 3 June 2023
13.	A Providential Life	30 May, 2, 3 June 2023
14.	A Providential Life and the Light	30 May, 2, 3 June 2023
15.	Providence's Deep Mystic Way, Unitive Vision, Baroque and Universalism	30 May, 2, 3 June 2023
16.	Direction and Destiny: Mission to Bring Peace to Humankind	30 May, 3 June 2023
17.	There is a Providence: Fulfilling our Destiny	30 May, 3 June 2023
18.	Providence and Influences: Key People arrive at the Right Time	30 May, 3 June 2023
19.	Providential Life and Works	31 May, 7 June 2023
20.	Pattern in Episodes	31 May, 7 June 2023
21.	Pattern like a Pine Cone	31 May, 7 June 2023
22.	Hermit in the Wilderness	31 May, 7 June 2023
23.	Shown my Future Direction and Destiny	31 May, 7 June 2023
24.	Slave of the Muses	31 May, 8 June 2023

		Date
25.	Keep Going	31 May, 8 June 2023
26.	Doing Good	31 May, 8 June 2023
27.	Family and All We Knew	31 May, 8 June 2023
28.	England and Europe	31 May, 8 June 2023
29.	The West in Decline	31 May, 8 June 2023
30.	The Light of the World	31 May, 8 June 2023
31.	Renaissance Man	31 May, 8 June 2023
32.	Old Age	31 May, 8 June 2023
33.	Booming Out	31 May, 8 June 2023
34.	Providential Light and New Powers	31 May, 8 June 2023
35.	Polymath	31 May, 9 June 2023
36.	End of Life	31 May, 9 June 2023
37.	Death	31 May, 9 June 2023
38.	Postscript, Gratitude: 23 Sonnets Sent Through in a Day	31 May, 9 June 2023
39.	Knowing my End	5 June 2023
40.	Looking Back on my End	6 June 2023
Volume 41: ***Agony in Arcady: Stroke*** (169 Sonnets)		
1.	Blood Clot	12, 25 June 2023
2.	Brain Stem, Locked-In	13, 25 June 2023; 30 April, 1 May 2024
3.	Nightmare	14, 26 June 2023
4.	Postponing	14, 26 June 2023
5.	Limbo	14, 27, 30 June 2023
6.	Quadriplegic	14 June, 1 July 2023
7.	Deep Sleep	14 June, 1 July 2023
8.	Project	14 June, 1 July 2023
9.	Pneumonia	15 June, 11 July 2023
10.	Not Long to Live	15 June, 1 July 2023
11.	Reunited	15 June, 2 July 2023
12.	Eyewitness: Bungalow	15 June, 2 July 2023
13.	Communication: Howl	17 June, 2 July 2023
14.	Crying	17 June, 2 July 2023
15.	New House	17 June, 2 July 2023

		Date
16.	Rose's Floor	17 June, 3 July 2023
17.	Genetic Flaw	17 June, 3 July 2023
18.	Shallower Breathing	17 June, 8 August 2023
19.	Despair	17 June, 20 August 2023
20.	Speechless	17 June, 23, 24 August 2023
21.	Stroking Beauty	17 June, 24, 25 August 2023
22.	Living in Uncertainties	18 June, 25 August 2023
23.	Tiredness and Quiet Despair	19 June, 25 August 2023
24.	Banned from Seeing You	20 June, 25 August 2023
25.	Walled-In Silence	20 June, 26, 27 August 2023
26.	Coma	20 June, 26 August 2023
27.	MRI	21 June, 29 August 2023
28.	New Spin	21 June, 30 August 2023
29.	Seizure	22 June, 1, 2 September 2023
30.	Melancholy	22 June, 2 September 2023
31.	Guard	23 June, 2 September 2023
32.	Level-One Rehab	23 June, 3 September 2023
33.	Pain	24 June, 3 September 2023
34.	Drawing to a Close	25 June 2023
35.	Sleeping Beauty	25 June, 3 September 2023
36.	Wounded Deer	26, 27 June 2023
37.	Recovery	27 June 2023
38.	Desperation: Shaken	28, 30 June 2023
39.	Calm	28, 29, 30 June 2023
40.	Resetting	3, 4 July 2023
41.	Infection	6 July 2023
42.	Distressed	7 July 2023
43.	Crying Out	8, 9 July 2023
44.	Counting, Memory, Hearing	11 July, 20 August 2023
45.	Key	11 July, 20 August 2023
46.	Bleak	12 July, 20 August 2023
47.	A Beacon of Hope	12 July, 20 August 2023
48.	Encouragement	12 July, 20 August 2023
49.	Crying from Pain	13 July, 19 August 2023

	Date
50. Keeping You Calm	13 July, 19 August 2023
51. Harrowing	14, 16 July 2023
52. Understanding Too Well	14, 16 July 2023
53. Care Home	15, 16 July 2023
54. Tears	18 July, 19 August 2023
55. Walled-In Wellness	20 July, 19 August 2023
56. Eternal Soul	20 July, 19 August 2023
57. Cleansing	20 July, 19 August 2023
58. At Cromwell's House, Ely	20, 24 July, 19 August 2023
59. At Ely Cathedral	20, 24 July, 19 August 2023
60. Return to Otley Hall	21, 24 July, 19 August 2023
61. Body like a Cell	22 July, 14 August 2023
62. Legal Consent	24 July, 14 August 2023
63. Arcady	25 July, 14 August 2023
64. Possessions	26 July, 14 August 2023
65. Grimace	26 July, 14 August 2023
66. Fragile	27 July, 13 August 2023
67. PBA	27 July, 13 August 2023
68. Bizarre	27 July, 14 August 2023
69. Aware Crying	27 July, 14 August 2023
70. Hospitality	29 July, 13 August 2023
71. Assessor	1, 13 August 2023
72. Athens	3, 13 August 2023
73. Unexpected	4, 13 August 2023
74. Goldfinch	23, 27 July, 4, 12 August 2023
75. Unthankful Hell	8 August 2023
76. Sunset	9, 12 August 2023
77. Raw in Arcady	10, 12 August 2023
78. Mangled	10, 12 August 2023
79. Lightning Strike: Oak Tree and Split Branch	10, 11 August 2023
80. Gone For Ever	10, 11 August 2023
81. Agape	12 August 2023
82. Kinks	12, 13 August 2023
83. Eyegaze Machine	15, 18 August 2023

		Date
84.	Low Blood Pressure	15, 18 August 2023
85.	Escaping from Locked-In: Talking	15, 18 August 2023
86.	Wildfire	18 August 2023
87.	Cornish Hermitage	18 August 2023
88.	Suffolk Fair Maid	18 August 2023
89.	Involuntary Groaning	18, 19 August 2023
90.	Belief	18, 19 August 2023
91.	Turning a Corner: Donkeys	22 August 2023
92.	Rehabilitating	22 August 2023
93.	Laughing	22 August 2023
94.	Nursing Care	23, 24 August 2023
95.	Conflict (+A + −A = 0)	26, 27 August 2023
96.	Debilitating	28 August 2023
97.	Triggering Regret	28 August 2023
98.	Unheeded Pain	30 August 2023
99.	Statues on Hope's Pedestal	30 August 2023
100.	World-Unity and World-Sadness Reconciled in the One	2 September 2023
101.	Hope	5, 7 September 2023
102.	Not Fully Locked-In: Walking Again	5, 7 September 2023
103.	Wisdom and Feeling Unite in Stillness	7 September 2023
104.	Escaping	8 September 2023
105.	120 Billion Connecting Brain Cells	8, 10 September 2023
106.	Blocked Motorway	8, 10 September 2023
107.	Care Home Ahead	8, 11 September 2023
108.	On the Right Path	8, 11 September 2023
109.	Assimilated Agony, Transcending	8, 11 September 2023
110.	Preparing to Go	8, 11 September 2023
111.	Avoiding Reporting	12 September 2023
112.	Sixty-Degrees Standing	12, 13 September 2023
113.	Three-Month Crying Blight and Plight	12, 13 September 2023
114.	Arcady Paralysed, Now Paradisal	12, 13 September 2023
115.	Infirm and Involuntary	14 September 2023
116.	Capacity	15 September 2023

	Date
117. Moving, Swallowing, Laughing, Balancing, Cycling – Escaping	19, 23 September 2023
118. Glassing-In Arcadian Landscape	19, 23 September 2023
119. Arcady's New Blight	19, 23 September 2023
120. War in Arcady	22, 23 September 2023
121. Atrophy: Faltering Together Following our Fall	22, 23 September 2023
122. Harmony in the Soul: The Music of the Spheres	26, 28 September 2023
123. Rescuing from Harm	26, 28 September 2023
124. Fountain	28, 29 September 2023
125. Eyewitness: Overcoming	28, 29 September 2023
126. Incapacity	3 October 2023
127. Fifty-Year-Old Pain	3, 4 October 2023
128. Determined Intent	3, 5 October 2023
129. Peace in Arcady: Stag	3, 5, 6 October 2023
130. In Arcady: Old Man in a Circle	5, 6 October 2023
131. Wilderness: Magpie, Free	7 October 2023
132. Independent Capacity Assessor Declined	10, 29 October 2023
133. Crying Despair	10, 30 October 2023
134. Court: Caught	10, 29 October 2023
135. Fall	12, 30 October 2023
136. Silent	12, 30 October 2023
137. Expectations like a Sea-Swell's Foam	13, 23 October 2023
138. Broken Ankle-Bone	14, 21 October 2023
139. Frustration	17, 18 October 2023
140. Chill in the Air	21 October 2023
141. The Way Forward	24, 26 October 2023
142. Recovering: Again at Peace in Arcady	24, 26 October 2023
143. In Arcadia: The Oneness of the Universe	24, 26 October 2023
144. Difficult	31 October, 1 November 2023
145. Strike	3 November 2023
146. Flemish Characteristics: Nothing's Certain	5, 7 November 2023

	Date
147. Speechless and Still, like an Infant	5, 7 November 2023
148. Palliative Care	7 November 2023
149. Death Setting You Free	7 November 2023
150. Defying or Accepting Fate	8 November 2023
151. Caring for All 'Yous' or 'Old You'	8 November 2023
152. Phases of 'One You'	8 November 2023
153. Occultation	9, 10 November 2023
154. Heroic Endurance	10 November 2023
155. Harmony and Bliss in Arcady	10, 11 November 2023
156. The Vivid Greens of Arcady	15–17 January 2024
157. Dream: Stag and Deer Grazing in Heaven's Arcady	18, 19, 22, 23 January 2024
158. The Old You's Back	20, 21 January 2024
159. Guard of Honour: Tribute to Heroic Endurance and Overcoming	25 May, 3 June 2023
160. Care Home, Struggling	30 May, 3 June 2024
161. DNR: Heroic Limit	30 May, 3 June 2024
162. Overcoming like Sisyphus	30 May, 3 June 2024
163. Sisyphus, and a Better World	4 June 2024
164. Overcoming like Shakespeare: Find a Way or Make a Way	30 May, 3 June 2024
165. Overcoming Two Hundred and Ten Resurrections	1, 3 June 2024
166. How to Overcome Locked-In Quadriplegia	1, 3 June 2024
167. Overcoming: Oval Soul Reflecting the Light like a Puddle	2, 3 June 2024
168. Overcoming Gloom with Soul's Brightness	3 June 2024
169. All Overcomings: Mind over Matter In Heaven's Arcady	4 June 2024

INDEX OF TITLES

Poems in alphabetical order, volume titles in italics

The first number is where the poem starts. 'See also' denotes other references to the poem within the book.

P

T

LIBERALIS IS A LATIN word which evokes ideas of freedom, liberality, generosity of spirit, dignity, honour, books, the liberal arts education tradition and the work of the Greek grammarian and storyteller Antoninus Liberalis. We seek to combine all these interlinked aspects in the books we publish.

We bring classical ways of thinking and learning in touch with traditional storytelling and the latest thinking in terms of educational research and pedagogy in an approach that combines the best of the old with the best of the new.

As classical education publishers, our books are designed to appeal to readers across the globe who are interested in expanding their minds in the quest of knowledge. We cater for primary, secondary and higher education markets, homeschoolers, parents and members of the general public who have a love of ongoing learning.

If you have a proposal that you think would be of interest to Liberalis, submit your inquiry in the first instance via the website: www.liberalisbooks.com.